I have a story to tell you

Seemah C. Berson, editor

Wilfrid Laurier University Press

WLU

We acknowledge the support of the Canada Council for the Arts for our publishing program. We acknowledge the financial support of the Government of Canada through the Canada Book Fund for our publishing activities.

Library and Archives Canada Cataloguing in Publication

I have a story to tell you / Seemah C. Berson, editor.

(Life writing series)
Also available in electronic format.
ISBN 978-1-55458-219-8

    1. Clothing workers—Canada—Biography. 2. Jews—Canada—Biography. 3. East Europeans—Canada—Biography. 4. Immigrants—Canada—Biography. 5. Clothing trade—Canada—History—20th century. I. Berson, Seemah Cathline, 1931–   II. Series: Life writing series

HD8039.C62C2 2010   331.7'687092271   C2010-903893-2

ISBN 978-1-55458-238-9
Electronic format.

    1. Clothing workers—Canada—Biography. 2. Jews—Canada—Biography. 3. East Europeans—Canada—Biography. 4. Immigrants—Canada—Biography. 5. Clothing trade—Canada—History—20th century. I. Berson, Seemah Cathline, 1931–   II. Series: Life writing series

HD8039.C62C2 2010a   331.7'687092271   C2010-903893-2

Cover design by Blakeley Words+Pictures. Cover photographs by Jose Carlos Alva (mannequin) and Lluís Torrent-Bescós (woman). Text design by Catharine Bonas-Taylor.

This book is printed on FSC recycled paper and is certified Ecologo. It is made from 100% post-consumer fibre, processed chlorine free, and manufactured using biogas energy.

Printed in Canada

I have a story to tell you

Life Writing Series

In the **Life Writing Series**, Wilfrid Laurier University Press publishes life writing and new life-writing criticism and theory in order to promote autobiographical accounts, diaries, letters, and testimonials written and/or told by women and men whose political, literary, or philosophical purposes are central to their lives. The Series features accounts written in English, or translated into English from French or the languages of the First Nations, or any of the languages of immigration to Canada.

From its inception, **Life Writing** has aimed to foreground the stories of those who may never have imagined themselves as writers or as people with lives worthy of being (re)told. Its readership has expanded to include scholars, youth, and avid general readers both in Canada and abroad. The Series hopes to continue its work as a leading publisher of life writing of all kinds, as an imprint that aims for both broad representation and scholarly excellence, and as a tool for both historical and autobiographical research.

As its mandate stipulates, the Series privileges those individuals and communities whose stories may not, under normal circumstances, find a welcoming home with a publisher. **Life Writing** also publishes original theoretical investigations about life writing, as long as they are not limited to one author or text.

Series Editor
Marlene Kadar
Humanities Division, York University

Manuscripts to be sent to
Lisa Quinn, Acquisitions Editor
Wilfrid Laurier University Press
75 University Avenue West
Waterloo, Ontario, Canada N2L 3C5

To Yaniv, Ayla, Matan, Noam, Talia, Noah. May the lights in your eyes always serve as beacons.

For Harold R. Berson, friend and lifelong partner

It is not your duty to complete the work;
Neither are you free to desist from it.
—Rabbi Tarfon, Pirkei Avot 2:16

Contents

Photographs follow page 112.

Preface

I HAVE A STORY—IN FACT, I have a number of stories—not about an important person or one who accomplished great feats in her or his lifetime. In fact, these aren't even my stories, but they were told to me and I want to share them with you.

There are always stories if you care to listen. Why are these stories different? What makes them unique?

I was an undergraduate at the time I heard Sidney Sarkin speak at a banquet, and I had a research paper to do. Sarkin was Jewish and what he talked about then, though it was a part of his life, was also a reflection of a larger picture involving more than one Jewish immigrant to North America. It reflected the transition of a people: the Eastern European Jewish people. After spending time with Sidney and listening to his stories, I was inspired to talk with more people from the needle trades. Soon after, I had a chance to do that.

I was fortunate enough to receive a scholarship, and in the summer of 1974, armed with a new tape recorder and brand-new cassette tapes, I said goodbye to my husband and four kids in Vancouver and took a plane to Toronto. I had names of Jewish garment workers in Montreal and Toronto to get me started. However, one needs more than equipment and names of people! I had grown accustomed to visiting Sidney, enjoying a cup of coffee, chatting with his wife, Sarah, and settling down with the tape recorder between us. In other words, I felt comfortable, at home, with him. In Toronto and Montreal I was a stranger to the people and the cities. Nonetheless, being younger then, I learned to find my way by bus and subway, and soon made many, many friends.

I was invited into homes and community centres. I was fed; at times I was even wined and dined. The people I interviewed freely gave me advice. I was welcomed by women and men in hospital beds, who were so glad to have a friendly face to talk to, particularly about a long-ago part of their lives that was filled with so much hardship and deprivation, and which no one—sometimes not even their children and grandchildren—was interested in hearing about. I am still touched by the pride in their eyes and voices as they opened little bedside drawers to show me their union membership cards and pension slips ... their credentials as contributors to society. Those contributions were not small; in the final reckoning, unionized garment workers were on the front line between 1900 and the beginning of the Second World War. Workers today must acknowledge their contributions because some gave their lives on the picket lines!

My fieldwork did not always go smoothly. Sometimes the electric outlet was dead; a fact I would only realize some five minutes into the interview when I noticed the tape wasn't going around! There were times when an afternoon of cards took precedence over talking to me. On one such card-playing afternoon at the YMHA (Young Men's Hebrew Association), one of the volunteers kindly introduced me as someone from Vancouver who would like to talk to anyone willing to spare the time. She promptly turned around and left. No one—all men—gave me a second glance. A man nearby finally got up and loudly said to the card players, "Elizabeth Taylor here would like to talk to someone maybe!" On occasion I felt I was being lectured to by my elders. "You shouldn't leave your husband at home by himself!" a man said to me, implying that my husband might get into mischief. Telling him that he had four boys to take care of didn't change his mind.

Yiddish, was not my mother tongue or that of my forebears, and I was concerned about conversing with this older generation of Yiddish-speaking immigrants. I need not have worried as by and large, they spoke in English. While some of them did occasionally lapse into a Yiddish expression or two when excited about something they were relating, their lapses gave their words the *tam*—the flavour and taste—of their Yiddish language.

Though my main interest was in talking with people who had worked in the needle trades, I did have the pleasure of talking to other workers as well. Were it not for the generosity of so many people, I would have been lost and these stories would have been lost and forgotten. So many who lived at home invited me in and shared not only their past; some spent their time with me. I was taken to dinner and the movies—that is how I saw *Blazing Saddles* in Montreal. Relatives and friends invited me to lunch or dinner to meet people who were in the needle trades. Some of these introductions were followed by invitations to offices and factories and, subsequently, to interviews. Others were so grateful to have someone to talk to about themselves. "Why would anyone want to know about my days in a factory?" I was asked. There was one woman who, even though she knew me personally, just could not talk about herself. She said, "There is nothing to tell you about my life. It was nothing important." When she did open up she had some interesting stories to tell.

※

Some of the stories in this volume are about lives lived in the Old Country, in *shtetlekh* (little towns and villages) and in cities, which many left to journey to the New World. In the minds of the Jewish immigrants there was no distinction between Canada and the United States. To them all, it was "America." "I am going to America. Hoh!" was the cry. Other stories reflect the early lives of these immigrants: where they arrived, with whom they lived until they found their bearings, what sort of work they did as a greenhorn, a newcomer, with no knowledge of the English language. Other stories speak of the struggles they had trying to make a living in the garment industry in this new country.

Many of the people I interviewed had lived and worked in Winnipeg (a major centre for the needle trades) and had been involved in the struggles for decent wages, hours of work, job security, and workplace minimum health and sanitary guarantees in that city. Their stories are horrifyingly unacceptable to us in Canada in the twenty-first century. I was told about conditions where one or two floors of needle workers, bent over machines for long workday hours, had to take care of their personal hygiene during very short lunch breaks in bathrooms shared by men, women, and young girls alike. These were the conditions, along with low pay and long working hours, that these men and women fought against and forced their bosses to change.

For these Jewish immigrants, there was no going back to where they came from. Today, unless they are political refugees, new Canadians can have the option of going back or visiting their place of birth. However, for the Jew arriving in Canada between 1900 and the 1940s, that choice scarcely existed.

Before my final year as an undergraduate, I was fortunate to have received a grant from the Institute of Industrial Relations, University of British Columbia, to travel to eastern Canada in order to do my fieldwork. Montreal, Toronto, and Winnipeg had been the centres of the clothing manufacturing industry during the period under review. Most of the Jewish immigrants who were employed in the needle trades were to be found in these cities.

I felt an additional impetus to get my work underway because of the age group toward which the research was focused: the majority of immigrants I wished to interview were sixty-five years old and over, and not too many of them were still around.

It has been almost forty years since I talked to these immigrants who had lived and worked in Montreal, Toronto, Winnipeg, and Vancouver about their lives. In all that time their stories have "noodged" me, prodded me. It is time now for their voices to be heard once again in Canada, in this country to which they came with all their hopes and dreams and which they made into a better place to live and work. The greater imperative is the sad fact that they are not here anymore to speak for themselves; but the nuances in their voices and the courage in their struggles can still be heard … if you listen very carefully.

So, if you have a moment or two, I have a story to tell you … in fact, I have a few stories to tell you.

Acknowledgements

BARUCH HA'SHEM! I am grateful to have completed this work, first in partial fulfillment of my M.A. thesis in 1980 and now in the voices of these Jewish immigrants. Why did it take so long? It is within the cradle of Jewish Ethics (Mussar) that I have found myself worthy of completing this work.

My gratitude abounds for the encouragement and positive feedback I have received from those I have talked to about this book. Twenty-five years ago, few in the publishing business and fewer still in the Jewish community were interested in this work. Times have changed, and with the appearance of another generation, so open and welcoming, came a thirst for Jewish historical data. My heart swells and opens in response. I thank you.

It is difficult to begin to acknowledge and give thanks to the many who gave of themselves and who made this work a reality. My expression of gratitude follows neither a chronological methodology nor a meritorious one. Each and every person acknowledged here stands equally tall and needs to be counted. I am forever in your debt. To Penny Goldsmith, for your confidence, for your finding my work praiseworthy, for encouraging me to send my stories to Wilfrid Laurier University Press in the first place, I cannot thank you enough. To Laura Moodie, thank you for your support and help and for your faith in me.

To Lisa Quinn, acquisitions editor at Laurier Press, now I can tell you that my mouth fell open when you asked me over the phone for the rest of my manuscript! I almost said, Huh? What manuscript? I had sent you a sampling and didn't expect a positive response. Thank you, Lisa, for your faith in me from the very beginning, for working on this book to make it a reality, for just being there. Thank you also to Leslie Macredie at Laurier Press, for your encouragement and help always, even when I was losing it, together with files! For your quiet patience and understanding, thank you, Rob Kohlmeier, managing editor at Laurier Press. Thank you, Kristen Chew, for your queries and suggestions during copy editing.

Thank you to Dr. Martin Meissner of the University of British Columbia, my sociology professor, now retired, who encouraged me to embark on the research that led me to this point. To Dr. Michael M. Ames, past director of the Museum of Anthropology, UBC, my supervisor and mentor, a friend who died too soon, my thanks to you always. To all those who entrusted their stories to me, I hope this publication will in some measure say thank you. I would like to say a quiet thank you to those of you in the academic world across Canada and in the United States who unhesitatingly responded so positively to this project when first I talked to you about its possible publication. It was your unqualified endorsement that filled me with confidence in the work I was doing. Thank you.

To the children and grandchildren of the storytellers: David Abramowitz, the Barrett family, Judy Charles, Gallia Chud, Faigie Coodin, Jana Danelle, Dorothy and Irving Grad, Laura Jacamovitz, Rima and Clive Kaplan, Sylvia Friedman of Outlook, Claire Osipov, Bernie Zuker (who died in 2009) and his wife, Christine Hodgson, thank you for all the time spent searching through family albums, making copies, emailing material in the format requested and entrusting to me the photographs used in this book. Unfortunately I was unable to get images of all the good people who told me their stories. I am deeply grateful to those who had faith in me and my ability to complete this work: Gallia Chud and her children, Gyda Chud and Rita Chudnovsky, the Kirman Foundation (through the good offices of Al Stein and Seymour Levitan), Claire Osipov, Stuart Ostlund, RBC Royal Bank of Canada, the Sidney Sarkin Estate, Rabbi Yosef Wosk, Harold Berson, David Berson, Joshua Berson, Saul Berson, and Adam Berson. Thank you for your contributions.

Thank you, Seymour Levitan. Your expertise in Yiddish/Hebrew guided me through minefields when working on Shaya Kirman's story and the glossary. Any mistakes in this regard are entirely mine. To Michael Kader my grateful thanks for providing your time and advice so unstintingly, as always. To Linda Thayer my gratitude for giving of yourself, your time and knowledge, your constant faith and friendship. *Hakarat Ha'tov.*

My family! Words cannot convey to you my eternal thanks for the encouragement, for the endless time out of your busy lives, for the many hours spent by some of you in order to bring this work to fruition, for renewing my faith in myself, in others, and in my work, and for reminding me to trust, to have *betechon* that all will be well, for coming to the rescue when a file I was working on flew off my desktop and I panicked, for your consideration, your dialogues and input, for just being there when needed. Thank you, thank you, thank you to each and every member of this great family! Some do need singling out for going the extra mile. Tamara MacKenzie, I humbly thank you for your love and quiet co-operation, for the times you helped me with the computer, even when you had much of your own work to do. I could work with you anytime! Number-two son, Joshua, what would I have done without you? Your smiles, your wisdom, your expertise in photography, the computer, your dressings-down, and your liftings-up—am I a better person for those? I think so! How do I thank thee, my husband, my life partner, father of our sons, David, Joshua, Saul, and Adam? When we both went back to school, I to university for the first time and you a returning student, with four kids to take care of and a house to run, I know I could not have done it without your help and encouragement at all times. You gave without reservation, always! It was you who took me to night school and helped me enroll. Thank you for looking after the kids while I was away in Montreal and Toronto to do my research back in the summer of 1974. Thank you for the *endless* hours (the first round in the 1970s) of transcribing the tapes of immigrants I had interviewed and then again in the summer of 2008, when I had to get all these stories into the computer for my editor— you did another marathon run of transcribing because some of the tapes from the '70s had not been transcribed! To work on this was a monumental task: transcribing cassette tapes that were thirty-five years old, of stories told by Jewish immigrants in an English of East European inflection … it was a labour of love. I cannot begin to enumerate the many ways in which I am grateful to you and will always be. *Todah Rabah.* Thank you, Harold.

Introduction

THIRTY-SEVEN YEARS AGO I had little knowledge about the Jewish immigrants who came to Canada, even though I am Jewish myself. My antecedents are not East European. My grandparents migrated from Persia (now Iran) and Baghdad in Iraq to India, where I was born and raised. I had vague ideas about what life had been like for these immigrants in the Old Country: anti-Semitism, the pogroms, the poverty, the struggles, the heroes and heroines, and their achievements. Listening to Sidney Sarkin speak at a banquet I was attending, I became interested in finding out more about these people.

At that time, Sarkin was in the process of writing his memoirs in Yiddish. He generously agreed to talk to me about his life, and we subsequently spent many hours at his home taping the stories about life in Lithuania, about his leaving home, his eventful journey to Canada, and the years he spent working in the garment industry, the trade union, and the Communist Party of Canada. The many hours spent together resulted in a sociology research paper. However, the major outcome for me was that it crystallized a desire in me to talk to many more people about their journeys to Canada in search of a new life and how they eventually found work in the *shmate* or garment business.

In 1974 I began to look at secondary sources on Canadian Jewish history, working-class struggles in Canada, trade union history, census reports, and other related evidence. What struck me again and again was that:

- 60 percent of the Jewish immigrants in Montreal, Toronto and Winnipeg were employed in the clothing manufacturing industry in the early decades of the last century;
- in any history of the Jews in Canada little was said about the industry itself (e.g., the sweat shops, the struggles, the working conditions);
- the histories and reports of the period under review were more concerned with quantitative documentation rather than a reconstruction of what life was like for the Jewish immigrant worker.

The historical record was incomplete, as the personal dimension was missing. References to institutional contexts were one-sided and impersonal. I asked myself: What was this history like from the point of view of those who had lived it? My interviews with Sarkin suggested a format for further research. As well, talking to Sarkin gave me a one-sided view because he was a cutter, an aristocrat of the needle trades and I wanted to talk to ordinary workers. I felt the need to reconstruct the history of East European Jewish immigrants from the perspective of their own memories in order to add a personal dimension to the impersonal records.

When I began my own study I decided to focus on accounts from the period 1900 to 1930 for largely pragmatic reasons, as follows:

- It was difficult to find anyone who worked in the trades prior to this time.
- Canadian census reports only begin containing dates, the numbers of immigrants arriving, their religion, language and occupation, and other similar information in 1911.
- Secondary sources dealing with Jewish communities in Canada are sketchy before the twentieth century because of the insignificant numbers of Jews living in Canada prior to 1900.
- The Jewish immigrants who arrived after the mid-1930s posed different sets of problems and reasons for their coming to Canada, particularly because of the situation in Europe prior to the Second World War.

Montreal, Toronto and Winnipeg had been the centres of the Canadian clothing manufacturing industry during the years under review. Also, the industry was still very much an entity when I set out to do my research in 1974. I was fortunate to be able to assemble the names, through friends in Vancouver and in the above-mentioned cities, of people who had come from the Old Country and had worked (or were still working) in the needle trades.

I needed to keep in mind that the people I wished to interview were unlikely to complete forms or questionnaires. Some of them could not read or write in English and, even if they could, the type of questions I wished to ask could not be answered in one or two words. Although I was interested primarily in people who had worked in the needle trades, I did interview a number of immigrants in other trades as well.

I initially wanted to discover why Jewish immigrants went in such numbers into the needle trades. I began my interviews with the following questions which I felt would allow people the room to unfold their life stories:

- Where did you come from and when did you arrive in Canada? (This was to establish why they had left their homeland.)
- With whom did you live when you arrived? (I felt that it was crucial to find out if the person with whom they lived influenced the type of occupation they went into. Was it a rich uncle? A revolutionary brother? A poor but religious family? Was the type of occupation found, and the position taken within that occupation, determined by the answer to this question?)
- What was your first job?

By asking these basic questions I felt I would be able to discover the reasons why a particular type of work was chosen. I wanted to know how various factors influenced choice of occupation, such as religion, language, skills, kinship, friendship, membership in organizations, and time of arrival in this country.

As part of my research, I visited public and private libraries and archives in Toronto and Montreal. In Ottawa I spent time in the archives of the federal government and of the Canadian Labour Congress offices, gathering data on labour and union activities.

Eventually, a shift in the focus of my work evolved for me out of my research. Instead of being concerned with gathering facts and figures to support what informants said to me and to bolster the conceptual framework with which I went into the field, I began to see myself as a funnel or channel through which the lives and struggles of my subjects could be written down. Initially, my priority had been to find adequate answers to the phenomenon: why had so many Jewish immigrants gone into the needle trades? Later on, the "why" was no longer important to me. Instead, my concern in doing this work became to portray the panorama of Jewish life at the turn of the twentieth century, both in the Old Country and here in Canada. Two years of personal illness (1975–1976) also worked to distance me from my research and academic life to the extent that I no longer considered my priorities as being paramount in my study.

> I was born, I have lived, and I have been made over.
> Is it not time to write my life's story?
> Mary Antin, Russian immigrant, *The Promised Land* (1912)

In reviewing my data on the oral histories of the immigrants from Toronto, Montreal, and Winnipeg, I realized I had somehow asked the interviewees to talk about their lives from the time they arrived in Canada—as though the years lived in Eastern Europe did not exist or have any bearing on their lives once they were here. I felt I had to know about the towns and villages and cities from where they had come. What sort of lives they had lived there? Had they exchanged one set of problems for another? Mostly, I believe, the real reason for me wanting to know about lives in the Old Country was simply because that world did not exist anymore. There is no more a Pale of Settlement in Eastern Europe, or anywhere else in the world, for that matter!

Consequently, the following summer, I was fortunate to receive a further scholarship to record the recollections of Jewish immigrants' lives in the *shtetlekh*, or the villages and little towns, of Eastern Europe. Some interviewees did come from cities and would have been resentful if these were referred to as *shtetlekh*, but the majority of those interviewed did indeed come from small villages.

By utilizing personal recollections, I hoped to portray, in all its richness, the experiences of Jewish immigrants as reported to me. These experiences are not the milestones in the lives of these people so much as the everyday, ordinary events confronting them in their struggle to live from day to day. Their experiences can be classified into three groups:

- the *shtetl* and the push factors: those factors which pushed the Jews out of their homes in Eastern Europe;
- "America" and the pull factors: those things which beckoned them to the North American shores; and
- their work in the needle trades, and the contributions needle trade workers made in fighting for—not better but, essentially *for*—Canadian labour laws and practices, such as the eight-hour workday, unemployment insurance, and more.

I chose these classifications because each in its own way, should be viewed first in order to understand how the Old Country played its part in pushing the Jews out, how "America" attracted them to Canada, and how these two factors influenced the lives of these Jews and ultimately their choice of occupation. One cannot, I feel, appreciate their fight for better working conditions without understanding the ideology within which these Jews were raised, and without being cognizant of the fact that they brought this ideology with them to this country, Canada, as part and parcel of their cultural baggage.

When I reviewed the oral histories of the almost forty people I had interviewed, I found the subjects were mostly concerned with talking about themselves, which is to be expected. However, male informants often juxtaposed their lives with political events, while female informants streamlined theirs with events closer to their persons. Men were always the doers, the actors, the makers of history; women were most often interested in telling me about what happened around them, even though they might have been as instrumental as the next person in "making history." For all of them, however, life was always hard. Each day was a struggle, but no one ever left it as being a struggle and nothing more. There were benefits, there were small rewards, there was the fight itself. The "givens" and those things we take for granted are the things they fought for and in most cases did without. On several occasions, men and women went to where they kept their little private things—letters, papers, photographs—and very proudly pulled out their union card and showed it to me. "See," they would say, "I've been a member for a long time and I still get a pension, not very much, it's only twenty-five dollars a month; but I get a pension!" Some cried as they told me about their "longing to go to school to get an education—to be able to read and write just a few words even."

Prior to their mass migration to North America, the majority of Jews lived in what was known as the Pale of Settlement, an area within Russia of about a million square kilometres stretching from the Baltic Sea to the Black Sea, and bound on the west by the borders of Prussia, Austria-Hungary, and Romania, and at its most easternmost point by the province of Ekaterinoslav. According to a Russian census of 1897, 4,899,300 Jews lived in the Pale, forming 94 percent of the total population of the Pale of Settlement and accounting for 11.6 percent of the general population of the area (Yehuda Slutsky, "Pale of Settlement," *Encyclopaedia Judaica*, 1971: 27). The Pale of Settlement began under Catherine II (1762–96) until the reign of Nicholas II (1894–1917). After the 1917 February Revolution in Russia, the Pale of Settlement, as an entity, came to an end.

The Jews were an homogenous group and yet they were not. They had their similarities, their differences, their idiosyncrasies. One of the idiosyncratic differences, for example, was what came to be referred to as the Gefilte Fish Line, which separated those who seasoned their Sabbath fish with sugar (the Polish Jews) and those who used salt (the Russian Jews). Each cook frowned on the taste of the other's! While they spoke the same language, Yiddish, there were variations in how certain words were pronounced. For example, depending on where they came from, some either said *shul* or *sheel* for synagogue. They believed in the same God but followed different schools of rabbinical thought: the followers of the Rabbi of Ger, for example, had nothing to do with the followers of the Lublin Rabbi.

The existence of the Jewish people as a continuous historic entity, from Abraham in ancient Mesopotamia to the Jews living in Israel and then the Diaspora (those Jews living outside Israel), plays an important part in both understanding and explaining the survival of the Jews prior to and during the period discussed in this book. What follows here is a very brief and broad history of how the Jews arrived in Eastern Europe.

The contribution of the Jews to Western thought goes beyond their belief in ethical monotheism. That a group of nomadic tribes were eventually able to forge such a document as the Bible stems, in great measure, from the fact that they were able to codify their one thousand to fifteen-hundred-year history of wanderings into a total unified structure. The accomplishment of the Israelites of that day was that they had evolved a method of recording— both written and oral—what one might consider to be the first *Whole Earth Catalogue*. This catalogue consisted of the Torah and the Five Books of Moses, plus the Talmud, which was initially transmitted orally and eventually transcribed into another set of sacred books.

The Sacred Books carried instructions on how to live a good life in the eyes of God: what health foods to eat, and how one should conduct oneself within the community. The sanctioning by religious edict of the Sabbath as a day of rest has been considered the first recorded piece of labour legislation. The wide variety of everyday activities which the Sacred Books implored the Jewish populace to follow in the name of God, covered a wide range of both spiritual and secular matters. The languages used were Hebrew and Aramaic.

Landless and nomadic for the greater part of their early existence, the Jews were admonished, in both languages, to instruct all their children—the poor, the rich, and the orphaned—in the teachings of the Sacred Books. This tradition has been maintained throughout Jewish history. The Talmud insisted on it, and the education of children became a part of the ritual of Judaism. The ancient Hebrew sages are purported to have said that the world is kept alive by the breath of school children, and that a town without a school ought to be demolished.

After the dispersion of the Jews from the land of Israel in the first and second centuries CE came the rise of Islam in the seventh century. The Arabs conquered Palestine in 638 and Babylonia in 642, and conquered the south of Spain in 711. Judaism outside of Israel and in the Moslem world continued to flourish, but under Arab rule in Spain had a Golden Age from approximately 900 to 1200. The forward thrust of Christianity eventually forced the Arabs out of the Iberian peninsula and subsequently the Jews, called Sephardim, were also expelled in 1492 during the Spanish Inquisition.

Small enclaves of Jews had been settling in the Rhine Valley for several hundred years before the expulsion of the Sephardim, and their numbers were increased by the immigration from the Iberian Peninsula. As Christianity continued relentlessly to march across Europe, the Jews migrated to those areas where a more tolerant view of their presence was accepted. The bulk of world Jewry finally settled in Eastern Europe. Even within the confines of this area, their stay was marked by persecutions and territorial confinement.

During their stay in the Rhine Valley, the Jews, called Ashkenazim, developed another language, known as Yiddish. This language came to life at the same time as Middle German but was written in Hebrew characters and possessed much of the morphology of the Hebrew language. Why did the Jews in the Rhine Valley, in the medieval cities of Worms, Mayence, Cologne, and Speyer, need a language of their own? The late Max Weinreich, a well-known historian of Yiddish, explained that the Jews of these cities chose to live apart from the Gentiles. They wanted to be close to the convenience necessary for a Jew to observe his religion: the synagogue, the ritual bath, the kosher slaughterhouse, the Jewish burial ground.

Yiddish followed the Jews to Eastern Europe, and this language became the everyday tongue of the Jewish masses. In order to teach the children Judaism, prayers were written in this language. Popular epic style poems and stories, very much typical of non-Jewish literature of the Middle Ages, were also written in Yiddish. Handwritten copies of these Yiddish works were circulated amongst the people until the paper they were written on literally fell apart. A continuation of the linear tradition and the multilingual approach was part of the mental luggage that the vast majority of Jewish people carried with them.

The eighteenth century saw the French Revolution and the Industrial Revolution. People were being freed not only from their physical bonds, but also from spiritual ones. Ideas such as the equality of human beings, reason above dogma, and conscience above subservience to church, began to predominate. The Jews living in Europe began to share in this freedom. But freedom came slowly. It was not until the nineteenth century that Jews were "emancipated" and the walls of ghettos in Austria, Belarus, the Czech Republic, France, Germany, Hungary, Italy, and even more places, slowly crumbled. To those Jews of Western and Central Europe who had managed to physically survive the onslaught of Christianity and who had not migrated to Eastern Europe, Judaism developed in such a manner as to easily accommodate and adapt to the evolving territorial nationalist ambitions of their host cultures. The Jews readily adapted to the cultural life of this part of the world and it is where German became the secular language.

For the Eastern European Jew, however, this was not a period of emancipation, and poverty was the common lot of the vast majority of the people. During this dark period, Judaism encountered Hassidism: a Jewish interpretation of God in a highly personalized and individualistic way that created a folk-type religion. Hassidism addressed itself to personal and intimate dialogues with the Creator and infused Judaism with a spiritually uplifting, joyful experience.

In contrast to Hassidism, the spirit of Emancipation attempted to force itself into the *shetlekh* and cities of Eastern Europe. *Haskalah*, meaning "Jewish Enlightment," was a movement aimed towards breaking down the destructive and imprisoning barriers of ignorance, backwardness, and strangulation symbolized by the ghetto. Its success was impeded, in part, by the fact that the advocates of Haskalah deemed Yiddish to be an illiterate and common jargon, despite its use as the mother tongue of the Jewish masses of Eastern Europe. The leaders of Haskalah were also concerned that the Hassidic movement was drawing the Jewish people closer to the womb of an obscure and isolated brand of Judaism, and by doing so was further isolating the Jews from the advantages of cultural enlightenment that was sweeping Europe.

The theme of return to Zion, to Israel, runs throughout Judaic literature. With nowhere to turn and hemmed in between Poland and Russia, the desire to return to Zion became very much more eloquent and plaintive. Hassidic scholars would use only Hebrew for prayers because it was the holy language and Yiddish was their everyday vehicle to verbal expression. To this language they injected their Messianic verve for Zion. Haskalah wanted to make Hebrew the spoken language of the Jews, saying that until the Jewish people had a homeland of their own with their own Hebrew language, there could be no saving the Jews from the obscure, bleak life of the ghettos. Out of Haskalah, Zionism began to emerge, even though it had not yet formed itself into an ideology. The proponents of Zionism felt that anti-Semitism would disappear once the Jews were settled in Israel under a mild form of socialism.

The growing popularity of socialism could not fail to attract wide segments of the Jewish masses with its promise of a better life here and now, a world of equal opportunity for all people no matter what their origin, and the eradication of anti-Semitism. All these items were on the minds of the people. The Yiddish language was eloquently used by the socialists in describing the new and better world to come.

Throughout this entire period of time, the Jewish community, as always, accepted its responsibility of providing education for their children. The vast majority of male children were enrolled in *kheyders*, Jewish schools, where they learned some of the rudiments of Hebrew, for liturgical purposes at the very least. The respect of the community was bestowed upon the scholarship of a student. The very best catch that parents could wish for their daughter was an aspiring young scholar, or one who had already attained a scholarship in his Talmudic studies. All this, despite the fact that the bride's father would probably have to support his son-in-law because scholarship was not very profitable. If the family was well-to-do, a girl learned to read and say her prayers. The first priority for a young girl was to know how to look after and manage a kosher home.

Yiddish started to transform itself into a viable crucible for the cultural expression of the Jews. Its literary endeavors came of age around the 1850s and continued to find a tremendous response amongst the Jewish people well into the twentieth century. It was the start of a folk culture of considerable literary as well as cultural merit and that continues to this day, although not as widespread.

The seething unrest in Eastern Europe created conditions whereby the monarchical rulers at the time found it most convenient to use Jews as scapegoats. The ensuing persecutions resulted in mass migrations of Eastern European Jews to North America.

The focus and thrust of the first dozen or so stories in this book is to present life as it was in some of the *shtetlekh* of Eastern Europe. In order to understand why Jewish garment workers in Montreal, Toronto, Winnipeg, and Vancouver did the things they did and felt the way they felt, it is necessary to understand the cultural baggage they brought with them when they travelled to this country: their language, their literature, their traditions, and how these played a vital role in shaping their lives in the new land. What they ate; where they slept; how they were taught; their daily triumphs and failures; their one-room houses with plaster walls and floors and their apartments with wooden floors; the dreams of mothers; family and community life; the struggles to feed themselves; their involvement in political activities; jail terms; escapes from one country to another—all these aspects of life were very much alive in their memories.

The memory of the Jew is long, and spans more than two thousand years. When interviewees spoke to me about their lives and their experiences, when they talked about pain and hunger, joy and marriage, they were recounting two thousand years of putting down roots and pulling up stakes; fleeing from one enemy to another; resting, multiplying, and moving on again. By talking about the dreams of mothers for their sons (and their daughters), about ideologies and philosophies, of how these pushed a vast group of people to question, debate, argue, accept, reject, and reshape their lives so drastically in so short a time ... by retelling these things, life as it was for the Jew in Eastern Europe should emerge, in some small measure, as a concrete entity, a reality, for the readers here.

Rose Kaplan Barkusky

Rose Kaplan Barkusky was born on 16 December 1907, in Vilna, Lithuania. A Kaplan by her first marriage and a Barkusky by her second, Rose's first husband, Ben Kaplan, was her first cousin. He was seldom called by his first name, even by his wife: he was always called Kaplan, or Kappy. He was born 1896 and died in 1962. Rose died on 15 December 2005, the day before her ninety-eighth birthday.

I DON'T REMEMBER anything about my childhood.

The earliest I can remember is when Kaplan left home for America. I remember the day he said goodbye to everybody. I was sitting on a table in the living room. He said goodbye to everyone else in the house. When he came to say goodbye to me, he started to cry and an aunt of mine said to him, You silly, you are saying goodbye to your mother, your father, your sisters and brothers and you are crying when you say goodbye to her. You'll still see her but it's doubtful if you will see your family.

That's all I remember from that particular time, that incident; and I was about six years old. My sister was lying in the bed and I was sitting on the table.

We always lived with my grandmother and grandfather, my mother's parents. In 1914, when the war broke out, my father passed away. I remember it was before Rosh Hashanah, or a Jewish holiday. I was playing out in the street with my girlfriends and children, and my grandmother called me in and told me my father died and my mother was screaming. Back in Europe, when a person died, they put him right away on the floor. And all I remember was he was on the floor, covered up. My mother got a hold of me by my hand and she threw the cover off that I should see him and my grandmother grabbed me away and started screaming at my mother, You shouldn't have done that!

I remember when the funeral of my father was going towards the cemetery, the Germans were coming into our city. Before that, when the Russians were living in the city, the Russian troops were raping and killing and doing things like that. I remember mother kept the door locked and someone kept us in and we were sitting all night and being afraid in case they'll come into our place—like into our suite.

After my father passed away, the war was on. The Germans came into our city and it was pretty good at the beginning. We had food and everything and they were very good to us. But then the hungry days came. We were blockaded—the Germans were blockaded and we had no food. And we had cards—ration cards. We got so much bread a week. We had soup kitchens and I remember myself and Abrasha Kaplan—my cousin—we used to stand in line from morning to get soup because Grandma lived with us and grandfather lived with us, and so on. The Germans and the Jews were together, but the Germans themselves didn't have very much food.

At that time I was taking piano lessons—my mother decided I needed piano lessons—from a Jewish young lady, and she had a German Jewish friend who was an officer in the German army and he was looking after prisoners-of-war and in our street there, where we lived, was a big dance hall and the prisoners used to be brought there for their meals and this German Jew was the chief overseer—I don't know what they called him. There was a piano there—we didn't have a piano—so I used to go there to practise. The German used to tell me I could go there and practise and he told his cook, his chef, that he should give me food to eat. This must have been about 1916. I was about nine years old. The cook, he made me a sandwich once of some kind of salami, bread, and butter and I ate it.[1] And that was the first time—not that we were strictly kosher—but it was the first time I ate such a thing. And I was so sick afterwards. And I came home and told my mother.

Anyways, that's what I can remember from those years. Then I had to give up my piano lessons because I couldn't go after.

In 1917, when the revolution came, the Germans went out, of course, and then we had changes of the government all the time. The Bolsheviks came in. Then they gave it over to the Lithuanians. Then the Lithuanians were chased out during the night and the Poles took over. From 1917 to 1918 we had changes of government constantly. We didn't know who was shooting at night and in the morning we'd have a different government.

After that my mother got married again in 1919, and then she had two boys and I went to school, to a trade school, to learn embroidery because that was very popular in those days after the revolution. Between 1919 and 1920, I don't remember exactly which year, the Poles took over our city and became the new government. So doing embroidering was a very popular thing because the fancy ladies liked to have embroidered underwear, embroidered handkerchiefs, and things like that. I learned that trade for two and a half years. I didn't finish because I started there in 1922 or 1923 and then my papers came to go to Canada. You needed three years actually to finish the trade. They took us in the school because we used to do the work for the ladies who wanted fancy things done. We were learning, and the school was getting paid for our work, so they made money to keep the school up. I learned that trade but it didn't do me any good.

Now the house we lived in was like an apartment block. It was different in Vilna, in the city. First, when I was small, we lived in a place which had three or four rooms; I can't remember. But the last one, after my mother remarried, we lived in a place where we had six rooms plus the kitchen. The kitchen was counted as a room there. It was a big apartment—two buildings—one in front on the street and one in the back. Between was a garden. We lived in the back one on the fourth floor; and eighty-two steps to go up! Bless her, my mother, she'll send me down to the store for salt. I'll come back with the salt; she forgot the pepper. I used to go about five to six times a day. But then I learned to go down on the banisters—to slide down all the way. But going up was marble steps: eighty-two steps to go up four floors. My grandmother meantime was dead by then. She passed away in 1919 when mother was remarried. We had typhoid fever, I forgot to tell you. I was sick with typhoid fever that time. Anyways she passed away, and my grandfather was with us.

My grandfather was doing everything—no trade, whose got a trade? He would dabble in horses. He would buy and sell, and he would go to the market and buy something and sell—just like that. He had no trade. My father had a trade. He used to make mattresses. He had a factory. But my grandfather, I don't remember him ever having a trade.

We were just two kids—myself and my sister—and then my mother and stepfather had two boys. Where we lived was in a big apartment block. We had already water. We had a bathtub and a shower. As a matter of fact, we even had a wedding of my stepfather's cousin. We had about 120 people in the house and we were dancing and having a good time.

I first went to a school I remember before the Germans came in. We had to burn all our Russian things and Russian books and that was when I was about six or seven years old in 1914. We had to throw all the books in the stoves there. Then I went to a Jewish school, to a real gymnasium—what they called it in Vilna.

In Vilna, was already advanced. These snaps [*looking at photos*] are either very old or from the villages and small towns. These are pictures of people who used to sweep the streets with this kind of broom.

Now, Vilna is in Lithuania. Actually it was supposed to be in Lithuania *before* I was born even, but when I was born it came under Tsar Nikolai.[2] In Vilna there was a university and it had nice buildings and homes.

One day in 1925 my mother came and asked me if I would like to go to America [Canada]. I said yes! Just like that. Then all of a sudden I got the papers and I came to Canada on 16 April 1925.

I went from Vilna to Warsaw. My mother went as far as Warsaw with me by train. Then she put me—there was a family that was going to Canada, a woman with five children, the oldest was my age, the youngest she was breast-feeding. She was going to her husband in Montreal, So my mother asked her if she would keep an eye on me. And she had another girl from Warsaw going to Canada, so she kept her eye on that one too. We went from Warsaw to Danzig,[3] which was the border, and the Canadian consulate was there. You had to go through all this washing and cleaning and what not. We had to go through all sorts of baths and delousing and cleaning and we had all sorts of things going on. Finally, I came to the consulate and he asked me what language I speak and I told him what I spoke. The interpreter was sitting there because it was a big immigration in those days; an awful lot of people were coming, a lot of peasant girls going to the Prairies. Anyway, he asked me and I told him I could speak Russian. So he spoke to me in Russian and then he says to me, How come you speak Russian so well? So I told him. I said, When I was a child I had a nanny who was Russian and I spoke only Russian. Fine. Anyways, he put the stamp on my passport and that was it.

From Danzig, we went to Southampton by boat. Everything was by boat in those days. We went by boat to Southampton and then the same thing happens: we have to go through doctors and all sorts of things. From Danzig to Southampton we went on a cattle boat and everybody was sick. But the other girl I told you about—the one travelling with her mother, her name was Rose too—and the two of us were the only ones on the deck. We couldn't stay below because it was impossible, so we went out on deck. We didn't have our own rooms on the boat, we were with others. We had cabins but so many in the cabin and you had to share it. I don't remember who I shared it with but her mother, the poor woman, was sick and the children were sick. It was rough. Three days on the boat and it was very rough. So we walked out on deck. I said to her, Rose I can't take it down below. Let's go up on deck. We went up on deck and on deck was the kitchen and a Polish fellow was sitting and peeling potatoes. And we couldn't walk on the deck because the boat was going up and down. And then I looked out on the horizon and there was a boat going too. And then you know she went up and she went right down like this and I let out a scream. So the man peeling the potatoes says What are you screaming … what's the matter? I says, I think the boat went down. I showed him there, there's a boat there! And I spoke Polish. I said, There's a boat and I think it went down! Oh! He started to laugh. He said, If you would have been on that boat and looked at ours you would think the same thing. I turned to Rose and I said, Let's go downstairs. The cook told us to take a lemon and chew on it so we wouldn't feel sick.

The boat was a cattle boat, a freighter. It was hauling cattle or something. I don't know what it was hauling but they called it a cattle boat. The food was potatoes and herring and that's all. We finally came to Southampton. From Southampton to Hull, Quebec, we were on a big boat. It was an American boat. And the sailors were Norwegian: a lot of Norwegian boys. And there were a lot of Jewish immigrants and it was very nice. We had music. We used to dance. First couple of days everybody was sick and crying and one was screaming, What did I need this for? In Jewish [Yiddish], they were cursing their husbands and their brothers, who had sent them tickets. Well, the next few days were all right. I think we must have been from England to Hull—it must have been ten or eleven days, I don't remember. But it was quite nice. I really didn't want to get off the boat because I had a wonderful time. And of course, one of the Norwegian boys was after me— a sailor was after me. And, anyway, he wanted to marry me and take me to Norway … and all that business. I'll never forget that. Rose and I, we used to laugh.

The Jewish Immigration was there at the docks and they put us on a train and we went to Montreal. Oh. But before that I was stopped at Hull. Everybody went through and one of the nurses there told me to wait here. I see everybody is going and I'm sitting there. I didn't know and I didn't speak a word of English and I didn't know what to do. Then she said the doctor wants to see me. I said to myself: I went through all the doctors I think in Europe. As a matter of fact I even went to a doctor before I left home. They had told me I had to have a doctor's certificate to say that I'm all right. Anyways, they thought I had a goiter. So they took me in and a couple of doctors there on the pier, somewhere, examined me and told me I could go.

I came to Montreal and there was the Jewish Immigration Committee, because I was all of seventeen years old, of course. In Montreal I arrived in the morning and they took me into a Jewish home and I had to wait until the evening when the train would leave for Vancouver, So, of course, the first thing they gave me was food, you know. It was Pesach time so I had matza. So I stayed there. They put me upstairs to lie down and have a rest. I didn't need to rest but I didn't know them. And then I felt funny already. Then I was sorry I had started the whole thing. I said to myself: What am I doing here? Where am I going? What for, what did I do that for? In the evening they put me on the train and seeing it was Passover she gave me matza with sardines on the train to eat. I got on the train. The Jewish woman told the conductor to keep an eye on me. She put me there where the conductor sits. The bench was a hard wooden bench. And I had a little pillow with me. Mother gave me a little pillow and a little blanket just in case I needed it.

I was sitting there and I had a piece of some kind of embroidery and I was looking through the window, of course. And I was sitting like this, and it took I think six days from Montreal with the train. As I was sitting there and the conductor tried to talk to me, a fellow comes up and sits across from me and starts talking to me in English. So one thing I knew: No speak English. When I said "No speak English," he kind of got suspicious that I'm afraid to talk to him. Where am I going?—he started motioning—so I told him: Vancouver. I didn't even know where Vancouver was. So he is going to Vancouver too and he talks and talks and I smile and I don't understand a word he is saying to me. Anyway, he walked away. I said sorry—I didn't even say sorry because I didn't know how. I wanted to ask him if he speaks any other language—Russian, German—he doesn't speak. He only speaks English. Few minutes later, about five to ten minutes later, there's a woman comes and she sits across from me and she starts speaking to me and I say, No speak English. She says to me in German: *Verstehen Deutsch*? I say, *Ja*. She starts speaking a little bit German. So I understood what she said. So I tell her I don't speak English, I just come from Europe. She said that the fellow sitting there asked me to go because he thought you don't want to talk to him!

On the train there were peasant girls going to Winnipeg, Saskatchewan, here, there. They are sitting and eating bread and salami and I'm looking at them—you know how you sit across on the train—and I am eating matza and sardines. In Winnipeg a Jewish boy comes up, one of the vendors who sell sandwiches and things, and he starts talking to me and he realized I was an immigrant and he talks to me in Jewish. He asked, You speak Jewish?

And I said yes! He says, I'm a Jewish boy too—not a good Jew—so he takes out a piece of sponge cake and he gives me: Here my mama gave me sponge cake. You have a piece too.

And I am looking out the windows: the snow and the mountains and the rivers and the way the train was going, I wasn't used to it. Anyways, I came to Vancouver on 16 April 1925. Kappy [*Rose's cousin and future husband*] was here already, since 1918. I didn't go to work for the Rothsteins. That was something they had to put down on my papers because in those days you needed to say you were going to work. Kaplan made papers for me so I didn't have to go to work.[4] He had a room for me right away. As a matter of fact, when he left home I was only six years old and he remembered me when I was six, so he thought he would need a nurse or someone to look after me! He did. He did! Because he didn't recognize me when I came off the train. I was standing there with my *rosinkas*, what you would call it—and he came with Mr. Katznelson and Mr. Katznelson walked by and said: I think that's her. And Ben said, No. Because he was looking for a little girl. Finally they came back because there was nobody left at the station and they realized it was me.

They took me to my room; Kappy was staying at the Katznelsons. I never went to work, as Ben said I didn't need to. I used to go hiking and climbing in the mountains. He never let me work; never did.

I arrived in April and we got married in September, had the three kids. And that was that.

Rose Gordon

Rose Gordon is the mother of Dave Barrett, NDP premier of British Columbia between 1972 and 1975. She was born in Koznitze, a shtetl, or Jewish village, near Odessa in the Ukraine. Rose was living in Vancouver at the time of our interview, and was a member of some of the same organizations that I belonged to.

I WAS BORN IN 1906 in a small village with very few Jewish people, maybe half a dozen families, right there by the water. My father's father and mother lived there. My father was born there but my mother was born in a big city. There was a cousin of my father's and my father's family and sisters. My father had about four, five, or six sisters. I remember every family in the village. My father worked in a mill. The name of the village was Koznitze, near Odessa somewhere in the Ukraine—it was on the border of Bessarabia.[5] We had a Jewish butcher—I don't know how in the heck he made a living—a small shop that sold things like *kasha* and such stuff—they used to bring it in from Odessa to our village; and the few families used to buy that. We didn't have a synagogue and therefore not much activities because it was a small village and a small Jewish population.

One of my first memories is when I used to visit my mother's mother. She lived in a big city and when I went there I used to live in the water. I loved the water. We were right on the Dneister [River], where I used to swim. As a matter of fact I played hooky one time to go swimming. I got a licking for that and never did it again. But, anyway, I used to go visit my grandmother, my baba, and once when I was swimming in a small water hole there I got an infection. I still have the mark. What cured it was a leaf my baba used to dissolve the poison—that is what they claimed in those days. Who had a doctor? Who had even seen a doctor? My mother never had a doctor for her children. The lady next door—if she made it in time, all right; and if not, my mother did it herself!

She had a miscarriage once. You know that Jewish people are not supposed to drive on Saturdays and Jewish holidays, but the rabbi told us that if you are sick, very sick, then you are allowed to because it's for your health. So we took a wagon (it was a sleigh because it was winter) and we put mother on it and my oldest brother and my dad took her down to a *felse*—there is no doctor. *Felse* here would mean like an intern, somebody who is learning. He hangs around a drugstore, apothecary is a drugstore, and the odd person who comes down to him—that's how he is learning. But I think he knew quite a bit because he sure did an awful lot for my mother.

But my mother would have a baby in the morning and at night time she cooked and she baked and she did everything. When my brother was born, he was the first son in the family. In Jewish families a son is very important. And when she had my brother (he is now in Los Angeles), a week before he was born she had the house spotless clean. She baked bread and buns and then the day after she was back cooking our meals. My mother never stayed in bed for nothing. It was a different world. The air was better, healthier. There was no pollution. If you didn't have something, you managed.

We had a garden, apples, pears, plums, strawberries, and also lettuce and great big tomatoes—you call them here beefsteak. The streets were not finished, not paved. We had neighbours all around us, Gentile people. We had big properties, lots of room. We could build yet some homes but it was the style then to live the way we did. Don't forget that I come from a very small village. Now my grandmother in the city had more rooms, but they didn't have lots of property with fruits and vegetables. My grandfather was a carpenter and he had beautiful hardwood floors. I had never seen such floors until I visited my grandparents.

My mother baked forty pounds of bread at a time and no one worried about getting fat by eating too much bread. We were lucky to have something to eat. We were healthy, believe me.

I used to walk two miles to a Russian school and two miles back. Then after school I went to *kheder* to learn to read and write Yiddish. Then by the time I come home, the day is over. It's time to go to bed. It's not like here where you take a shower, where you have a tap and a bathroom and everything. There the bathroom is outside and there's no shower. You have a tub and you warm up the water on the clay oven. You sit in the tub and you take your bath. When we were small we had to take baths together but when we got a little bit bigger we couldn't do that. We had to take turns. Then for Passover my mother had to clean the house, all the way through: the walls, the floors. We only had one room: kitchen, sleeping, everything was in one room. From that room there was a little other room where you kept your barrels of water because we had no water in the house. You had to go down a few blocks to get the water and carry it on a wooden pole, like that. Where did you get that picture? [*Rose points to a picture I have of a man carrying water.*] It brings back memories for me. Yeah. Yeah. That's the way we carried the water. You see, every day we used to bring water like that. But when Passover came, I don't know why, but my mother had a special barrel. It was used for nothing else but for water especially for Passover. And she used to fill up that barrel every second day because if you went with those pails and maybe somebody else is there with bread or something—you had to watch it.[6]

Our house was spotless clean. Nobody had any bugs or anything because you see my mother used to have a tub—the same one we used to take a bath in—and she used to soak the clothes in there and wash it out real good and then go down to the water and wash it again and hit it on the stones and bring it back and lay it on the grass to dry it, because it was clean, the grass was clean. We didn't have a line—didn't know what a line meant. Inside the house my mother used to have a special stuff that she used—not paint—but it's like whitewash—on the walls and the floor. We had a sort of attic where my mother kept the Passover dishes. Before Passover she used to put ten chickens in this attic and feed them and make them good and fat so there will be lots of chicken fat for Passover because you need a lot of fat. And kosher! The biggest rabbi could eat in our house! We could never do anything wrong. Before the Passover holiday my mother used to take everything off from the windows. Wash the windows clean. We had to turn our pockets inside out to see if there was any bread. My mother used to make her own preserves, her own jams. It was lots of work there. But here it is nothing.

We were three sisters and two brothers and we lived far away from a synagogue, but my whole family used to walk down to the synagogue on Saturdays and Yom Kippur and Rosh Hashanah. We used to go down and stay with my grandparents. For Yom Kippur my mother used to bring all the food along for us kids only, as the adults were not allowed to eat on that day.

My father was a foreman in the mill. It was a flour mill, and they used to bring the wheat to the mill where there was a great big wheel that used to carry the water and run the mill. We had very, very good connections with the Gentile people. They were Ukrainian people. My dad was always good to them and they were always good to us. As a matter of fact, when the revolution broke out there was lots of times when we had nothing to eat but the Ukrainian people sure paid us back: they were very good to my Dad and us kids. I went to school with them every day all of my life. I also went to Jewish school where my uncle used to teach me; but that was only once or twice a week.

The revolution broke out and they started to kill us; started to kill the Jewish people. But my dad was so close with all the people there that they did everything to save us. They dug a hole—just like a grave—and we were there for two weeks. And for two weeks they bring us food every day. They put boards over the hole and covered that with straw, so if others come, they wouldn't know we were there. This was in 1919, 1920. We were all small kids but everybody knew they had to keep their mouth shut—and it was for two weeks! We used to go out at nighttime and they used to bring us the food and also to sleep wherever we could find a place. We couldn't go back to the house because they would have killed us had we gone back there. That was during the time of [Symon] Petliura and all those bandits.[7] I remember one day standing—we had all kinds of people who went after the Jews—but this Petliura was really something. He—I mean not he but his gangsters—they came in, I was standing with a bunch of kids with whom I used to go to school. None of them was Jewish. And those guys come along with long knives and they asked: Is there any Jews in this neighbourhood? And everybody said: No. No. And I was standing right there and they said there were no Jews here. Then after, when the bandits went away, one kid said to the other, We should have told them that Rose is Jewish. And one guy who was standing there slapped him right across the face and said: What do you mean? Rose is one of us. She is all right!

You see, my dear, it wasn't the ordinary person. The ordinary person had nothing to do with it. The ordinary person tried to help you. But then it got to a point when we had to leave home and we were very fortunate because our place in Bessarabia was just like Vancouver and North Vancouver with the water in between; and the local people, our good friends, they took a little canoe with paddles and sent us over to the other side with a few little things which we could take with us.

We went over and we went from Talmud Torah[8] to Talmud Torah to sleep. They fed us there, all the Jewish people tried to feed us—we were the whole family. Then we came to a place, they call it Kapresht, in Bessarabia. It's a small little town and it was there that I went to learn how to be a seamstress—which I never finished but I went to learn that. My dad tried to do what he could. He helped everybody so he could make a living for us all.

At the time we had nobody in the US or in Canada, nobody nowheres. The only one we had was a brother in Israel. He had gone to Israel in 1920 and so we didn't have him with us. We remained in there and did all we could to get by to have something to eat. And then it started—the talk about going to America. You see, we didn't know about Canada. To us it was America.

[*Rose shows me a picture of people standing in line for bread.*] That's what I did too. I stood in line for bread in Romania after we left home because there were too many refugees all over the place and they couldn't take care of so many people. We weren't the only ones. We were at the border, right by the Dneister, and it was not such a hard time to go across but we had a hard time to get food. We were almost the first ones to cross being so close to the water, so we were trying to go to bakeries to get a bread or something, because we were all small children. I'm the oldest of the whole bunch—there was five of us—I wasn't even seventeen. I was eighteen when I came to Canada and we were there four years. I would say I was about fifteen and I'm the oldest except for my brother who went to Israel.

We did housework, took care of children, we did anything we could to have enough to eat. Then we managed to get to Bucharest and there there was a place—you would call it here, an army place—[*Barracks? I suggest.*] Yes, and we were all there, hundreds of us slept in one room. And it was like: here you put up an extra table with a board right across—and that's where you slept—hundreds in one room. Outside there was a stove, the old-fashioned stove that you used to put wood and coal—and there were so many people and nobody had a chance to get near the stove. Sometimes they used to argue about who is next, and who is what, and—excuse my expression— the bedbugs ate you up because there were so many and very little room for laundry. If you were lucky, some bakeries used to come down with a load of bread and *throw* it at you and if you were lucky you grabbed and maybe you had one. If you didn't, you didn't. I remember standing in line for bread and I passed out and I never got my turn.

Then the Hebrew Immigration Aid Society [HIAS] asked the people if they had somebody in the United States (meaning also Canada). Well, we didn't have nobody nowheres. If people had somebody in Canada then HIAS would try to find your relations.

They found out if you had relatives, if you knew the city in America or you had a name—but people changed their names. They had long names and the Immigration changed it. But HIAS was able to find people who sent *siskarten* and if you were lucky, and the American or Canadian family was rich, they would bring you over. We had nobody at all so we were fighting our own way.

In 1922–23 they tried to get organized and get all the people together who had nobody in the US or Canada and by 1924 there were 350 of us, in the first bunch, that got together to come to America [Canada]. They took us in a little boat from Bucharest—it was a cattle boat. The 350 of us had nothing except what was on our body—nothing else: no food, no clothes, nothing. And they give us an interpreter who spoke seventeen languages and we took that boat from Bucharest to Constantinople. It was the most horrible thing you have ever seen in your life, the cattle boat! There was no place to lie down. You were sick. It stunk. Your clothes were filthy. You were … Anyway, when we did get to Constantinople, what we did have on us they threw it in the machine to get it disinfected. And when they brought it back to us … it was worse than before.

Then they took us in a French boat to Marseilles and that was heaven because it was a real nice boat. We were in third class but it was very good and we met some Jewish people who worked in the first class in the kitchen and they used to swipe an orange or a lemon or something, to bring to us; and it was a treat.

In Marseilles they put us in a Canadian boat and it was the filthiest, the *filthiest* boat you had ever seen in your life! It was just the most horrible thing and I am thinking how can Canada have anything so filthy? The interpreter made us go on strike three or four times on this dirty boat: to not eat the food. But everybody was hungry and they were laying around all over, sick, sea sick, even myself. We were so sick! You had nothing to change into and you smelled a mile away. You couldn't help it. It's not because you wanted to. This was the condition. We got up from the table many times. We were on this boat for a whole month. This boat took us finally to Halifax.

When we got to Halifax, the Jewish organizations met us. I don't know about other people but my family didn't have one cent to our name, just what we had on us. My dad and mother worked. How are we going to live? What are the children going to eat? What is going to happen?

The Jewish organization met us and put us on a train. They brought us sandwiches, they brought us something to drink and they gave us some fruit. They gave us some *gum*. We start to chew. We thought we were going to die because we couldn't swallow it! You know, we were not used to this in the country.

From Halifax to Vancouver—each stop they made, so many Jewish people got off. We were the last ones and the only family to get off in Vancouver.

Everybody was scattered all across the land and we were the last family to get off here. And there was a very famous man, very wonderful guy, Rabbi Pastinski, who met us at Great Northern Railway station on Main Street and he took us to 700 block on Keefer Street, where he had rented a house for us. There was no furniture, nothing in the house; but the Jewish people in Vancouver, the community used to stick together then and whatever they had they divided: this one brought a table, this one a bed, etc. And it was just before Passover. My mother was very kosher, so they bring three kinds of dishes: for milk, for meat, and dishes for Passover. Everybody brought something and we got organized. The Jewish community—all those people—were very good to us. They couldn't have been better.

No language. My father couldn't speak. None of us could. My father had no trade. They tried to teach him to go with a horse and buggy. He tried but it didn't work out. Then my mother was a marvellous cook; so she took in roomers and boarders—mostly boarders for food to eat. Then I went to work for seven dollars a week. I was learning how to be a seamstress—I never graduated from that because I couldn't speak the language.

My mother came here with tuberculosis, which she had from the time we left the Old Country. She wasn't a pushy kind of person and if she got anything she gave it to the children. She didn't eat but she gave it to us. And when we got to this country she died. She was sick for two years in a TB hospital. Then my dad took it very badly because they were very close. After my mother died he was in a sanitarium for five years—just the time when the children got on their feet a little bit and we could have given them some pleasure. Anyways, my parents went a long time ago.

I would just like to say to you: being an immigrant and having a son become the premier of British Columbia is pretty damn good!

Haskell (Harry) Ullman

Haskell (Harry) Ullman was born in Dagda, Latvia, in 1898. Harry and his wife left from Staraya Russa, a resort near Novgorod, and immigrated to Winnipeg, Manitoba. In later life, he and his wife moved to Vancouver, where their two children resided.

Harry was an avid stamp collector and had some rare stamps in his collection. I was invited into their home for this interview, and we talked at the kitchen table. His wife Nina hovered around, pinching dead leaves from house plants, doing little things, keeping an ear open to Harry's story ... and sometimes interjecting! Harry died in 1986.

AT THE TIME OF THE Russo–Japanese War in 1904–5, when I was seven years old, I remember I used to go to the market and see huge displays of pictures and illustrations about the war. I remember it as vividly as sitting here talking to you. In October of that year the Tsar gave forty-eight hours' liberty to all. That was my earliest memory.

We were poor like a church mouse. Absolutely nothing to eat whatsoever. We lived in a small one-room house or cottage, as you would call it, in Dagda, Latvia, where I was born. There were eight of us. Two had died when they were small. I had a brother who was tall, almost six feet (I can show you his picture), and he was a revolutionary. Mind you, I have to make it clear. When I say revolutionary, in those days it had a different meaning. Today revolutionary to me is a bastard. (Maybe I shouldn't say that!) But in those days it was most necessary to be involved in the revolution.

When I was nine years old I went to learn—in those days until the end, Jews tried to be a tailor; and in those days when you have nothing to pay to teach you, so we went to the farms—not to learn to farm but to learn from an older tailor. I went to learn the trade from an older man. In those days we used to work for nothing for three years: to learn and also to do house work and other things.

[*Nina interjects: You see, the tailors used to take young people into the trade. So whenever they went to a farm and they got work, they settled down. In the meantime they got a little experience. You see, they were practically like slaves, working for nothing.*]

The small towns and villages did not have enough work to keep a tailor busy. So he carried his sewing machine on his shoulders and went from farm to farm. If there was work for him to do, the tailor would stop at the farm from one week to three weeks, depending on the size of the family. Farmers had material that was made on the farm. It was very seldom that they bought material in the cities. And so these young boys, starting around eight years old, helped the tailor, doing all kinds of work. It was a blessing for a mother who didn't have to feed the boy all week long. In between doing chores, he learned the trade; and this took anywhere from two to three years. In those days, you made a contract—not in writing but verbally—and that was it.

I didn't do any housework and chores as we were a little bit more progressive already and we used to come home Fridays and go back on the road again Mondays.

I had two older brothers in the US—one in New York and another later in Philadelphia. The one in New York wrote to us saying that if we could raise sixty rubles he would send us a *shiftcarten,* a ticket for the journey. They bought *shiftcarten* on credit. In those days to make sixty rubles—you might as well tell us to jump to the sky and get something!

To go back to the man with whom we made a contract to teach me how to sew. My older brother in Dagda, who was a good tailor already by now, says to me: Haskell, we'll rent a sewing machine, a hand sewing machine (if you remember those machines), and we'll go to the farms and we must save up this sixty rubles and then I'll go and then I'll send for you. That was the way it was then with the Jewish people.

But I gave my word to the tailor, and so I went to him and told him what my brother wanted to do. The man, who was a nice man—he lives today with his daughter in Winnipeg—said, All right, your contract can be broken. Go with your brother, Joseph. And I did. And we went. We had an auntie who had a sewing machine and we paid her a ruble a week rent for the machine. My brother used to carry the sewing machine and I used to carry all the things: the parts, the scissors, cotton, iron—the old irons with coals.

It was eighteen to twenty pounds which we carried on our backs! Friday we used to come home and Monday back on the road. And we did this half a summer and a whole winter.

On the farm the farmers fed us. We still ate kosher, we didn't eat meat. We had our own spoons, plates and other things which we carried on our backs. There was bread or bagel, butter, milk, tea. That was enough. And we saved up the sixty rubles! And in 1913 we sent Joseph off to America.

It took him almost a year. He had trouble along the way. It wasn't like travelling today. We lived in a small town, about seventy-five miles away from Dvinsk in Latvia. Dvinsk was a big town and there was an official, an agent with whom you could make a deal, that for so much and that much he would take you across the border. You didn't need a passport because a passport to go outside Russia used to cost twenty-five rubles. So there was no way we could get one. There was further trouble along the way: his luggage was lost; he was sent over to Germany (it was in those days different in Germany than like now), where he stayed for a few months until, finally, he made his way to Philadelphia.

In October 1916, my class was mobilized. I was eighteen years old and I had to join the Tsar's army. What I did to not go into the army! I tried everything. I had a brother, younger by two years. I went to see a man who had a small office who gave out birth certificates and passports and so on. There was a lot of corruption there then, naturally. I remember we paid him forty rubles, by then it wasn't quite the value as a few years before, but it sure was a lot of money. We paid this man the forty rubles and he gave me a passport in my name but with my younger brother's age. So I didn't have to go into the army but I had to leave town. In a small town everyone knew you; and the fact is that we had a big boy in our town who was an informer and when he saw you on the streets he would say, You must be eighteen or nineteen years old. You have to go to the army! Yes, he was Jewish also. And unfortunately, this was the way. So when I got my passport the man said you must leave this place.

I had the money to travel with but where could I go? I had never stepped out of the small town except in Dvinsk I was once. So I hired a man with a horse and buggy who used to come from fifty miles away to our village. We had no trains. There was a train—from one side it was about twenty-seven miles and there was the Front—it was already there—and the other way it was fifteen miles to another train station. So, I don't remember how much I paid him, and he took me the fifteen miles to the railroad station in a not very big town called Shaybish. There my future wife, Nina, had relatives, so

I went there and stayed—I don't remember—three or four days. I told them who I was and what I'm doing in those days, in 1914 when the war started.

By 1916, the war [World War I] was going no good for the Russians; they were being killed by the Germans by the thousands. A cousin of mine got his left arm shot off in the first weeks of the war. You see, they used to make the slugs for the rifles, and these slugs when it hit you it used to explode. It used to explode so that his bones were running piece by piece. His bones were shattered. He was kept in the hospital close to a year. Then when my cousin came home we saw what had happened to him.

The war was bad right from the beginning and nobody knew what to do. All the Jews were spies. They must let the Germans know and that is why the war was no good for them, for the Jews. So they came, the Russians, it was a Jewish holiday and everybody was in the synagogue. They took all the Jewish people to the railroad station and put them into cattle trains and sent away deep into Russia.[9] In those days, Jews were not permitted to live in the cities and big towns without a permit.[10]

So I was in Shaybish for three or four days even though the Jews were not permitted to live in the big towns, but because of the war people freely moved around. Let me tell you, those Jews didn't have to go to America where gold is like mud in the street. Gold was there in the city. But we didn't know. Nobody knew.

When I came to this town there were people there, refugees some of them. I don't remember, but my wife's aunt lived there with a large family, boys and girls. It was a full house. They asked me questions, like what are you doing here? I tell them that I came here, I have no place to go, I don't know anyone. Maybe someone knows an address or name to help me. So finally, I cannot remember how, but I was brought a piece of paper with a name and address in Orenburg, in the Urals. Do you know your geography? It is six hundred miles from Moscow and it was damn cold there, damn cold! I went to that town of Orenburg and to the address they gave me. An elderly woman lived there—a nice-looking woman—with two beautiful girls, grown-up girls, and one boy.

I come in and we start talking. I tell them where I am from and how I came to them. And the woman, her name was Sorah, says to me: You sleep here in the kitchen (on a bench, a small bench) and tomorrow my boy will go with you to the Jewish Refugee Bureau. The next day he took me there, right in the centre of the town—it is a capital city—and they start asking me questions—have you got money? I said, So far I have enough for a week, maybe two weeks. What do you do? I said, I'm a tailor. I'm looking for a job.

So they sent me a few streets further to a refugee tailor, one from Vitebsk—this is Vitebsk, a capital city.[11] And I start to work. It was now late October, probably November and I worked until February 1917 and then the revolution came—the February Revolution came.

When the revolution came, of course, then naturally, everything was free—meaning free of state restrictions—and everybody could talk and do whatever they wanted. It was nice—the nicest feeling I have ever felt in my life—but then I was actually nineteen years old—but still my passport said two years younger. Then when the Freiheit Svoboda—that means "freedom"—came [in 1917], I had a comrade from a small town ... he was also from a small town but he worked in my home town and we were comrades. And somehow fate had something to do with this. My comrade went to Krakow and wrote me a letter to come there. I had been working all this time so I bought a train ticket and I went to Krakow. The weather was like California, not like in Orenberg where it was so terribly cold.

Krakow is a bigger town and there are thousands of Jewish refugees there and I felt it to be a nice town. It wasn't cold. I went to see my comrade where he worked. He had a room in his boss's house, where he worked. He took me in his room and his boss took me to his shop and gave me a job. And we worked and we lived. It was fine. This was the end of the summer in 1917 and Alexander Kerensky was appointed provisional governor.[12] And then they start again: the call to the army. Well! So we had to repeat the Tsar's business!

My comrade was older than me, not much older but a year is enough. You are cooked! [*Harry laughs.*] Then we come across another trouble. A band of Jewish boys—not an organized one—used to go around at night and when they met other young boys, they would start to ask for money or they give you a good licking. In the end they gave you a good licking and they used to take away your passport. You see, they knew if you were a young man and not in the army then you must have a good passport and this was worth millions—never mind millions—it was worth all the money in the world. Why? Because the army would take you away and you were *gone!*

Well, my comrade went away. They took him away. He couldn't wiggle out and I was left alone. I hated fighting and I hate the business of fighting, even today, and I was running like from hell. So from Krakow, again, where could I go? From our small town where I come from, there was a girl, a friend, who lived on the other side of the house with two tenants. We knew them. And I knew she lived in Kubishov (they renamed it Samara after the revolution), close to Siberia. And I came there and went to see her.

She lived in two rooms with two kids and two girlfriends. And again begins the same story. I stay here, I look for a job. There were no shops anymore. I mean the big shops were out of business. There was a shortage of everything, especially cloth. I remember distinctly that it was wintertime and there was nothing. I couldn't find any work. One time I found a big shop and I went in. Do you need a tailor? I asked. The man says, What can you do? I told him.

You see, in the big shops in big towns, it wasn't like in small towns in small shops where you make a complete garment. In a big shop there was sections. Here in Canada we have sections too but entirely different. When you made a topcoat you don't make a jacket. When you made a jacket you don't make the pants. When you made the pants you don't make a vest. In other words, every craft was a separate thing. But I could do everything. And this they never heard of, that a man could do the whole thing. That was something. I remember he put me to work. The boss himself was not a tailor. He was a cutter and the main manager.

Now in our little town, back in Dagda, we were bad tailors. We weren't good tailors. We used to work with cotton material. We were afraid to touch a good piece of cloth. The boss here gave me some cotton from which to make a pair of pants and I made it the way I used to in the old town. He examined it to see the way I had done it. Remember, everything had to be made by hand. He looked at it and threw me out! He didn't like the way I had made it. This was not a Jewish shop. The factory boss was a convert from Jewish to Gentile. There were a lot of such people.

And again, what shall I do? I don't have a job. But I have a little money. People used to go from house to house asking for work. I came to a house. I went in there. The man says, What can you do? I said, Everything. He gave me an overcoat lined with fur and that's another story. There are so many stories … I can keep you here for days and nights!

I believe you interviewed Max Dolgoy [*Harry's future brother-in-law*]. He was my comrade, and in small towns a comrade is sometimes better than a brother. Now it is a different world. Max had an older sister [*now married in California*]. There was a boy who liked this sister and when she left to go to Canada, this guy went crazy. So he says to me, Come over, come over. I already knew Max and so I went over. [*Harry starts to laugh and can hardly stop.*] And so I noticed this *tsatskle* (a toy, sometimes a little cookie). I noticed Nina. And that is when the trouble started! No. No. We fell in love and all that! We got married. We have two girls already by now. And then I had to leave town again and Nina left town after me; she went also to Staraya Russa.

It's a big story how I came to Canada. We could correspond with the people in Canada. So once came a letter that they will send us papers to come to Canada and we should try—it took us a year—this was the end of 1928. The trouble started with me personally. The situation was like this. First, I knew distinctly that they wouldn't let me out. Second, I was a well-known revolutionary there. I knew the Tsar and I knew the life of the Jewish people under the Tsar. And I had a taste of the bloody communists there. The life we lived there was so miserable that I would do anything—especially when you are so desperate your mind becomes nothing; your heart is taking over. And I had a family. I had my two girls already. So what should I do? If I start and they don't let me out—I'm also cooked. And that's no good.

I had another comrade and I knew where he lived. And we had the discussion whether we should start to leave or not? If they don't let you out—you don't envy that person. And there was nobody to ask because if you did they would think you were a traitor. Finally, I decided I would go. I sent them a letter to Moscow, to the Russian-Canadian-American passenger company. And they sent me the information, the bible on what I should do; everything. I did everything, word by word, they told me about. The case was sent away.

Now our town, Staraya Russa, was a resort town, and the people used to come from all over Russia. A girl rented a room upstairs from where we lived. And I lived downstairs. And you send away the case, your application, and then you wait. Now the *shiftcarten* from Canada was only good for a year. The time had passed and they sent us another paper, they extended it. Then, oh yes … Nina had a cousin who was in the [Communist] Party and I asked him, You don't have to do nothing but can you find out where my application is? You see, sometimes, they put your file under the cloth that is covering their office desks and so it gets forgotten. But he couldn't tell me anything. How could he?

And then, this same cousin was going to Moscow to the university to learn. I received a postcard from him that I should go to my capital city, to the commissioner, where the case is. I went there and I talked to them. They gave me some applications to fill out. I filled this out and finally I received permission to leave Russia. We did everything that we could—like if you had five rings you could only take one. I had two watches, so I sold one. You could take one item apiece. We came to buy *shiftcarten* in Moscow. They looked at me like I was crazy. Who comes to buy a *shiftcarten* in Moscow? So then again I was scared to death. It was unusual. These *shiftscarten* were a thousand rubles a card and one card for the two girls, that's three thousand rubles. I had exactly three thousand rubles, exactly. If I knew now what I knew then, I would be … nevermind! I bought it and they give me the *shift-carten*, three, and they sent us away to England. We stayed there ten days and then the boat to Halifax.

Muriel Grad

Muriel Grad was born in Kovno (now Kaunas), Lithuania. She was married in 1921, and followed her husband to Vancouver, arriving on 26 March 1927.

I had known Muriel Grad for a long time when we got together for this interview. She came over one September afternoon in 1974 and, over tea and cookies, we talked. She died in 1982.

I WAS BORN IN KOVNO in 1900. My mother was a dressmaker, a dressmaker what is making trousseaux for brides; and my father was a cabinetmaker, first class. So I start to work. My mother wants me to learn how to work to do sewing. I start to learn when I was ten years old. We were five children in the family. We were three girls and two boys. Before the First War, I was twelve years old, and I was already a good sewer. I was working with my mother. She had six girls all the time working with her. When the war broke out, I was fourteen years old. We were driven out from our home by the Russians. The Russians thought the Jews would stick with the Germans and sell out the country; so they sent all the Jews out from Kovno and all the area around there.

We went to quite a few cities before we were settled. We finally came to Astrakhan.[13] And there we were four and a half years. We have left everything behind in Kovno. I was working there on everything: sewing, on boats, washing, cleaning the boats, fishing, packing the dry fish in the sacks. I did everything what I could. We were four and a half years there and my father says he wants to go back. So we went back and we came back home and we didn't find nothing. The Germans were there for a year with us and we were hungry. For a whole year we were starved—nothing, just one meal a day. And after, when the Germans went out from

23

Kovno, so the Lithuanians came and we find a little bit work there and we were all right.

When I was a child I didn't have time to play. I didn't go to school. I had a tutor and I didn't like him. So I didn't have schooling at all.

Kovno was the capital city of Lithuania. Lots of Jewish people lived there. We didn't have pogroms. We had very good neighbours. Polish neighbours. They liked us very much. Everything was okay and we lived a very nice life. But when we came back from Russia we didn't have nothing—everything we left behind, was nothing. My father had closed up the house with boards and when we come back after four and a half years—everything was open and everything was gone—everything.

I used to go and help my mother every day when we worked. We had three bedrooms, a kitchen, and a dining room. That's all. And you had a wood stove, no coal. We had water, running water. I used to wash in a tub and I used to take the washing to the—we lived not far from the river, the Neman—and I used to rinse there the clothes bring them back and put it in the attic to dry. It was more than a ten- to fifteen-minute walk and I used to carry the clothes on my shoulders—you know how the Chinese people do?—and this I did every week and I was washing everybody's clothes.

We had a well at the corner of our street from where I used to buy the water, five pails for a penny. And I used to carry this back, on my shoulders [*we look at a picture of a man carrying pails hanging from either end of a pole*], to the house which was two blocks away, where we had a barrel and I would fill it up. When I was washing the clothes, I had to have a lot of water. This was back in Belarus. I didn't do this every day. When I filled up the barrel it lasted a couple days. And we had water. I spoke Russian fluently and I had friends there and they liked me.

I was working hard all those years since ten years old. My mother had some girls working there. My mother used to go to the house of the ladies to get the material—the ladies they didn't trust her; maybe she'll take it off a little piece or something for herself. She used to go away for hours. And I used to be home and I was young. I was just ten years old. I wanted to go and play. But this German girl my mother had used to run after me. After meals she hit me, she said, you have to learn, your mother told you to sit down and do things, by hand, on the machine. Oh yeah. My mother used to make nightgowns for trousseaux. So you have to make buttons—buttons from here up to the shoulder—and for men she used to make dress shirts that had fifteen buttons. And on the cuffs on the side, on the front, and you had to make one in here to keep the underwear; and buttons here for a collar to button—fifteen buttonholes and every buttonhole had to be just so. We had one sewing room and a table and everybody sits around.

When the Jews were driven out from Kovno in 1914, some were left in different towns along the way. Right from the beginning we stopped in Rovna.[14] There they put us in boxcars like cattle. There were so many you couldn't even move. And they locked us up and didn't even let us out—not until we came on the station. Then they opened the door and we went and we got hot water to make some tea or something. Some people in the town they brought us something to eat, to greet us. They brought some bread and butter and something else. They were very good to us. They knew we were passing through.

This took many, many hours. By the time we came to Rovna, which was our first stop, where we got off for a couple of nights, and then they send us back on the boxcar to Poltava, in the Ukraine. Just too many people there.

We came to Poltava. We went into town. We did anything we wanted. We were not quarantined or anything. We were there six, seven months. We were all Jewish families that they bring together. Jewish people from Poland and some of them came there with disease, so they quarantined the whole lot, for miles and miles.

We were there six or seven months in Poltava. We came there and they put us in a barracks. In that time, in that year, was rats in there. Rats! I'm telling you they were so big! My mother used to sit there nights and watch they shouldn't bite the kids. My little brother was only two years old. I could speak Russian good so they find a job for me helping at a dentist office—and I worked there for quite a while. Six, seven months in there. I was fourteen and working as a receptionist. I didn't have to do nothing—just to tell the patients to sit down and tell the doctor, and I used to clean the instrument in the morning when I used to come in. They liked me. I did a good job.

After being in Poltava for six, seven months, the Russians asked if we wanted to go someplace else because my father didn't have very much to do there and then there was the rats. They said if you want to go, we'll send you to Astrakhan. And so that is how we came to be there. The journey was more than two or three days. We did a lot of travelling. No water. No nothing. At every stop we had to do it! We managed. I was very fast. When the train start to stop I was there right away. I was the first one to get something—water, or hot water, or anything. We didn't have to buy it. They gave it to us for nothing.

We were in Astrakhan for four and a half years. My father wanted to come back to Kovno. No, we didn't have to buy tickets. We just got on the train and started back. When we got to Smolensk we were six weeks staying in the train. We couldn't go anywhere. We slept and ate in the boxcar. And cooking—we were cooking outside something with wood. We went into the town. We had to find something to eat. The train is in the town, it is Smolensk, and so we went to the store to buy something. Every day was an exciting day … you are meeting so many people!

We went through the revolution. It was a terrible time to be there. You couldn't even go outside. We were living in our house. There was shooting from the windows upstairs. They were fighting: the Red Army and the White Army.[15] It was a bad time. But we managed. My father was very good friends with people there, one was a baker, he used to bake big breads and he used to give it to people to divide it for everybody, the neighbours. My brother was younger so he wasn't in the fighting, but he was working. He was managing there working with fish. In the city you need fish. There was a lot of movement going on at that time. Oh, my gosh!

So finally we came back to Kovno in 1919 and in a couple years I met my husband there. In Kovno we had roomers staying with us, and he used to come to visit the roomer and so we got acquainted. Well, we did the same things that young people like to do. We went to a movie. We pass the time, walking and talking like you do here, the same thing. We got married then and I had two children and I stayed with my mother.

We had a synagogue just across the street. My father and mother used to go for the holidays, for the Sabbath, but they were not strictly religious. My wedding was outside in front of the synagogue. I had a veil, I had a white dress, and there were a lot of people there, about twenty or thirty people, just friends. We did not go away after the wedding.

My husband when he came to Kovno was working making wine in a distillery. He knew how to do it. So that is what he was doing. And I was sewing with my mother. And my mother after she stopped sewing, she had a stall with dairy things. I used to come and help her.

Every day was market day. This is open markets—like open air. But hers was a stall inside a store and I used to help her out. And my sister at the time was at home and after we had a girl in the house, a washing girl. So I used to go and help my mother every day.

My husband came first to Canada. I came in 1927 with my two children. I was pregnant when he left and so my daughter was only two months and my son was five years old when we arrived here. On the way I went to Hamburg. I was in Hamburg to get on the boat and there was some mistake or something with my papers and I was two months waiting there with the two children. In Halifax, when we arrived, we had to go through immigration. I didn't have any trouble—just my eyes: the immigration officer he didn't like it. One eye was a little crossed because when I was young I had a fever; so he didn't like one eye crossed! But they let me go through with the children.

We came here and it was very bad. We didn't have no work. We came straight to Vancouver. We lived on Georgia Street. My husband had his father here and his six sisters and three brothers—nine altogether. So we lived with them for a while and we moved out after into a small apartment. There were not many Jewish people here—only about five hundred or so.

My husband didn't have work. He hurt himself. He fell down and hurt himself. So it took him quite a while—and that's what it was. When I came I couldn't go out to work as I had the two children to look after. Then I got pregnant right away and had my daughter. I worked in the house looking after the kids and sewing for them. In Vancouver I couldn't do dressmaking. There were no factories here at the time.

During the Second World War in Poland, they suffered more than in Lithuania, but after the war the Lithuanians were bad. They start to join the Germans. My mother and father were killed. I'm talking after the war. My sister was probably killed. My brothers' two children were killed. The Lithuanians killed lots of people. I came in 1927 and the war broke out in 1939. I brought my sister over here after the war. She was in the camp, four years in the concentration camps, she was lucky to be alive. So I helped her. I worked. My children helped me and I send them every month a parcel there to Europe. She had twin girls and now one is married and has a daughter here in Canada.

Years later I was working in dresses, here in Vancouver. I worked at Sweet 16, upstairs in the factory. [*Coincidently, at the same time I was working for Sweet 16 in the office.*] I worked also in Fitwell for twelve years, and after I went to Winnipeg where my daughter got married, I worked there in Jacob & Crawley for twelve years until I retired.

I worked thirty-four years after my husband died. He died very young. He was forty-one at the time, in 1942. I worked as a dressmaker and pants maker, for men you know, with all kinds of straps for the military uniforms.

And that is my story.

Fanny (Baba) Osipov

Fanny Osipov, née Swartz, or "Baba" as everyone not her contemporary called her, was the mother and mother-in-law of dear friends of my family and like a bubble, *or grandmother, to all of us. No one, but no one, could bake bagels, and knishes and varenikes like she did, even up to the days before she died in her eighties, with nary a grey hair on her head! She was an example to all of us who knew her. Baba Osipov died in August of 1988.*

I AM COMING FROM—it's a city, a big city, Nikolaiyev, right next to Odessa. When I was four years old we had a pogrom. (For whom you are writing this—they know what a pogrom means?) And the pogrom which started, for three days they come and they kill and they take away just from the Jews. And we were hiding in a corner of the house. Next door to us there was a little grocery store which belonged to Jews. They made a mess there. The oil and the flour and sugar—they threw everything on the floor. I started talking to my father: what are we sitting in the house, they'll come here. Let us hide—I was four years old—let us hide under the bed. For a long time people were laughing at me! Next door we had a neighbour who was Russian. He was a fine man. He said to us, If something happens, I'll put a stepladder to the cellar. You come and I'll take you in. See, they didn't go to the Russian people, just to the Jewish people. And we were in the neighbour's house, hiding for three days in the cellar. He brought us milk and bread and when we came back after three days, our house was a mess. All the windows were smashed, lots of things were taken away—the good things. And not only did they take away, they were drunk and they break everything.

This was in 1905, the start of the Russian Revolution.[16] That's what the Tsar started, saying that it comes from the Jews and that is why they made the pogrom. And after three days everybody came back to their homes and started again living. And that is what life was until something happened again.

We had three rooms: a kitchen, one bedroom, and another room. We were just two kids then. My father was a driver. He had a horse and cart and he used to sell seltzer water as well as all kinds of pop for some of the stores. That was his life. He was very religious. He made a living. He didn't have much but we were not starving. The thing is, my father came from a little town. He was born in a little town. You see, Jews were not allowed to live in cities like Nikolaiyev—only those Jews who were citizens and had a permit. But my father made a living there and so he thought he would stay. The police came. In those days everyone had a passport, papers, and they must register with the police. The thing is that you could give the policeman five cents, ten cents, and he lets you stay. But every month he came, and my father paid him up. There were lots of people who lived like this over there.

When I was ten or eleven years old already, I remember they were so tired, the Jewish people were very tired. They had to pay up always and they always knew what would happen if they didn't. It was at this time that a Jewish family read in the papers that if anybody wants to come to Canada, they'll be given land or farms for nothing. A man went to Winnipeg, Canada, and he went to the city and he started working there. He worked mostly as a peddler. You know what is a peddler? Others went and they start writing letters to their families. Meanwhile people in Winnipeg started to organize, like a society, and this organization lends money to people so they can buy papers—*shiftcarten*—to bring the family to Canada. When you started working you paid up every month the money you borrowed. And that is what happened to my father too.

We was four children by then already. My mother was a sick woman. Wait. I'll tell you what happened. All the family couldn't come. He, my father, went first; he went first and then after he saved a little money, he took out *shiftcarten*—papers, papers—my father will pay them up and then he will send for us. I was maybe twelve years old and I had a sister about ten, one who was eight, and one was a little girl, maybe about two years old. She was a baby when my father left. It was very hard for our mother to take care of all the children. My father had an uncle in Poland and I was sent there to stay with him and help him in his work. He had something like a coffee shop and sold ice cream too and I was helping him.

All our papers came and the family was to come to Poland and we would all leave together. Then it happened! My mother, who had the money and the papers and everything, got pneumonia. In those days there was no penicillin and she got double pneumonia and she died. She died and we were left alone, four children! The papers are no good. Two sisters went to live with one family and the others with someone else. There was another family going to Canada. So we sent the papers back so my father could make up new ones and we could travel to Canada with this family. Again all the papers are ready. I was in Poland. My uncle said the children will come to Poland and he'll take us to the boat. My sisters came and just then starts the war. You know, the First War, 1914!

So we couldn't go. We were stuck already! What happened? We were in the city called Brest Litovsk and in this place there were, like, big generals, and they said they were going to fight. The head of these generals was a German and the Germans were all over the place then. Then it was announced that everybody could go on the trains—no charge, you can go anywhere for free—because in Brest Litovsk there will be fighting and everybody will be killed. So we are four children; it was summer; we are with no clothes, bare feet. We went to the station with my uncle and his three kids. And we are running. Everybody is running to the trains. We get on the train, we pass by about five or ten miles. I look around for my uncle and his kids. No uncle! No kids! Where were they? … They put him in one place and us four children in another.

We go ten miles or so and we are alone. People said to us kids, the youngest is two and a half, Where do you want to go? You can go wherever you want, there is no charge on the trains. And I said, We are going to our city, Nikolaiyev. It is far to go there. So we went on the trains. There were lots of people there, everybody is going someplace. Sometimes we went for half a day and the train had to stop—the soldiers had to go on. We were in the middle of …? Nothing to eat. How to wash? It was like running from the house. We went to farmers and begged them for something to eat. And on the train when we came to a little stop, a little town or a city, people came and they brought some food. In the meantime we don't know where the uncle is. We left him. We couldn't find him already and since then we have had no news of him.

We came to Nikolaiyev. It took us two and a half months. All the time on the train, day and night, not washed, not dressed, just in the same little dresses. Good it was summer. We came to our city. I had another uncle over there. He had a factory and made candies. I was already fifteen years old. I went to school and learned to write and read and I helped him. You know, he couldn't write. He had a big factory. They came for orders. I could write and I could help them. At that time my two sisters were with my grandmother and another sister was with my auntie. We didn't have letters. We didn't have word. The years passed. My sister was working in a shop. The other sister was sixteen and she could do something but the little one, she was so little, she was in a foster home—in a home, you know, because the auntie was very old and she couldn't take care and so my sister was there in the home.

Meanwhile now I am seventeen or eighteen. I start going out. I met the man who would be my husband in another year. I had a girlfriend in Niko-laiyev who had a brother in the Russian army. She also had an older brother who was a teacher of dancing and she was the piano player. She played the music and we were coming there to dance. Then, after her brother came home from the army, we met at the dance. It took about a year or so and then we were married.

His family had a printing shop and they belonged to the Left. The war at that time was against the White Russians and these White Russians were in our city. An underground printing shop was started and they began print-ing leaflets. I used to take bundles, which I would wrap with a towel and hide in my coat; and I went to places to drop the bundles. One place I had to go to was a house in the middle of many others—all of them closed inside a gate. Here there are maybe twenty to thirty families living and there is a man at the gate. At night it is closed and you must have a key. One night as I came to this gate and just opened it, I felt my leaflets—it was winter and very windy—I felt the leaflets, oh *tot-tot-tot-tot*, falling down! What should I do? I wasn't afraid. So I opened the gate and I sit on the floor; and I tie it up and then I went there to the house. The people in the house saw I was very pale. They said, My, you are lucky! We could get killed! That is what we were doing. One time the police came to the house but they had a back door and the people ran away, including my husband and his older brother. But the police took away everything.

Life in Nikolaiyev was very hard for the Jewish people. They couldn't go to the beautiful places there. They were not allowed. We were not in a ghetto. Our entertainment was today at my house, tomorrow another house. Some-one has a piano, there's dancing, we make our own entertainment. We just played together: enjoying, dancing, singing, and that's what we did for a long time.

After I got married I had a son, his name was Velvel. My husband was again taken into the army and I was left with this little boy. I became sick with—not measles, not chicken pox—oy, I forgot the name! You have it here in Canada—it's a rash and it's very catchy and you go around with scabs—

it is worse than measles and chicken pox [*possibly smallpox*]. Anyway, I couldn't stay at home. They took me to the hospital. Meanwhile my little boy became very sick. He was two years old and he got the measles. You are not supposed to take someone out of the house. It was chilly weather already and they took him to the hospital.

When I came ... shall I tell you what happened in the hospital? You want to hear this? When I came to the hospital there were two people in one bed. On one bed! One on one side, one on the other. There was so much sickness! I was quiet but the other one in the bed was very wild. She nearly killed me. You know when you are sick in the hospital, as soon as your temperature is gone you go home. They need the bed for someone else. And they came and I was weak and they said you are okay. They shave your hair and say, You go home! There is no one at home. My sister-in-law lived with us. The hospital has a telephone but there was no phone at home so I couldn't tell them I am coming home. I went for my clothes. Somebody took away my shoes, took away my dress. And what did they leave? A coat. At the time I went to the hospital it was cold; and now it was warm. I haven't got any money. The hospital is far, like from one town to the next. I thought, well—at that time there were street cars with horses—I thought I'll go inside, I'll tell the driver that I haven't any money. I could talk!

Nu, you see I was with a coat on, without shoes, my head shaved, so when I came into the street car, the man thought I was from the crazy home. He was afraid. He said, Get up! I told him that I am coming from the hospital but he was afraid. So, Get up! Get up! And so I went. I got off. I start walking home. It was in the morning, nine o'clock. I walked and I sit. Where do I sit? Near someone's house, on the porch. But they come, the people who live there and they say, Get up from here. What are you doing? Well, it was two o'clock when I came home. My brother-in-law was there and he didn't recognize me! He said, For who are you looking? I said—his name was Selma—I said: Selma, it's Fanny! Oy! They took me in and ... at least I was home already.

And then the time was very bad. There was not enough food. My baby passed away. I went to look in the hospital. They said that he passed away. I asked, Could I see him? And they put him in a room, you know, for the dead people there. I wanted to see with my own eyes. So I start begging. I go to the door and the man there said I couldn't go in.

Nu, I am sick. I thought, if I found him, what can I do? What can I do? But at least I wanted to see him with my own eyes. I start begging and crying and so he finally opens the door. He opened the door and I went inside.

The smell … I start looking … the man saw that I was shaking. He took me out. I didn't find my son, Velvel. Let me tell you, if you went in, you would pass away. I still remember this: from the floor to the ceiling were men, women, kids. There were so many dead people. There was no food and many sicknesses. They didn't have the time to bury everyone. Yes. That was life there then.

In the meanwhile the war stopped. My husband was still in the army and I am alone. I went to the market—selling, helping, doing something to make a little money. There were tables spread with things you could buy. I had a few cents. You could buy a pound of bread, a few pounds of this or that, whatever you want. I went with my few pennies. I said I want a pound of bread, the man cut me a piece and I thought, holding the bread, it would be for me, my sister-in-law, and for the very old grandmother who lived with us. A nice woman. I thought for everyone there would be a little piece of bread. I went two blocks and from the back a boy came and grabbed it. Right there on the street. You see, I didn't realize that you must to hide this and put it in a bag so nobody should see it. People are starving and they have a chance—because I am holding the bread open so you can see. This was right after the war. You see kids running around on the street. Bread. Bread.

When you are starving you are swollen in your stomach, your feet. People are on the street begging. In some families there were four, five, ten people, lying in the house, dying there. It was a time of starvation. So the boy grabbed my piece of bread. By the time I looked around, he had finished eating it. That was also what life was.

Organizations in America and Canada sent people to look for family members. My father gave our name and address and a man came to find out if the family is alive. Then he wrote a letter back to my father to say that he found his daughter. At the time I had four sisters. The little one was in a home and the two in the middle were again sick and they died in hospital. So I was left with the little sister. My father sent me a parcel of food from Canada: one hundred pounds of white flour. What will I do with white flour? I sold it and got five times that of black flour. He sent cocoa and chocolate. I sold some of it and, meanwhile, I had something to eat. Lots of Jewish people had food like this. My father thought we were four sisters and he sent four pairs of shoes. I need one and the rest I sold. I have money to eat, to live, to buy food. The Russian people started up again. They were jealous. They came again against the Jews. They say we have everything.

My husband came back from the army and he started looking for a job. The time was better. Then came the revolution, 1917, 1918, 1919. I had a letter from my father. He said we can come to Canada but we would have to apply for the papers from a farm. We had to be living on a farm not in a city. So we moved on to a farm where we lived for several months. At that time, if you wanted to come to Canada you had to show you were a farmer. They didn't want city people. The Russian people are good people; they are good-natured people. When you live with them and you are good to them, then you find out. They couldn't read. They couldn't write. You could bring a paper and read it for them.

My son Louis was born on the farm. I didn't have a doctor. I had this woman. We had one room and this Russian woman whose farm it was, was crazy about him and he called her *Chochow* [Auntie] Paula. She had one cow, and every day she hid a glass of milk for him. She had enough for her family, but she would give him the milk every afternoon. He would go to her and say: Auntie, I think the cows are coming already—meaning he wanted milk. Meanwhile we made the papers there.

My husband, myself, my son, and my little sister left from Nikolaiyev. It didn't take long. We took the train to Riga and a little ship from there to England. In England we took a big ship to Canada. My father had made all the arrangements and we had nothing to worry. My husband could talk a few languages—he was a printer and had to know other languages. We came to Winnipeg and met my father, who was a very religious man. When he had left Nikolaiyev I was only nine or ten years old, and when I arrived in Canada I was twenty-eight already. My sister didn't remember him. She didn't know him! She was only two when my father left. We lived with him for a while but we couldn't stand it. We are not religious. We never went to the synagogue. So he moved out. He would come to visit us and just drink a cup of tea from a glass.

My husband found work. He made good wages and we start saving. We bought a house and then our second son, Oscar, was born. There were lots of Jews in Winnipeg and for us a new life began.

Abe Smith

Abe Smith was born 10 December 1898, in a little village about eight miles from Gomel [today Homyel], near Kiev, in the Ukraine. He arrived in Canada in March 1925.

I had known Abe and his wife Rose Smith for many years by the time I interviewed them in their Vancouver apartment on a sunny afternoon in 1974. Abe Smith died 18 May 1991.

I WAS BORN IN 1898 in Gomel—actually, in a little village about eight miles from Gomel. I lived there all my childhood. It was a little village and there were a lot of peasants. The peasants lived in their houses and we lived— it was our house but it was the landlord's territory, in a compound, like. We had a whole house to ourselves. The peasants were generally nice to us. Not all the time. They were hooligans you know. The landlord had cows, so we got milk from him. The water we used to get from a well and then later we had a pump to get the water.

We had seven brothers and two sisters.

I went once with a Gentile friend off mine—supposed to be a friend!— we went to swim and he tried to be smart and he grabbed me in the back, and we were naked you know, and the water wasn't clean, too—the cows used to go in there—he tried, he tried to drown me you know, in a joking way, but I see he means it, so I hit him in the face like that and I hit right in the eyes and he falls down in the water and I ran out and I was running, without clothes, over an orchard, across the highway, to run home, and I got rid of him. I must have been about ten years old then.

By trade I was a watchmaker, so I was allowed to live in any city in Russia.[17] So I lived in Kiev. There I met a fellow. He was a German fellow and was working for the secret police, like. And we used to go out every night, you know, for walks in parks, to talk and other things. (I want to tell you, when I was in Kiev three or four years ago, I went to that park where we used to go and meet.) So one time that fellow comes to me and says to me, There is going to be tonight a pogrom. And he says, The pogrom will start at twelve o'clock and all the streetcars and the buses will stop and the pogrom will begin.

I lived in a place where Gentile officials from the government were in that same place. Anyway, twelve o'clock at night, I climbed on this place where was a lot of green stuff growing. I push my head under and I don't hear nothing. I was glad but I was disgusted. I came next day to that fellow and I said, What the hell are you trying to pull? You told me there'll be a pogrom, and this and that. He says, There was a student, Golboff was his name, and he's in charge of to make that pogrom and just at the last minute he changed his mind and he called off the pogrom. So that's why there wasn't a pogrom last night.

But once—I'll tell you a story—when I was going on the boat in the spring to Kiev, there was a women dressed in black and she was sitting by me down there and she was going, "Oy, oy," and started talking like she had nightmares. So I woke her up and I say, You are troubled by something? That's why I woke you up. She doesn't know me and I don't know her. So she tells me a story what the bandits did. You know the bandits?[18] The bandits were on the boat and they took her father and mother and they tied down the hands on the back and they throw them in the water. And she looked like a Gentile, that girl, so they let her go. They didn't know what her connection was. So she thinks about what happened to her father and mother and she cries and has nightmares. There were a lot of other things like that going on.

I'll tell you something else. I remember, when I was a little kid, in our village there was a pogrom and they put us, you know, they put us in a stable, with horses. We were like hiding there. And the pogrom happened and I didn't know nothing. I was hiding. And the next day, or morning, everything went back to normal and it was okay, you know.

At one time, we lived near a farm, like a dairy farm and my father used to get milk from the dairy, and other things. So once, one fellow came in with a big piece of wood. He came in and he hit a Jewish fellow there in the head. I was sitting there and the whole … the pillow was all in blood and everything else and then, and then, the same fellow grabbed a big stick, was a nail it that … and … and he came on and he wanted to hit my uncle. My uncle was always six feet tall, you know, and my uncle grabbed the stick from him and he ran away. My uncle ran out of the house. And my mother opened the window and started to call for help. So the fellow says, We are not going to touch you. You are nice people and we are just after the city Jews!

In 1905–6, I was there, I was just a kid. It was not so nice then. The pogroms was on, there was parades and fighting in the streets, the army was shooting. I was living in the village near Gomel. Well, I'll tell you, when this revolution started I was just a kid, I was going in the street and I see the police—you know the police in their uniforms, the officials—they were running; they were running away in a taxi pulled from horses, you know. And the community, the people, they tore off the *pogony* [epaulets], the braids like the army for the Tsar are wearing, like with three stars. I couldn't figure out what was happening. I was just a kid. And the officials are trying to run away and the people jump on them and they pull all the gold buttons from the coats. That was when they overthrow the Tsar, you know. I was in Gomel at the time and it happened there and I witnessed that and I remember when Kerensky came in and the people were going in the streets and they were singing the "Marseillaise" and everything else. That was very nice. So there were lots of good memories and bad memories then.[19]

In our village, the landlord's daughter—I used to go out with her, you know—we used to take out the white stuff from the corn and make a beard. We used to play like the theatre. And I was playing her father. So once we went into the woods for a walk and it started to rain and she went under a tree and she got scared and she called me under the tree and I didn't want to go under the tree, so she was crying. After that we went back home. We were very friendly, the whole family. They were very nice people. They were not Jewish. That landlord was a very nice man, that when the revolution came, the government told him, You're a nice fellow and you were nice to the peasants and did good things; and if you want to remain here we'll give you land just like the same as we give to the peasants and you can produce vegetables and take it to the marketplace to sell. It's all yours. And he did it like that. The government was very good to him as he was not nasty to the peasants.

Harry Smith, my cousin, already had relatives in Canada, and they wrote and said to leave the gymnasium, the school, and learn the watchmaking trade. Harry went to a fellow who was one of the best watchmakers, not only in our city but in the whole province. The watchmaker couldn't take in more than three boys at a time to learn. When Harry left for Canada after apprenticing/working for nine months, I took over his job. I apprenticed for three years. We had to pay the teacher. We worked three years for nothing and still we had to pay the teacher! That is how I became a watchmaker.

The relatives in Canada sent us tickets and visas and so we came here. My father said the house is worth money and so he gave me some money and I paid it back to him later on. We came to Calgary and my father bought a dairy. I went to work in the dairy but my brothers didn't. They didn't want to work with the cows. My brothers worked in pharmacies.

When we got our tickets and papers from Canada, our journey began. From Gomel we went to Moscow, because they sent a letter saying we must come there. When we came to Moscow, the visa between Russia and the other countries had expired. So I went after them and I said, You got to give us our visas, we are a big family, ten, twelve people. We haven't got … So the man said, Keep quiet. Don't give me money. I'll get your visas. So I gave him some money. We got our visas. We stayed in Moscow for about two to three weeks and after that we went to Riga, where we took a boat: one small boat first, and then we took a big boat to Montreal, and from there a train to Calgary. This was in March 1925.

I will tell you the story about my name. My uncles, my mother's brothers, were Shumiacher, but my father's name and my name is Sholomenko, and all the Sholomenkos are related. That was our name. I bumped into a fellow when I went to see my brother who was in the army in a certain place, and a nurse tells me in the hospital there is so-and-so by the name Sholomenko. I look and I don't see anybody and I come back and tell her there's no Sholomenko there. So she takes me to a room and there's a fellow with a beard in bed and his name is Sholomenko. So I ask him where he is from and he says Kostukovich, which is a small town where his family was established. So he was a very far relative but he was a Sholomenko. So if you bump into a Sholomenko he has to be a relative—no monkey business.

So when I came here to Calgary my name was so long, and I was opening a shop, and the man said, That name will never go on the window. I had an uncle (you know Harry Smith; well, his father was my uncle) and he came with Harry to Calgary before anybody else. So Harry's father went to work in a lumber shop and the man asked, What's your name? And he answered, Shumiacher. And the man said, Never mind, your name is Smith. So he became Smith! And so then when I came in—I have a cousin in Ottawa and his name is Shalom. Shalom is a nice name. I didn't know what Smith is. Now there was a certain time here in Canada when I registered my name that I could register by any name I wanted. So I like the name Shalom but it was already too late. I had registered my name as Smith. And so I am Abe Smith!

David Shaya Kirman

I interviewed David Shaya Kirman (he was Shaya to all who knew him) at his home in Vancouver in 1974.

Shaya Kirman came from Wlodova, Poland, which is by the River Bug, near Lublin, Chelm, Zamosc, and Goray, and not far from Warsaw. He was never short of stories to tell. Even though Yiddish was his mother tongue, he could still spin a good tale in English. During my visit, Shaya showed me the Yitzkor book from the Wlodova and Sobibor gas chambers, which had been recently published (Yitzkor books are books of remembrance created by Holocaust survivors to memorialize the places they've lived in). We looked at photos of his father, who was a painter; of Shaya in a play called Shulamith; *and pictures of others, some still alive.*

I sadly recall visiting Shaya Kirman in hospital a few days before he died in 1982.

MY FATHER WAS A HANDWORKER. A handworker is not a worker which works by somebody. He is self-employed and somebody could work for him, and he belongs to the handworkers union. You see, if a boy wants to apprentice, after he finishes his apprenticeship, he goes to this board—the *zect*—and they examine him to see if he could be a self-employed handworker. And there you will find different kinds of professions. [*He points to a photo.*] This is not a shoemaker, but he makes the top part of the shoe. He's a *kamashenmakher*. And here's a tailor; and there's another tailor. My father was a sign painter; and here's a capmaker. [*He points to another photo.*] Most of them were tailors. Some was for men—men's tailor, and somebody was for womans, ladies—a *damske*. A *damske* couldn't make a costume for men.

My first memories was going to the *kheder,* that they took me to the *kheder.* The *belfer*—you know what a *belfer* means? A helper to the *melamed,* the teacher. A little boy, a helper—that's a *behilfer.* He used to go to bring the kids home and took them to the *kheder,* you see, like you used to do to our kids. [*I used to pick up Shaya Kirman's kids after school, along with my own, and drive them to Jewish school.*] There was no car, you had to take them when they were small; you had to carry them. Every child went separate. And the first time they took me with a *tallis.* So I was about three years old. Not like today. Three years they took me the first time to *kheder.* And then I learned a few years. They made an agreement with the father from the child: I'll give you my child for *zman. Zman* is six months from Pesach to Succoth, and then from Succoth to Pesach is another *zman.* The *melamed,* the teacher, used to come after *zman* and the father paid him for the *zman.* And then, if my father liked the *melamed,* then he gives me to the same *melamed* for another *zman.* If not, he went to another *melamed.* But the *melamed* used to come every month, every two months to the home to examine the child. And the father used to sit this side; if the father didn't like the *melamed,* he doesn't teach him good, so he went to another *melamed.* So I was with the first *melamed* maybe three *zmans* and this was called *dardeke melamed,* the first grade or primary.

Then the primary *melamed* hasn't got more to give me so we went to another level *melamed* and start to learn *khumesh.*[20] You see [in] the *dardeke* you learn the alphabet: aleph, bet, gimel, and to put together words. And then in the higher *melamed* we used to learn to *davn,* to pray already. You see, for myself, after *khumesh* and Rashi,[21] I was learning another few months with this *melamed.* So this *melamed* hasn't got more to give me. By now I've had two *melameds* already.

Now I go to a third *melamed* and I start to learn Gemorrah—this is Talmud. So my father doesn't like this *melamed.* So I learn there a *zman* and my father says to the *melamed,* Moishe, I see I don't like the way you are teaching my Shaya. He is able to know better. He has a good *kop,* a good head. So my father looked around for a better *melamed.* And this next was a good one. I started to learn Tanakh.[22] Most *melamdim* don't want to teach Tanakh. You see it is going deeper into the study and the Orthodox *melamdim* was against it. Tanakh was more progressive, you know. The same thing with the Rambam.[23] Most people don't want to teach Rambam. They don't want to learn Rambam even.

So I learned with this *melamed.* I was learning already Talmud, Tanakh, you see. Every Thursday you have to know the whole *shiur,* the whole lesson. I used to learn good; mostly by heart. So I had to work. It was not like today. The pupil has to work, if not, some melamdim used to *shmays*, hit you with a *kantshik*, and pull your *peyes*, your sideburns. There was a *kantshik* on the table, and instead of a wooden handle, some would have a foot from an animal, the leg from—how do you call it?—a rabbit. And they would pull the *peyes*, you know, the side burns. You know what *kantshik* means? A leather whip. The *kantshik* was on the table all the time with a pointer made from bone, ivory. They used to take it from the corset. The bone, they called it fishbone. It was flexible. And they used this to point with, what is called a *taytl*. The first time, with a small child, you say, what's that? That's an aleph. Here take this. Give me *ashtokh*, a poke, at the aleph. So the child was to take a poke at the aleph, a poke at the bet. Then they used to take a *groschen*— like a penny—and say, *der malekh*, the angel, *vet varfn a groschen*. If you learn good the angel will give you a penny. So the *melamed* would drop a *groschen*, so the child wants to learn good.

When I finished with the Gemorrah my father says, I don't know what to do with you. There was now in town a higher-level school known as a yeshiva. It was a *kloyz*, not a synagogue, not a Beth Hamidrash, it was a *shtibl*. A *shtibl* is like a Lubavitch, a house of prayer and learning, you see. (But here, in Vancouver, the Lubavitcher *shtibl* is nothing. They are coming together only on a Saturday to *davn*, to pray.) In the *kloyz*, in the *shtiblekh* there was a *rov*. There a rabbi is called a *rov*. And the Hassidim used to go to this rebbe. There was the Gerer Rebbe from Ger, the Tovler Rebbe, the Sokolover Rebbe, Lubliner Rebbe, and many others; and all the rebbes they used to have Hassidim—followers. One Hassid doesn't like the other rebbe. Only his rebbe. Your rebbe is nothing. Every rebbe had his own Hassidim and the Hassidim they had a *shtibl*—like a synagogue, but a small one. Only these Hassidim, these people, used to *davn* in this *shtibl*. Like the Lubavitcher in the Lubavitch, they don't go to other *shtiblekh*. And these rebbes used to come from time to time to visit. And they give them little money for this.

Near our house, side by side, there was a *shtibl*—Mezeritsh *shtibl*. There were two *shtiblekh* together, like—it was one house but divided. One was a Partshever *shtibl* and one was Mezritsh. The Partshever Rebbe and the Mezritsher Rebbi were brothers. Their father was the Bialer Rebbe, you see. So the Partshever Rebbe and the Mezritsher both divided two halls. So in our house was a wall with the *shtibl*. So I went to learn to this *shtibl*, private, by myself. There were more boys learning. If I didn't know something so I asked my *khavr*, my partner. So we used to learn together, without a rabbi, without a *melamed*. We used to learn the whole day. But in the morning and in the afternoon the Hassidim used to come to *davn*. But in the middle of the day we used to learn and sometimes at night too. This is called *mishma*, at night, after midnight. *Mishma* means the night is divided in three *mishmorim*, in three parts. So many hours the first *mishma*, so many the second, so many the third. So I learned the first *mishma*. Then I went home; around the second *mishma*, some others would come. So there was learning the whole night. So in each session we would have five to ten boys. We used to learn by candlelight.

I remember now in our house we used to light the first kerosene lamp, and we used to make low, low the fire because it cost money for the kerosene. We would see almost nothing! And we used to learn by this light. When I used to learn at home I have to make it a little bit lighter; and it was smoking and stinking from the oil. And sometimes it wasn't kerosene; you put some kindling from wood. They used to sell wood which had sap—it's called *pimsinholts*—all the woods which has sap you call *pimsinholts*. That's the same wood, gopher wood, what Noah made the Ark with. And we used to buy whole pieces and we used to cut out where was the sap and we make kindlings, in small pieces, and with this we used to make the fire, you see. It was like matches. It was matches but it was expensive. I used to go to a neighbour with a cover from a pot, which was clay—my grandmother used to give me two covers—and I used to take a little coal, live coal from the neighbour. I used to blow it, blow it, and run, run quick and put it in the oven. We used to put more coals on top of it and that's how we made a fire. We used the wood coals for the samovar also. When there was no kerosene in the house, we used to take the kindling—the pieces of wood—to burn the lamp.

Later, when there was kerosene, there were different sizes depending on the glass—a No. 3, a No. 5, a No. 8. Then there was a No. 12. Each glass was different. The nice, fancy ones was elegantly done for the rich people. And when you had guests you used to put the big lamp which was called a *blitzlomp*. You know what's meant, blitz? A thunder and a lighting—that's a blitz. And you called a big lamp, *blitzlomp*.

Mostly on Sabbath nights we used to have guests—*feters, mumes*, you see—so they put the *blitzlomp* on. They served from the samovar some tea served with *gerhakte* sugar. It was a cap of sugar called *hitl* sugar, and from this *hitl* sugar you used to cut pieces. And you got small pieces of sugar called *goske* sugar, small pieces. The *hitl* sugar was better, it was harder. Russia had this sugar.

In the meantime, my father was working for a long time in Warsaw, and he took my mother and me and my brother to Warsaw. This was before the First World War. I was still a little boy. I was maybe ten years old because I was learning for myself already in the *shtibl.* In Warsaw I went back to Talmud Torah to learn, and then I went to a yeshiva. I had long *peyes,* and when I went to the barber, I used to hold it up here so he would not touch it. I remember my father told me, Whatever you want—you want to be a rabbi?— it's okay with me, but you have to learn, you have to know everything. I went to school, in the public school, but I didn't study there much. Mostly my father used to teach me at home. My father was born in a village, a *shtetl,* he went to school with non-Jews, so my father, he knows a few languages perfect—Russian, Polish, German, Hebrew, Yiddish, Aramaic. All the handworkers, the self-employed, used to come to my father to make the bills for them to give the customer. My father was an *apotheka* and used to work in a shop like a drugstore but for prescriptions only.

I was now in Talmud Torah and then yeshiva. In my free time I used to carry lunch to work to my father. My father was working with a master, not for himself then. And one time he was working in the Yiddishe Germaynde— it's the Jewish community centre, there was a *kehilah,* a community council, in Warsaw for the Jews. There was working Peretz. He was secretary for the cemetery and used to sell burial plots. I didn't know Peretz. I used to read every week in the paper was a column written by Peretz. It was called *Mayn Vinkele* [My Corner], that was the title. And my mother told me, You want to go and see Peretz? I say, what's Peretz? That's the man who writes the column in the paper, she said. There was a paper called *Haynt* [Today]. I said yes. So she gave me lunch and she said, Go there to the Yiddish Germaynde, Grzybowska Gas, Grzybowska Street No. 26, and there Peretz is working. So I went there, there were workers, there were painters, all the doors were wet from paint. I still was in a long *kapote,* you know. So it was written in a piece of paper in Polish on the door: Be careful, is fresh paint. I could read and write Polish at that time. So I took the two ends of my *kapote* and I'm walking carefully, so, so, and I saw a man. It was written here a *karke-teyler.* A *karke-teyler* means a man what allots burial plots. I see a man, he's sitting there, with a big moustache. I didn't know that that was Peretz. So he comes to the door and he took me by the arm, he pulled me in, and he took from my hand the *shtapl.* I was with a basket like this, with the lunch. He took me with one hand. And he told me, Please come in.[24]

In the meantime, from the other room, my father saw this scene, so he comes in, and he tells Peretz in Polish, This is my son Shaya. And to me he told me in Yiddish, *Dos iz Yitskhok Leybush Peretz*, the writer, which you read every week in the paper, his column *Mayn Vinkele.* So I thought, Peretz, I thought he was a man with a beard or something. And I saw here a man without a hat, without a yarmulke, he looks like not a Jew, he's with a big moustache. So my father told him that I'm learning; I'm learning good and I could sing. So Peretz told me, I'm not writing for big people. I'm writing for you too, for little people, for kids. (I wasn't bar mitzvah yet.) Then Peretz told me, After your bar mitzvah, when you will be a little older, you'll come to me. I'll take you in Arzomia—Arzomia was an institution, it was a choir there. Peretz organized it. *Arzomia* means song. It used to be Friday-night gatherings of artists with discussions and singing. It was a choir, Arzomia. So he told me, When you're a little bit older you come to me, and I'll take you to Arzomia.

Nu, when I was a little bit older I didn't went anymore to Peretz because Peretz died already in 1915. Then my father came back from work, so he brought me on a postcard, a song written by Peretz—"*Dray Neytorins.*" [*He sings a few bars of the song.*] He brought me one song and another song from another writer. [*This song appears in Shaya's copy on page 49.*] My father told me, Shaya, Peretz give it to you, he gave this for you to learn. So I have this still and it's something to be very proud about. Yes! You see that was how I saw Peretz. Only once. I didn't see him anymore. I used to see him along some street when he went to work. I knew the house where he lives.

Then it was the war, 1914. It was no work, my father … there was no money. I want to help. So I went to the street to sell candies, fudge, which I buy in the factory and sell on the street. Little boxes like that, they sell for two or three kopeks. We used to scream out to try to sell the candy on the street. So I and my two brothers (I had an older brother and one was younger by four years) used to do that. It was near the house, it was a bazaar, a marketplace. We was standing near the bazaar, sometimes thieves they grab the candy, sometimes they took away from me, and I come home with nothing. It was a bad time.

In the meantime my mother has another child. What's going to be? So my father, who was a painter, he started working by a master—a master means he hired many people, a company, a big firm. And they send you here and there. He has to come every morning. So my father used to talk to the *balebos*, a Mr. Epstein was his name. He was a nice man with a beard, a religious man, a *frumer.* He used to come to see the work how it was every few days. He had sons and they used to go around. It was a good place. There was always work—summer and winter—because mostly painters wintertime is nothing to do. But he holds, he keeps the work, you see. For example, in some house we could work a little bit later. He saw that the windows were closed so people could work in winter inside. So he keep this house for wintertime and in summer there is other kind of work. So by him it was always work. So my father talked to him, he said, Mr. Epstein, I don't know what to do. It's wartime and I can't make a living. Maybe you can take my Shaya for to help, to do something. He said all right. So he took me. My father doesn't want to make me a painter. But, in the meantime, he said, Come, it will be a better time and maybe you will do something else. So I started to work. There were no cars to go. We used to go to work, walking, sometimes with a tramway—a streetcar. But the streetcar used to cost money. Sometimes when they gave me money for the streetcar, I walked and took the money.

The first time I went to work, there was a pushcart, a two-wheeler. And they put all the stuff, ladders, cans of paint (not cans like you have today). It was cans with dried paint—powder—which we used to mix ourselves. And they'd give me a piece of paper on which was written this and this, you have to put in there, a district, a number, giving instructions: where to put the stuff. And we used to push this through all the streets of Warsaw for miles and miles. I start to work and they paid me half a ruble. A half a ruble a week, you see. My father used to make twelve rubles. Then little by little I start to work and I can't remember how long it was. Then they paid me one ruble already.

It's a funny thing. There was in Warsaw a doctor. He was very bad. And we used to work there painting his house. The doctor would watch you, see how you are doing, so he would chase you out, through the house, and he would throw you from the steps. Yes! But not me! The best worker could work there but when the doctor looked at him, how he is doing, he would get angry. So nobody wants to go to the doctor to work. So I come in one place, I see a few workers they are whispering about me—to send me to the doctor. I know how to do the work by this time. They have to paint a ceiling for the doctor in a *kabinet*—a doctor's *kabinet,* the place where he took his patients—the examining room. We used to paint only the ceiling. Why? Because the walls were paper. It was expensive wallpaper. So there was the foreman there. He told me, Shaya, you go over there—number this and this street—to the doctor there. You have to paint the ceiling. So I thought, to paint the ceiling, that's nothing! Now my master, my boss, would go in every house in which we used to work. There was already a ladder standing. There was a ladder, there were some cans with everything what you need in the place. So the caretaker had the keys; he gave me and I took it. I mixed myself this white powder with everything, and I came up to the doctor's and I knock. He opened the door and look at me like that. He says in Polish, What? I will not talk to a snot-nosed kid like you! So I said, I want to go back. I didn't want to paint there. So he told me: Come here! Could you make this ceiling? Oh yes, sir, doctor, yes. He says to me, See all this what's standing here is to stay. Not one drop must fall on the furniture, not one drop. And the walls is to be like it is.

There wasn't like it is here. Here you come to the house, you put canvas on the floor and cover everything. There we had nothing to cover with. If, he said to me, you make this ceiling and it wouldn't be one drop, I'll give you for beer—how do you say it, a tip—of half a ruble. He would give me a half a ruble tip. Half a ruble? I'm earning a half a ruble a week. I went downstairs to the water and I washed the ladder clean. Took off my shoes and I put my cap on.

Oh, I must tell you. Before I went to the doctor's house I stopped in a place where my father was working. My father was a foreman there. He asked me, Where are you going? So I told him, They send me to the doctor. Ooohh! he said, Okay, now remember when you work you close the door so nobody can come to see you. If the doctor will see you he will chase you out. So I did like that. I took the ladder and I cut a piece of rag I had in my pocket and I'm holding my cap like that in my hand and I paint so the paint won't fall on the walls and floor. It was with brush, no rollers. I came to the ceiling, sometimes it's a drop, I went down and I wipe it up. And I made the ceiling and I took everything down, down, down. And I look around to see if everything was clean. And I opened the door. Okay, that's it, finished. So the doctor come in with a flashlight. With a flashlight he was looking! Then he put his hand in his pocket—I think maybe he has a revolver or something—and he took half a ruble and said, Here. [*Shaya pounds on the table.*] And he said, What's your name? I told him. He said, Remember, if I need some work you will come. No other people. I took the half a ruble and when I went back, I stepped into my father there. He asks me, *Nu,* what's …? I said, I did it! My father said, And he didn't tell you nothing? And he takes the half a ruble, he looks at it. He gave you half a ruble? And the workers were there and they asked, What's the matter? So my father told them, That doctor gave Shaya half a ruble for beer—a tip. So all the workers they start to pick me up and chuck me around, and said, Ho! Oh!—and they took away my half a ruble. I didn't see where it went. They took away the money and they sent a boy, and they brought vodka and they was drinking and I was drinking because I am the man who did the work for the doctor. For this reason they drink from my half a ruble. I didn't know it was from my half a ruble and when I found out I start to cry. Then they give me back. That is the story.

The next time I went to work—to the doctor, where I was working—I went to the kitchen and I saw there was the maids, and the wife from the doctor, they are painting by themselves in the kitchen. They didn't know how to paint a straight line even! The maids know that the painter uses a string but they don't know how to use the string. So I am working and I start to work; and I became a painter. I used to work each time more and more. Then the war, and in the meantime, one child of mine had died … oh, there are better things to tell you!

At that time I had a grandmother in Wlodova still there. It was very hard then when it was under the German Occupation in the city at that time. We made some papers and they took us back from Warsaw to Wlodova. And then we start to work. My father started to work by himself and I used to help and I worked there. In 1921 it was an epidemic and my mother died. She was thirty-four years old. It was a typhus epidemic after the war.

Oh! I forgot to tell you. I went from house painting to sign painting. The sign painters, the last time I was in Wlodova, they didn't let young people in to work. If I want to look, to see how they do it, they wouldn't let me. They sent me somewhere else. Go here, go there, bring me that, bring me this and when I came back, it's all finished. They want to keep it a secret for themselves. I want to see how they draw, how they work, how they paint it. A long time ago we used to make signs, not only to write letters but to paint figures, something; for example, a shoemaker, who used to make a boot, we used to paint a boot, a ladies shoes, different things. For a tailor we used to make suits, with a man, a face. Sometimes for a poor tailor you make a scissors with a tape. But you know why? Most people they couldn't read. The peasants from the villages they couldn't read. They see a boot—he's a shoemaker. That's why we used to make pictures. One time, so when I was in Wlodova, in our town, I was a sign painter already. Sometimes I helped my father. He was a sign painter too. And then my mother died; it was not a year after, and my father gets married the second time and I was left in the house. We had an old house, and my father went from this house to his wife there. The wife had another house. And I was left over with my grandmother, and my younger brother, and another two children. We were four brothers. When my mother died, there was a child at the breast already—small one— and I remember the last words that my mother said to my father, Yankl, *hit op di kinder!* [take care of the children!]. That was her last words.

When my father got married the second time, my grandmother don't let us go there to him. I was still working with my father. He paid me something. The kids were with me and my grandmother (my mother's mother). She had seven children and they all died. My mother was the last one. My mother was fifteen years old when she got married to my father and he was twenty-five. My grandmother was fourteen years old when she got married and my grandfather, my mother's father, was twenty-nine years when he died. My name is after him.

My grandmother raised the four of us. She hasn't got money. She used to sell apples in the market or some other thing. I used to work—I was a painter then—a better painter than my father. I used to paint signs and drawings; and it was a good piece of work. So it was that my father sent the people to me. People said why do you have to work for your father? You can work for yourself. So I start to work for myself. And I used to take care of my grandmother and the three children. And my father used to still give me work—better work. He would say, You go to Shaya, he'll make for you.

It was a small town, our *shtetl*. My father and I were not the only painters. There were other painters. So it was not much work. And I didn't want to take work away from my father, you see. Most people, for pity, you see for pity, they give me work, not my father. So I don't want to have it like this. So from time to time I went to Warsaw to work. And Paula was born in our town [*Paula was Shaya's future, second wife*]. I remember when Paula was born. I was with my father in their house when they made a banquet, like a party, you know. I want to take a look at what this little baby looks like. It was Paula! Then Paula's parents went to Warsaw to live. They lived in Warsaw. I don't know how old Paula was when she went to Warsaw—maybe a few months old. And when I was in Warsaw I used to come to their house to visit; sometimes for Shabbes or Sunday. I know where they lived. Her father was a sheet-metal worker and had a small store and they used to sleep there upstairs, like a loft. I was there the first time in 1928. She was just a little girl. She was nine years old. I used to come there. I know that my father and her father used to be colleagues. I used to work for years in Warsaw and then come back to Wlodova with a nice hat, with a nice suit, with a nice tie; sometime with a valise. I'm coming back from the big city! People look at me. I come from Warsaw! Mostly we used to come for the holidays: Sukes or for Pesach. And my father used to meet me with a *droske* [a wagon, in this instance]; he brought me home. It was Yom Tov. Sometimes I am staying in Wlodova again and I start to work. Then there was no work and I went back again to Warsaw. So a few times I went back and forth.

The last time I was working in Warsaw my master was different. He was a drinker, he took money from clients, he hasn't got money to buy paint, we couldn't finish the jobs. He was a bad man. I was working in one place, and in the middle I didn't get the materials, and the owner buy me the material and I finished it. And he pays me the money. I told him that the master doesn't pay. So he paid me the whole money and he told me, Why do you have to work for this guy? You start for yourself. I'll give you clients. So I start to work for myself in Warsaw. By now this was 1936, just before the war started, and that's another story!

Der Feter Itche

My Uncle Itche
Learned tailoring.
And now he makes old cloth coats
Look brand new.

He descends on a village
With needle and thread;
Hangs out a sign
"Clothing fixed here."

Uncle sits on the table
Simple Turkish-style;
Ripping, turning coats
And patching over patches.

When he has patched up one village
He goes on to another.
Till by his hand
The whole district is sewn up.

[Repeat first verse]

Translated from the Yiddish by Seymour Levitan

Der Feter Itche by M.Kulbak was hand-printed on parchment by David Shaya Kirman and given to me when I interviewed him with the understanding that I should use it in my work.

Rose Smith

Rose Smith was born 17 July 1899 in Gomel (now Homyel), Belarus, in the Ukraine. I interviewed Rose one afternoon in 1978, at her apartment in Vancouver, surrounded by the pieces of old furniture that she had cared for over many years.

Rose came to Canada with her husband, Abe Smith, whose story appears earlier in the book, and two children in 1925. She was a kind and gentle woman. Abe, suffering from Alzheimer's disease, was unaware of her passing when she died on 21 September 1982.

I COME FROM GOMEL (today it is called Homyel) in Belarus—it is not far from Minsk and on the way to Moscow. In the old days there were so many pogroms and my childhood was terrible. The pogroms, it happened all the time and I didn't understand what it's about. They used to raid father's house. Then they used to put a bomb on the street and it used to blow up— and it was always on our street! They want to kill an enemy. It was all against the Tsar. Like one shooting the Tsar in Kiev! A student shooting right there in the Opera House![25] Then you must have read or heard about the Beilis case.[26] They used to say that in our matzas we used to mix in blood! Somebody killed a kid, a child, and they blamed it on the Jews. Every time, just before Easter, somebody used to kill a child to just make provocations against the Jewish people, till in the end, the King, the rabbis, and important people from all over the world gathered and they had a meeting and they studied so much and found out that it was all provocation against the Jews.

I remember when I was living in a house in our city and there were Catholic people next door and they were very religious. We lived together, we were very good friends. and her daughter-in-law came over and I had my one baby at the time, Leo (who was killed later in World War II in Italy), and I said to her, I am going to swear—and they knew how much I loved him—

I'll swear with his life (and they loved him very much), I'll swear with his life that there is no blood in the matza. Her son who worked already in the post office—he understood it—and he said to his wife, Don't talk nonsense. He understood that it was full of nonsense about the Jews using blood in the matza! Anyway, by the time they found out what's what there were pogroms all over the place until they cleared it up. And when I was a child it was very hard, very hard.

In 1925 my husband's family—he had a sister and a brother here [in Canada]—and we wrote to them that we want to come here. I didn't know where Canada was because I had nobody here. I had no family here. I had a sister, of course, and nieces and nephews, a whole bunch of them in the Old Country and I correspond with them. I hear from them very often—from my sister, specially. I still have people there.

Once the hooligans came to my Dad's store. He was going to Papindrov and he just wants to close it up before going. They told him, Don't close the store. They are going to burn it. They are going to burn the whole city. So we had a doctor, an eye doctor, who had a clinic—he was a socialist himself—so Dad phoned him. He was very friendly with the doctor, and said, What shall we do? The doctor said, They are not going to touch the hospital, so you just come here. So we went there overnight. The next night it did quieten down and then we decided we were going to run away. We were going to run away because they said there would be other pogroms, you see.

My grandpa, my mother's father, he was a rabbi and we decided we would go there. He was a rabbi in a small town where everybody liked him, where they didn't bother him. We went there and on the way there we picked up everybody. There was no train to take. We had a wagon, a buggy, you know. We were all travelling in the wagon from Gomel to Grandpa's to hide ourselves—our whole family, my cousins—especially one of them who got beat up terribly when he was a younger man. Grandpa lived in a very small town, Nesavitche. Gomel was a big town already.

Life was very complicated and it was a very bad childhood. It was cruel, and ... nothing to talk about. I don't want to discuss those things. It is better to forget about them. Hooligans just came from the road and beat people up. Then when the Jews went to the station, to run away, there was a man who said, Look what's going on! And he was a Red (a Communist, you know), and he had buns and he give us buns. There were so many Jewish people trying to run away from the city, the station was full of them. I remember the taste of those buns! Some people couldn't stand it. I don't know who he was but he was a very nice man, the one with the buns. Not all of the

Russians were bad. There were good people. There was lots of hardship, lots of hardship.

Pogroms were nothing. I remember my mother was there in the store and suddenly they just come in and say they are going to take prisoners from one prison to another and everybody start hammering with the doors, to lock up the stores, and run home. And there was a prisoner, a Jewish guy, a Bolshevie, in chains; and they drag the prisoners from one place to another— I don't know to where—Siberia, I suppose. My mother had a nervous breakdown and came home and Dad had so much trouble. My Dad's store— they used to buy fish from different countries—it was the only store like that, beautiful, beautiful.

They did not destroy the city of Gomel, so we came back because there was nothing there in the small village where my grandpa lived.

I was able to go to school. They used to take just a small percent of Jewish kids. Then they decided that they would open a Jewish school and a Jewish woman, she opened up a school for Jewish children and Gentile children. And so it meant the Jewish kids went to school after that. I did not work. It wasn't something for me to do. All the money my father had went for our education.

In those days, in university when you finished with a gold medal, you can go in a city like Leningrad where Jews are not allowed there unless you were a worker. A worker was allowed there and those who were finishing with gold medals like my brother-in-law. He got a gold medal, and my oldest sister too, and they went to Leningrad. She got married there and Father went to a whorehouse to sleep over when he went for the wedding! Otherwise they wouldn't let him stay anywhere. He had no choice. And he slept over there because he wanted to go to the wedding. I don't know what happened but my father was a stranger and the poor guy, you know, he had a beating.

The situation was not very good there for the students. The first time we went to see my sister and brother-in-law in Leningrad they were still alive, but the second time, not.

My husband and I left the Old Country in 1925, when his brother immigrated to Canada. I met Abe ... well, I was the best-looking girl in the city and he was watching! He saw me. He saw me coming out of a dairy store and he went in to ask them who I am. And they told him that my Dad had a store from seeds, beets, flowers, and all kinds of things. You see, Germany used to send all this in January and we used to open the store for a few months. We used to supply all the seeds to all the factories and my father was a specialist. And he was also a *shochet*. He also had the education to be a rabbi too but he didn't like it. So he had a store, he had a feed store, he was selling seeds for flowers and vegetables, and he was a *shochet*, but he never had money. He was a poor guy.

So Abe saw me coming in the store and went to find out who I was. At the time he needed a place to work—he was a watchmaker—so when he saw our store was open he tried to get a place to work in the store. But he didn't want to rent. So his father came (he was renting in the same place as my father), and he came to tell Dad that he would be responsible; he is going to be responsible for Abe. Dad has to leave town for business when the season comes, so they decided for Abe to work there. And that's how I met him. So then already he used to come to the house! I didn't pay attention! That's all.

As youngsters we had a lot of things happening in our town. There used to be a travelling theatre that used to come through. They used to come from all over. First the students played a whole summer on a big stage. I was going to theatres when I was fifteen and buy standing-up tickets because there was no money to buy a seat. So I used to stand and then people would feel sorry for you and say, Go on, and used to tell us to sit down. But it was lots of fun. We used to enjoy it so much.

When we got married there was no wedding. We went to the Justice of Peace. We didn't have a regular wedding. Who had money for weddings? Oh, there was a rabbi—I'm telling you, a progressive rabbi—and we all had so much fun, you have no idea. And they brought ten old men—ugly to look at, you know—to be as witnesses. I couldn't help it, but I'll never forget their faces! We got married in 1918 at the end of the First World War, 19 December. We are married sixty-two years!

I never look back. Sometimes it is not so funny looking back. It's hard. It hurts. But we were all looked after very well. The houses didn't have water—you had to take it on your shoulders—to fill the bathtubs ... it was always very comfortable. Even though we never had a cent yet we always lived in a beautiful place, always. But it was tough. My father did a lot for us but he died very young.

I came to Calgary in 1925 with my husband, Abe, and our two children: Leo and Mary.

Nina Dolgoy Ullman

Nina Ullman was born in Dagda, Latvia, in 1900. She came to Winnipeg with her husband, Harry Ullman (whose story appears earlier in this volume) and their two daughters, Gallia and Bebbe. Nina worked as a dressmaker in Winnipeg for many years before she and her husband moved to Vancouver. She died there in 1991, a month short of her ninety-second birthday.

Interviews with Nina's brother, Max Dolgoy, and her sister, Bertha (Dolgoy) Guberman, appear later in this volume.

I REMEMBER WHEN I WAS A CHILD—there were so many of us— six in the family, brothers and sisters. I had an older sister. We were living in a tiny place with our grandparents and it was on a big, big hill. And we lived in a small little house and underneath the house was sand and clay. And the yard—it was a big, big yard and water was running all the time. I don't know how you call it but it was like a waterfall. And there was a well and the whole little town used to come to take from us the water. The water was so beautiful, so clean. I had an uncle who used to look after it. He used to make sure the water was clean. He used to bring a big barrel every year and clean it up.

My grandfather wasn't such a generous man. He didn't want to share the water. My grandparents used to have a porch and we used to play there. I remember the door used to make so much noise. My mother was a very good-natured person and so she used to tell the neighbours that my grandfather is not home and they should come and take the water. This I remember.

We were small kids—what did we know? My grandmother was very, very strict. They had a shelf, you know, and on the shelf was certain dishes— I don't know what you call it here—it's like silver but it's very heavy. They use it here but not for dishes. [*Pewter? I offer.*] Anyway, my grandmother used to have it and I should have to clean this. So we used to go with my older sister to clean this by the waterfall and we had to make with it certain patterns—so you can't imagine because you have to take this and make like this, a line like that and … So I talk to my sister that this is not a good thing.

Let me explain what we used to do. We would take the sand and the clay and make all kinds of little pottery. It wasn't hard. Somehow we used to make little dishes, little pots, little cups, and we used to go with my sister to the rich girls and they used to give you a kopek, maybe two kopeks. After a while we decided that was enough and we start to go with my sister to all the dressmakers in the yard and pick up little pieces of material and we used to make little clothes. We needed something to do, you know. And also we used to make little dolls and sell them. This was when I was six or seven years old. When I was nine years already, my mother gave me to learn the trade. There wasn't such a thing as schooling, you know. In the Russian schools, Jewish people they would not accept at all.

When I was eight or nine years old, my mother gave me to learn a trade. So there was a dressmaker from whom you learned to make dresses; and also there was men's underwear, which also had to be made by hand. So she gave me to make men's underpants. I had to make buttonholes and I was very good in making buttonholes. I remember I used to say, Oy. Oy. If I'll grow up and I'll have to make men's underwear, then how will I take a measure? And I came home and I start to cry. My mother say, Why are you crying? I said, Mummy, I'm not going to, I don't want to take a man's measure. And I didn't want to go.

So anyway, the woman from whom I am learning, said I was so good and she liked me. I used to make all the stitching and buttonholes—and just for nothing. And I cried. I said, Nothing doing. So my mother decided that if I am so good she will put me with another dressmaker that makes clothes, dresses, suits, whatever it is. And she asks for some money. Such a little girl, who would pay her? You see, my mother had to pay for three years for my sister's training. Three years and you get nothing. So the dressmaker didn't want to pay for me. But they took me to try out. I was a small little girl. I could do very well on the machines. So my mama made a bill: ten rubles for a year.

The whole little town went crazy. They couldn't understand. Such a little girl and already she is making money. Ten rubles a year! The second year I got thirty-five rubles and the third year I got fifty rubles. By this time the war [World War I] already broke out.

So when the war broke out I was training. I got together with another girl and opened for ourselves a business already. Can you imagine that? I think I was about fifteen years old! The war started and it was very, very bad and we had work up to here [*indicating her head*]. Ours was a small town, a *shtetl.* The army used to stay in our town and we used to go from one government to another government [*depending on which country's army was in residence*]. It was so complicated, you know, for younger people to be in small towns. You have no idea.

When the army used to come into the small towns, the *shtetls,* they used to go to the farmers and confiscate all the cattle, and when they brought in the cattle into the city, so somebody had to take it closer to the front. So all of a sudden the soldiers used to run around the city and anyone who came into the city, they caught you. So they caught me once and I was to go out and drive the cattle for fifty miles, seventy miles, twenty miles; and when you come to this place, they let you go back home and they catch somebody else.

So they caught me and I start to cry—this was in Dagda, the fighting was there, the Germans were there, the Polish soldiers was there, the Red Army, and whatever else you can think about was there! Anyways, they catch me and he is running after me and he's holding the stick and my mother start to cry and she start to beg, She's a small little girl. She doesn't know anything. She said, You know what? I have my son. Take my son. And my brother went in my place. And I didn't have to go. I was lucky. So my brother went fifty miles one way—thirty miles by foot—to drive the cattle.

At the time, we were living in a double house: one side my grandparents and one side us. Once my father took us to hide from the Cossacks. So we had to go—it doesn't matter where you go, you have to cross a bridge, and the bridge was where all the soldiers were. So we rented a little boat and we crossed the river. And our house is right by the river. You go out and you jump right away in the river. And we went and there were so many farmers who were good friends. They hide us for a day or so and after it is all quiet down we would come back to our town.

So on this day I went to a farm with my girlfriend and her father, who knows these people very well, and he tells the farmer that he would like we should stay for the day. He said, I am going into the fields. And a little boy, about two or three years old who was living there, said, No I'm not going to stay with the Jewish people. They'll kill me!

Wherever we went, nobody is left in the houses. So a whole day we were in the bush. There was no food whatsoever. We were picking the berries to eat. So a whole day we were there and the father said, You stay here in the bush a little while and I'll go in the road and I'll see if somebody we know will come by and I'll find out what's happening.

And all around from the farms they came, the hands, in big wagons, they all came like it was a pogrom. And the Cossacks didn't come and we were about twenty miles from the town and we went out from the bush to go home. And it started to pour with rain. It was pouring all the way down and I remember only one thing: I opened up the door to our house and I fell down between the doors of our double house and I don't remember what happened after that. When I woke up two days later they had the doctor—I don't know what was the matter with me—but that's what happened.

You see, all the grown-up young Jews, about sixteen, seventeen, eighteen years old—they had all left the small *shtetl* and my mother said that as long as she lives she wouldn't let me go away anywhere on account she was left with only three children.

So this is the story. My father, whom I had never met until I came here, had left in 1905 for Canada because he didn't want to become a soldier in the Russo–Japanese War. And the war was very bad and they start to count his years—how old he was. So he came to Winnipeg in 1905 and left my mother with six children and he didn't leave a penny! But my mother was such a woman … you know what it means not to have anything to eat? My father stayed in Canada for three years and he came back and he left again. That was when he took the three children. So my mother said she wouldn't let me go away, not for anything in the world. So she had the three children during the war—no money, no letters, no anything from my father.

One day, all of a sudden a woman came over to our place and they start to talk about going to Canada. You know, I never saw a train in my life. I never knew how a train looks. The train was about twenty-nine miles from our small *shtetl* and you had to go by horse and buggy. And I came to the station with the train and this woman promised my mother to put me on the right train. And so I started my journey from Dagda to many more cities from the Ukraine to Russia to Latvia until I come to Canada. My father, my brothers, and sisters were in Winnipeg, and that is where I went.

Sidney Sarkin

✻

Sidney Sarkin was born in Vilna, Lithuania, in June 1903. Sydney came from a rich family, whose members were not only "captains of industry" but also owned a bank. However, when Sidney came to Montreal, he wanted to begin at the bottom rung and work his way up. His life was devoted to the union movement, and he rose through the ranks to hold some of the higher positions in the executive of the Amalgamated Garment Workers' Union. In his later years he wrote and published his memoirs of the Old Country, in Yiddish. A second book, translated from Yiddish into French as well as into English, still awaits a publisher. Sydney died in 1985.

I spent many, many hours at Sidney's apartment, taping much of his life. Besides being a unionist, a Communist, and an "internee without cause" at Camp Petawawa during the Second World War, he was a closet artist who worked in wood. Art was a hobby he begun at Camp Petawawa, where he found a piece of wood and a piece of glass and with them made a box covered in intricate carvings.

The following story is only a small part of Sidney Sarkin's life and involvement in the garment industry and trade unions.

DURING THE FIRST WORLD WAR, the family in Canada was looking for ways and means of getting us over. They made proposals that we should go to Siberia, from Siberia to Japan. They tried everything under the sun. But things were impossible because of the Russo–Japanese War. The family also tried every which way to get in touch with us. When the war ended we were the first ones in the city of Vilna, where I come from, to receive from the family our travel tickets and also an official permit from the Government of

Canada to come here. Canada at that time had no representatives in Lithuania because Canada was part of the British Empire.

As soon as we received the tickets and money for our expenses, the British Consulate helped us with our passports, even though we did not have birth certificates. They advised us to immediately leave Lithuania. Our tickets were booked to leave from the port of Le Havre, France, so we had to get a transit visa also from France. This was the beginning of 1920 and the British consulate undertook to get it for us. The consul failed because France at that time never recognized Lithuania and so they refused to give us visas. At that time, there was also trouble developing. Poland tried to extend her territory and occupy parts of Lithuania, especially the city of Vilna, where this British consulate was situated. So he kicked us out because this could take place any day! He told us to immediately leave and get out of Lithuania generally.

The consulate advised us to go to Berlin, the capital city of Germany, and there we should get in touch with the British consulate or ambassador, with whom he will get in touch; perhaps they will be successful in getting us permits to sail from Le Havre. So we went to Germany, as it was not very far from us.

For the first time in my life I saw the world and the way it looked! When you have lived in a town like Vilkomir, like we did, and then you find yourself in a leading city in Germany, well, your eyes are opened. It was the end of the war and, after the Treaty of Versailles, we could not go directly to Germany through Poland. We had to take a ship. However, we arrived in Berlin and there we were faced with a general strike. It was 13 March 1920, Easter, when the Kapp putsch took place. This was an attempt, a *coup d'etat*, to overthrow the Weimar government.[27] Wolfgang Kapp, a right-wing East Prussian civil servant and fervent nationalist, was the leader. The government issued a proclamation calling on Germany's workers to defeat the putsch by means of a general strike. We arrived in Berlin at that time.

For the first time in my life, you know, I learned as a youngster, that if the workers want all life to come to a stop that they could make it happen. I saw it before my very eyes! Everything was stopped: transportation, water, electricity, communication, all the stores. It even became a joke that the Chancellor couldn't wash himself when he got up in the morning. Everything was cut off—as if you had pushed a button. And at this time there was great hunger prevailing in Germany because of the loss of the war. An announcement was made in our hotel, a general strike had been declared, and that there would be a demonstration by all the workers at 10 a.m. in Berlin.

We saw a million and a half people marching twenty-five abreast, just like the German army did, using their special step—that is how they marched. Police dispersed: you couldn't see one anywhere! Each group was led by its own leaders, with their red bands on their arms. And they marched through all the main streets of Berlin until they came to the Kaiserhoff, which means the Kaiser Park, which occupied tremendous grounds. You know, Berlin was once a wonderful city! And there in the park, special tribunes were set up for the speakers—there were a minimum of forty mass meetings going on. With this general strike, they finished the putsch of Kapp and the Weimar took over again. However, they didn't like the spirit that had developed which was evident in the strike. You see, there was a left wing, which was led by one named Karl Liebknecht.

Liebknecht, together with Rosa Luxemburg and Clara Zetkin and others, formed the first groups of the Left under the name of the Spartacus League [*Spartakusbund*]. Luxemberg and Zetkin were outstanding women who were known throughout the labour movement worldwide. One came from Poland and the other from Lithuania. They were outstanding leaders, agitators, propagandists, speakers, and writers. Lenin carried on discussions with them for years. These people tried to follow the example of the Russian workers in establishing the equivalent of soviets[28] in Germany. However, when social democracy came along, they found the only way to stay in power was to cut off the heads of the left-wing leadership. That was the time they killed Karl Liebknecht, Rosa Luxemburg, Clara Zetkin, and others.

To get back to when we arrived in Berlin. Everything was on cards, which were used for all kinds of materials, even the sale of food, one's necessary daily food. And the bread! When you tasted it, you didn't taste wheat but grass. It was a good thing that we had brought with us four loaves of bread from Lithuania. When the hotel boss saw it we offered him a taste. He couldn't get over it. So you can imagine what the situation was like at the time.

We visited the British consulate and they told us to see the ambassador. He tried to get in touch with the French ambassador. He tried for a week, hoping he would change their opinion to let us through; but the French refused. Well, my mother was terribly disappointed; but as far as my brother and myself were concerned, we had a good time. We had a chance to see Berlin. For the first time in my life I saw the most outstanding museums. To me they were at that time outstanding! A terrific impression was made upon me by the biological museum. I had never imagined there could be anything like it. The city itself was wonderful. There was a district known as the Unter Den Linden, which is something like the Notre Dame de Paris district and much nicer. They had ice arenas where the seats were around and there was skating and actual shows. And there were theatres too.

We were there a month. The ambassador did everything he could. Finally the Cunard Line agent, with whom the arrangements had been made here in Canada, informed us that we could sail. The family in Canada had done everything necessary for us. After all, my uncle controlled Maritime Packers Ltd. And they were millionaires. So because of them and because my father had citizenship in Canada—he was a British subject and had come here in 1904—all arrangements were completed.

We left Berlin under the instructions of the Cunard Line and were able to sail from Antwerp, Belgium. It was interesting to travel through Germany by train; and out of Berlin I took with me—I was lucky enough—a good bag of experience and discoveries that I had made. This added to the ideology I had absorbed in Lithuania. Words and phrases became to me flesh and blood, proof of all I had been taught, like the general strike, the demonstration, speakers and all the rest of it.

We came to Belgium. There was nothing to complain about it. I was satisfied. Mother was again disappointed, you know. She wanted to see her family and then she was tired generally. She was also afraid that we would never reach Canada. For us, again, it was a new experience, in a new country. We stayed in one of the finest hotels. I'll never forget even the name of it: the Max Hotel, it was called. The owner's name was Max. He was at the same time the burgermeister, the mayor of the city and he became an institution during the Second World War during the occupation of Belgium by Germany. He was a terrific fighter, because as a mayor the Germans tried to win him over, but he fought back every attempt that they made. So he became an institution terribly respected. Wherever you went you heard the name Max.

For the first time we had wonderful quarters and for the first time we tasted white bread. Ha! Ha! It gave you the impression that Belgium never suffered one iota during the war. The breakfasts and the dinners and the suppers were outstanding. We were amazed. When we arrived there, we went after the bread, you see. So the waiters stopped us. They said, Don't do it. There is some more coming. All kinds of dishes are coming. But we had been away so long. It had even been a long time since we had tasted our own black bread.

We had a good time. We spent most of it going out and sizing up the city. Oh. I forgot! We also stopped on the way in Brussels, the capital city of Belgium. There we were two days and I had a chance to see the city. It had a very fine zoological gardens, which made a great impression on us—after all we were people from Lithuania. Both Brussels and Antwerp—wherever you turned—there were corners with stands of chocolate sellers, like the way you find ice-cream sellers here. In Lithuania we had very little chocolate, and in Belgium there was such a variety of it that I couldn't grasp the fact that there could be anything like it.

In Antwerp, we walked around and visited first the centre and then the district around us. We used to say, Another few days and another few days and we'll be sailing. So we were careful not to stay out too long or too late. In one of our walks, we came to a district where it seemed two languages were being spoken. We thought there were some Jewish people there because the expressions sounded familiar. It was not long after that when we continued our journey to Canada.

On arrival from the Old Country, immigrants were first taught how to make a home for themselves, to get a job, find work. In my case I had an alternative. My family was well-to-do and wanted me to have an education. However, coming from a socialist and revolutionary background, I felt I must immediately go into the workers movement, join a union, and become a proletarian. Members of my family in Montreal were owners of a number of clothing factories, and two jobs were held open for me and my brother on arrival in 1921. I rejected the offer with much thanks and my family finally conceded that I should go my own way.

I started working for Rubin Brothers, cousins of mine by marriage, as a sweeper at five dollars a week. My main concern at the time was not to be misunderstood by my fellow workers. Being a cousin of the boss immediately put me in a category apart from them. Also we had just arrived from Saint John, New Brunswick, where my mother's sister lived. The family having wealth, I was dressed in the latest and best fashion! It aroused the sentiments of the workers when I used to go and wash myself; that such a nice-looking fellow, so well dressed, is being treated by his cousin in this manner: as a sweeper! And I was tickled pink because, you see, that meant I had made contact with the workers. The women, the girls, used to watch me going into the washroom and used to hand me a towel to clean myself. That is how I broke the ice. They did not look upon me as the boss's stooge but as one of them.

I made the same impression on the cutters, the aristocrats of the needle trades. In connection with the needle trades at that time, there were regulations prevailing as far as the cutters were concerned. The contract with the cutters is part and parcel of the collective agreement. It allowed one assistant to every ten cutters. Everyone who came from the Old Country, unless he already possessed a trade, started by sweeping in the factories. From cleaning the floor, your next position was message boy to the cutters. If you showed promise and were destined for the cutting room, you moved closer to the handling of the scissors by cutting undercollars. Then you became an assistant cutter and finally a cutter. From sweeper to cutter, in those days, it took a period of five years.

The cutting room at Rubin Brothers was made up of a section of nine men, the majority of whom were Jews, with one Englishman and one Frenchman. Amongst the Jewish cutters there were two brothers named Barkin. They had both come back from fighting in the First World War. One brother had applied at the outbreak of the war to join the Navy. On the application form, he had to fill in his religious denomination. He was terribly disappointed to find out that Jews could not enlist in the Canadian navy! They could join, fight, and die in the Army, but not in the Royal [Canadian] Navy! The man had grown up in Canada and considered himself a Canadian, and it was consequently a great disappointment to him. This was my first acquaintance with honest-to-goodness Canadians and we became close friends.

The friendship helped me along towards the cutter's table. After a month of sweeping, I became part of the cutting room. I was allowed to chop, that is, to cut cloth and the undercollars of the garment. As I have already mentioned, the apprenticeship period was five years. However, in my case a concession was made *and* with the consent of the union. If you are not listed as a cutter with the union, you cannot accept a position as a cutter.

During the 1910–20 period, the clothing industry as a whole was moving slowly into the hands of the Jewish people, not only in the numbers of workers employed but also in ownership. For example, there was an English firm which employed fifty cutters, which was unheard of, and fifty cutters in those days produced, that is, cut thousands of garments per day. They used to pile the cloth up, some twenty to thirty high, and cut them with electric cutting machines. The English actually had the monopoly of the cutting trade; but it was beginning to shift. There was keen competition from Jewish-owned small shops, which had lower overheads, greater production, and brought down the price of the garment.

Thus the larger firms could not compete. Also Jewish workers tried their damndest to get their sons into the cutting trade instead of being operators [*workers on sewing machines*]. Through begging the bosses, and also because of the fact that they were faster and more productive than the average, it finally came to a point where they managed to get one of their sons into the cutting room. Thus, in the period between 1921 and 1924, the English were practically cleaned out of the cutting rooms.

In Toronto, however, the cutting trade was firmly held in the hands of the English, and they employed every means in their power to keep out Jewish workers. As late as when I became a business agent, that is, an officer of the trade union, in 1935, there were only three Jewish cutters out of approximately three hundred. As far as the other operations in the clothing factory were concerned, the Jews held the absolute majority, both in Montreal and Toronto.

The period of the 1920s was a time of organization, because during this time the workers in the industries had grown to great numbers. For me and people like me, it meant the organization and consolidation of the left-wing progressive forces in the trade unions, political fields, and the mass fraternal organizations on the cultural front. It meant the organization of the unorganized workers, the struggle and movement toward industrial unionism, the struggle and movement toward social and labour legislation, the building of the political arm of the working class.

Although at the time there was already a developed trade union movement in Canada, however the basic industries, heavy industries (outside of mining), where the masses of workers were concentrated, were not organized. For example, the textile industry was an open citadel; a citadel of open shops [*not unionized*] and company unions. The automobile industry, which had developed by then, also was unorganized. In the needle trades there was the beginning of the dress industry, which by the mid-twenties developed into one of the largest industries in the trade, not only supplying markets in Canada but also overseas. Thousands of people became employed in the needle industry. In the East the organized miners of the Maritimes in Nova Scotia were affiliated with the International Mineworkers of America. They were District 26. In the West there was District 80. But the steelworkers and other heavy industries were unorganized.

These then were the main tasks facing the left-wing movement. It required the organization and consolidation of their forces for an immediate program of action. On the basis of this, the Trade Union Educational League was formed, an arm of the left-wing forces. Their aim was, first of all, to consolidate their own forces, expand them, and at the same time work out plans for the organization of the unorganized on the basis of industrial unionism against craft unionism. In the first two years of establishment, over fifty thousand workers had been unionized!

The organization of the unorganized was led by a number of trade unionists and I was one of them. I was involved in the co-ordination of the left-wing forces in the needle trades, which covered all aspects. At the same time I attended meetings, consulted, and advised on campaigns in practically all the other industries with which they had established contact. This was all done under the auspices of the Trade Union Commission. Lectures, classes, mass meetings, campaigns, etc., were all part of my work.

In those days the leadership devoted all of its time. We worked from morning till night—to the early hours of the morning at times—running from one meeting to another. The remuneration was next to nothing. As a matter of fact, every one of us contributed part of our salaries to these things.

The structure of the Amalgamated Clothing Workers' Union, in a broad sense, was based on industrial unionism. It embraced every phase of the men's clothing industry. However, one could not compare the task and contribution of the cutters to any other operation. They only cut and nothing else. They had nothing to do with the rest of the work. Then there were the general operators, who were only concerned with the construction of a coat and there were many aspects to this. The operators' local was the largest. Here the bulk of the workers were found. There were also the pants makers. The making of a pair of slacks, as compared to a coat, was a thing by itself. It involved different operations, though less seaming. There were pockets, zipper, and that was all. The vestmakers—this was a bigger job—because the construction of a vest involved more labour than pants. Thus you had a cutters' local, a pants makers' local, a vestmakers' local, etc. For example, a French Canadian could belong to his French Canadian local or to the cutters' local, if he was a cutter. Each group was formed around its specific tasks. Each group had its own business agent and organizer; therefore, each group was able to discuss and decide upon its own particular beefs and policies. Each local had its own executive, which dealt with its problems, and which was concerned with the administration of its own local.

Six months after I had started working in the cutting room (I had moved from sweeper to assistant cutter in one month), I applied to become a member of the cutters' local. It was not so easy for an assistant cutter to get into the cutters' local. With help and friendships I had developed, and the relationship I had established with two cutters in the shop (who had a fine record in their local), I appeared before the executive of the cutters' local and was finally accepted. I became a full-fledged member of the Amalgamated Clothing Workers' of America!

Two years later, by the end of 1923, during the period of elections, I ran as a member of the executive, and I was the first assistant cutter to be elected to the executive board. With this appointment, my general activities outside the life of the trade union organization began.

About six months after my election, the general executive board member of the Amalgamated, who visited the different cities and markets from time to time, came to Montreal. When he saw me, a youngster on the executive, he turned to the executive meeting and gave them a lecture on the degeneration of the cutters' union in allowing an assistant cutter to be on the executive. He concluded his remarks by saying that this was a precedent, and a very bad precedent, and should be done away with. However, the whole executive stood up against him and I remained on the board.

It gives you the psychology at that time, although it was nearing the end of that period because, in a few years, it was practically gone: the end of the general approach and psychology of the cutters, their relationship, their outlook as to who should be in the leadship and who should have a say in the affairs of the cutters throughout the US and Canada. This was carried over from the former organization, the United Garment Workers, whose basic philosophy was based on craft ideology.

This was the background of the Amalgamated and, when I joined, the cutters were known as the aristocrats and were clothed as such. They used to wear striped pants, very fine dark jackets, a vest, and through the vest a golden chain and watch. This period came to an end when the Jews started coming into the trade and one found little evidence of that period of the striped pants.

The relationship which existed between the owners and the cutters was different from that which existed between the owners and the rest of the workers. The cutters were treated better and with respect, and had amongst them an understanding that so much was to be produced and no more. If someone went over the production agreed upon, one was called to the union executive and fined. That was the kind of control which existed. And the bosses couldn't do a damn thing about it! I was a fast worker and there were a number of cutters who were very fast; but in order to keep themselves within the quota, they used to kill time by going umpteen times to the washroom; or sit down on a bolt of cloth with a box of chalk and sharpen the pieces. There were fifty-two pieces in a box.

This vividly portrays the difference between the cutters' condition and the life they enjoyed and those of the operators. Even at that time the salary was forty dollars a week for a cutter. In the cutting room one seldom found anyone aged sixty to sixty-five years. After the age of fifty you were looked upon as being through!

On 15 June 1922, the very first agreement in Canada was signed between the Associated Clothing Manufacturers and the Amalgamated Clothing Workers' Union. It is not an impressive-looking document, but it is a landmark of its time. What is important is that such a document was finally agreed upon and signed.

In 1924, trouble developed in the shop where I was employed. The shop was a union shop and was owned by my cousin. The union, through the shop committee, demanded action and I participated in my first strike. It was the winter of 1924. I was on the strike committee of the shop. On the picket line one met scabs, gangsters, and squads of mounted police. I don't want you to misunderstand. It was not the Canadian Mounted Police. It was the local police and they were mounted. It reminded me for the first time of Cossacks! The horses were well trained to use their hoofs to push back the people on the picket line.

The cause of the strike had its basis in three developments during that period:

- The development of that disease of contracting
- A move on the part of the clothing manufacturers to run away from the unions by moving out into the country
- The Catholic church's inducements to manufacturers to move out of the city by offering all kinds of concessions: no tax payment from five to ten years, cheap labour because farmers were employed, and so on.

The contracting system is a disease as far as any industry is concerned, but especially as far as the clothing industry, because the character of the industry permits a few people—two or three—to get together with their families and take work outside from the inside shops, undertaking to produce the garments cheaper than the cost to the inside manufacturers by working all kinds of hours within the home. It is from the conditions of the contracting shop that the term "sweatshop" originated. You see, an "inside shop" was an established shop or factory; whereas an "outside shop" was where a contractor takes out bundles of clothing and contracts with the manufacturers to do the work. This was always in the contractor's home, under miserable conditions, long hours, crowded into a small room, very little or no pay, because they are learning the trade! Hence the term "sweatshop"!

In that given period, contracting had become a menace to the general conditions of the tailors. It was a basic problem. This was one of the reasons of the 1924 strike. For workers to go out on strike in those days was bad. If you went out in winter you were confronted with the prospect of starvation, as well as standing in freezing weather on the picket lines. There was no strike pay. Strikers existed on handouts and collections of kindly people. If the strike was prolonged, you and your family suffered deprivation. This was one of the main reasons why strikes were broken: the workers could not go hungry for too many weeks at a time!

Another great problem, which existed in Quebec particularly, was the army of scabs which were brought in by employers. All sorts of methods were used by the workers to get rid of scabs, because the scabs endangered the workers' bargaining position. Employers also used gangsters and the police. There were bloody fights and workers were beaten up. As though this was not enough, they faced court injunctions, sellouts by top leaders, and, in some instances, defeat. Nonetheless it was these militant workers who won union recognition, reduction in working hours, and wage increases which today the labour force takes more or less for granted.

I was, of course, an ardent picketer and it was in this, my first strike, that the trouble with my leg began because I had to stand for hours in freezing weather. [*Twenty years later, after years of pain and suffering, Sidney had a leg amputated.*] After six weeks of cold, hunger, scabs, police brutality, the strike was lost. This company then moved out to Victoriaville, away from Montreal, and only the cutting room remained in the city.

Similar problems were faced by other workers in other shops. The progressive and left-wing sections of the union called for action to eliminate the contractors. A division or difference of opinion developed between right- and left-wing sections of the union. Although there was much talk about the problems of contracting at that time, the right-wingers were never willing to take action against it. As a matter of fact, they proposed that the union organize the contractors so as to bring about collective bargaining and agreement with them, which had never been worked out. The contracting problem from then on became one of the scourges of the industry and undermined the conditions and livelihood of the people employed in the clothing industry.

Two hundred and eighty people were employed in the shop where I worked when it was moved out to Victoriaville. They all lost their jobs. After the strike was lost I did not go back to the cutting room, which had remained in the city. I joined the ranks of the unemployed. Through family ties I had the opportunity of getting work in an open shop. However, I could not bring myself to work in a non-union shop, and for months I was breadless! I didn't have a job.

At that time, another cousin of mine, Samuel Hart, owned one of the largest shops in the city of Montreal, which was also an open shop. His wife, Mrs. Hart, was a very fine woman and used to visit me quite often. She used to, in a very nice way, ask me to go out to work. She said there was a place open at Samuel Hart and why don't I go out to work? She said that nobody was going to interfere with my ideas and thoughts. And so on ...

I went up to the union, told them my story, and said that it was up to them. If they gave me a working card, meaning an official acknowledgment to go to the shop, then I would. But without a card I would not go. So it became a joke at that time: the union issuing me a working card to work in an open, non-union shop! But from the point of view of status and the relationship with the workers, I felt that it should be done.

Finally, after three months of being without work, I started at Samuel Hart's in the trimming room. This was by now the beginning of 1925. In this shop there was a large cutting room employing some twenty-five men. Within the first few weeks I felt I couldn't breathe. I felt cramped and suffocated. No one bothered me in my work. After three weeks or a month, the general manager of Samuel Hart called the workers together to hear a speech, the sum total of which was that times were hard and that none of them should be surprised to find in their pay envelopes, comes Friday, a cut in wages of $2.50 to five dollars a week! He explained that this was happening in union shops and, after all, they must be competitive.

Well, I nearly busted when I heard his speech. I couldn't swallow the self-rule of the open shop, where workers could not express an opinion about the conditions. So I went to the back of the trimming room and told the foreman, who was a nice fellow and I had nothing against him, that he should accept my resignation. The foreman said, What the hell is the matter with you? You have not been touched. And this was true. I had not been given a cut in wages. When I received my envelope my pay was intact. But I couldn't look at myself. You know what it means? I'm favoured in the shop because I'm the boss's cousin. He too, plain and simple foreman, couldn't figure it out. He said to me, You are working very easily here, right? So why leave? And he went in and reported it to my cousin, who didn't come to see me but Mrs. Hart called me and asked, Why? I packed it up and left the job. They couldn't understand and I did not blame them.

Organizing the unorganized was not the easiest way to make a living in the 1920s and 1930s. The Canadian government and the Canadian people were afraid of the spread of the October Revolution, the Russian Revolution. The 1919 Winnipeg General Strike had thrown a deadly fear into the government to the extent that every capitalist and every bourgeoisie in Canada was looking under his bed to make sure there wasn't a Bolshevik there! Consequently, every form of binding, spreading, broadening the trade union movement, organizing the unorganized, was looked upon by the federal, provincial, and civic administrations as revolution. Not what you have today, the right of organization, that all you have to do is call upon a labour board to take a vote in a shop—who is for and who is against!

In those days it was just the opposite. The might of the whole state, the police, all kinds of intimidation, arrests, charges of conspiracy, were the order of the day. And you never knew when you were going to be picked up. We were picked up upteen times. We were thrown into police headquarters and that is my own experience. No such thing as a cell, but a general room with a few cots and you had, pardon me, the urinal running right through the middle! Some of us were beaten up as well.

I am going to jump ahead now to the period during the Second World War when the treaty between Germany and the Soviet Union was concluded. The political atmosphere prevailing at that time in Canada was that the left, the Communist Party in Canada, was considered as a partner to the position of the Soviet Union. There took place the internment of all kinds of subversive elements like Germans and enemy aliens. Besides the Germans the Italians were interned, and a number of left-wingers. The Communist Party was declared illegal under the War Measures Act, which can be considered now, as it was considered at the time, the greatest injustice which was carried through from the point of view that no charges were laid. People were picked up, among them a number of trade union leaders, officers of organizations. That was also the time when I was one of those trade union leaders who was arrested without any charges. We were not given any hearing, we were all buried in the Montreal post office—those who were arrested during a given night. We were kept for a night until the next day, when we were transported to the St. John's military barracks. I can recollect the scene that given morning when preparations were made not knowing where we are going to be sent and a thorough check was made of those interned. The officer in charge, when he came to my name, asked me if I am Italian and I said, No, I am not, and he said, What are you doing here? That is exactly what I told him I am wondering about, what am I doing here? I'm Jewish. I'm not Italian. I'm a Canadian citizen. He said, Go ahead. Go home!

It happened so that one of the Red Squad at that time was around in attendance and this man stopped the officer in charge. [*The Red Squad was a squad they had for years in the province of Quebec, with the specific task of moving against communists and revolutionary activities.*] The Red Squad said to the officer in charge, Never mind. This fellow is a very dangerous element in the trade union movement! And that is how I was stopped. I was shipped along with the Italians and Germans who at that time were interned.

From the St. John's barracks we were taken off to Petawawa, in northern Ontario, where the government at that time had established internment camps on the same pattern as those of Hitler. They were Hitler camps! There were three of us from Montreal amongst the hundreds of Italians. The Italians were the largest group. Also interned at that time was the leadership of a fascist movement that existed then, one of them named Adrien Arcand. I had never been told where we were being taken. Finally I arrived in Petawawa. There were some huts already finished and occupied by Germans previously interned. And more huts were being built. We were billeted in different huts.

At that time I was suffering from a disease called *thromboangiitis obliterans*, or Buerger's disease [*gangrene in the foot or leg caused by loss of blood supply*], and my legs were inflamed. After distribution of work and jobs, I was not included in the work where they were clearing trees for lumber. I was given other jobs, like raking the compound. No communication, little or no mail was allowed. The mail was heavily censored, and even then kept for weeks before we got them. The compound was surrounded by barbed wire— electrically charged—and you had posts of elevation towers. We were given uniforms that were plain with a red patch on the back so the guards will be able to see who you are. Beyond the wire was a nice little lake, and we were warned that if we were caught touching the wires we would be shot.

In charge of the camp at that time was an outstanding democrat— "democrat" in quotation marks—a Colonel Pence: a true-blooded Nazi! He gave a good reception to the Arcand group. He even took advice from Arcand's proposals as to who is a communist, who is a left-winger, that he doesn't want to stay with them—he wanted them out. Colonel Pence agreed with him, you see.

I'm relating this from the point of view to give you an example of the general atmosphere that was prevailing at that time among the people who were placed in charge. They would have been better suited in a Germany than in our particular democratic country!

We were in the camps for months without any charges being laid against us or told why we were arrested. In the records of the RCMP you will find that they *always get their man;* however, they failed during that period because, while they were after the communists and the Communist Party, they weren't successful in getting even one of them!

Mr. Shano

Mr. Shano was born in 1884, and was almost ninety years old when I interviewed him in a nursing home in Montreal in 1974. It was one of his "good days," the nurse had said, when I came to speak to him.

A nursing home is not generally a quiet place to talk. Sometimes a lot of banging went on and sometimes music erupted from a piano nearby. There were many periods of silence during this interview, when Mr. Shano forgot the question or even my existence. He could not remember his wife or her name or where she had worked. I did not press him. At the time I felt he had earned his quietude.

I WAS A SMALL BOY in the Old Country; what could I do? My father was already in Canada for four years. So I came here with my mother.

Sometimes, sometimes, I can dream up something about what I had … I think I was instrumental in saving a man from being sent back to Europe because he didn't have a place where to stay here.

I was a boy then, going around selling newspapers here in Montreal and in the two-months vacation that we get from school—I went to school here—I used to go down to the wharf and onto the boats and sell magazines to the sailors and so forth and so forth. Once, when I was on the boat, I met a Jew who was to be sent back to Europe. It didn't take long. I came down from the boat and I spoke to a man who was here, he's a Consul from Mexico, a Jew—I forgot his name now—and I told him about the Jewish man who was going to be sent back to Europe. He didn't take a half an hour and the man was gone. [*Mr. Shano laughs as though he were part of a conspiracy.*]

That time I remember; but that's not the question. The question is that he got free. That means I was instrumental in saving his life, from sending him back! I was a boy then, going around with papers, you know—that's about every bit of seventy years ago. These things you really can't forget. This man happened to see me on the main street in later years and he recognized me. He didn't know what to do with me! [*meaning* for *me!*]

I remember I was born in the year 1884 and I remember things like in 1896 when Wilfrid Laurier was elected the first time to the government.[29] That's what I remember. I think it was in the month of April. I was selling papers then. There are a lot of other things and when I'm rested then everything comes into my mind.

I went to school here. I must have been twelve years old when I left school in 1896. I had to help my parents make a living, so I went into the needle trades because I didn't have anything else to do. That is plain and simple. I was working in men's clothing—working in men's coats. I used to sew sleeves. Later I was the head operator. I think we worked forty-nine hours a week. I started to work at 8 a.m. and we worked until 6 p.m.

I was once going into contracting. In contracting you get bundles of work from shops, parts of a garment, and you are working in your apartment or house. But contracting didn't pay me. It was no good.

I remember I worked in a place called Solomon Brothers for twenty years. At that time I it wasn't a bad salary—I think it was about sixteen dollars a week. I was considered the fastest man in the city!

[*I asked Mr. Shano to tell me how he met his wife, what was her name, when he got married.*]

That is hard to say. That is hard to say.

[*After a long pause, he continued. I asked him if he would like me to come back after he had a rest.*]

What would be gained by it? My memory is not so good ... I think I can remember that there was a strike in the needle trades and I helped to settle the strike. What was the reason? I was working for a new businessman, a Jew, in a new factory, and he didn't have many customers. And the factory went out on strike. Everything stopped off. So I went in to the manufacturer, the boss. I said to him, Look, you are new in the line, in the business. I have a suggestion to make to you where you can fill up the stores. On account of the strike, if you settle with the workers, even though you lose, little by little you'll at least gain something. You'll gain customers. And that's the way it happened.

So I went over to the union, I told them that the place is giving, is settling, that this company is settling this strike. So, you know, even though it was a poor rate we got, at least we won. The man that I was talking to, the boss, he was getting customers. He couldn't get customers before because as a new business it is very, very hard. That is the way it worked. So I was instrumental in a lot of things there.

[*I asked Mr. Shano how old he was, and he said,* You try to give me a guess! *My guess fell short!*]

Me? I am ninety. It will be around the month of February, I will be ninety!

[*Mazel Tov, I said.*]

Sam Greenberg

Sam Greenberg is not his real name. His life was not an easy one. He came to Montreal in 1912 from the Old Country with his father, after his stepmother died.

I interviewed him in Montreal in the summer of 1974.

IN THE OLD COUNTRY, life was very hard. It was so bad that my stepmother, who was a nice woman, got sick. She was having her change of life and she was sick. She wanted to go to the hospital, but they didn't take anyone unless they had an accident. So in order to have an accident she jumped down from the roof and killed herself! You see she wanted to go to the hospital and we could save her. But she made a mistake and she died!

I got married. My wife never worked. She doesn't want to work and I can't go against her. She came from Europe also. She was a sick woman all the time and I didn't have very much work either. At that time it was hard to get a job. It was a crisis and people went around looking for a job and it took me sometimes three months, four months. I used to work in different kinds of contracting shops.

The contracting shop was no good because I worked in a contracting shop and they used me for $2.50 a week. I used to work hard. I was young. I was worth more than that but they paid me so little. What could I do? I worked then for Oliver & Sons. I used to go in seven o'clock and work until eleven, twelve o'clock at night—all week. At that time I made about five or six dollars a week. But the boss didn't want to pay me. He had a brother who used to always fight. Sometimes he used to take until three weeks before I got a dollar from him. He didn't want to pay me at all. But I couldn't help myself. At least the dollar or two that he give me was something.

You see, this Oliver had a shop, a sweatshop, but he didn't pay the workers. He used to keep the money himself. He got the bundles [*made up of pieces, like pockets, sleeves, etc.*] from the factories and we used to work for him. There were about a dozen people in the shop. But the thing is, if you came to payday, he says he hasn't got no money! How can you eat?

There was one man, he was a veteran, who also worked for him. He was the head operator and he was a big shot; and when it came to pay he says, Pay me what's coming to me. The boss says, I haven't got no money. So the man said, You're taking money from the manufacturer, why don't you give me [something] for a living? I don't get out of the shop until you pay me. The boss says to him, I haven't got. And one of his brothers wanted to go fight with the worker, who said, I'm not afraid. If you fight with me—eye for eye and if you don't pay, I'll knock the whole thing out.

So they paid him but the others, we were weak and he didn't pay us. What could you do? Sometimes I got two or three out of him. It is coming to me at least five or six dollars and I used to get only two or three dollars! Sometimes I got nothing. What could I do? I worked till eleven o'clock at night.

After that—later on—I worked in different places. Others used to make a living but I worked for three or four, sometimes five dollars a week. Then I went around for a whole year and I couldn't get a job. My brother-in-law took me into S. Ruben and gave me a job there. There I had a chance, as the foreman there was good friends with my brother-in-law, so he gave me a chance to work until eleven or twelve at night.

I was doing everything there. I used to make anything that they were short of. If somebody didn't come in, so I used to replace for them. The others were making around twenty-five dollars, but not me. Then I got on better. After that job I got a job at Freedman & Gabby. That was good. I was making about thirty or thirty-five dollars a week. I worked for Levine & Son—also a good place. There I used to make thirty dollars a week and I was fast like anything. It was a lot of money.

Then I got sick. Of course I was already married and I was about forty-something years. I got sick on my foot. I couldn't walk. I took aspirins. I tried my best but I couldn't do it. I came to the Jewish Hospital and they bandaged it around and they covered it up. But the whole foot was no good. The doctor told me, Take it off. It's no good anyways.

It was TB, tuberculosis, on the bone. So they took it off. It was a year and a half, I think, that I couldn't work. We lived on Clark Street. We paid sixteen dollars a month rent and somehow we managed.

I got married when I was about thirty—maybe a year or two less. I could have lived with my father but I didn't. I could have helped him out. At the time bread was five cents—it was cheap. You used to get a box of tomatoes for thirty, thirty-five, forty cents—a whole box of tomatoes. Potatoes was also forty cents a bag. No, less than that. Meat was also cheap. You used to get some meat for free. It didn't come from the butcher. My father used to go downtown to buy a big bag of bread, you know, a day old. He used to pay fifteen, twenty cents a whole bag. He used to come home and we used to have it for a week or so. We would put it in the stove and cover it up.

I was involved in a strike at Weinberg, a big strike. Also at Kellers—though not so big. Weinberg used to give a lot of trouble at that time. And we had a lot of strikes. I can't exactly remember most of them. One strike—it was at Greenson's—I was involved. I used to take off many people ... that means, I used to come in contact with the people that were working. I was the chairman of the factory, you know, and I spoke with the bosses. The boss would say, I'll give you everything but I wouldn't make a contract with the union. I says, We can't do that business. The only business is that we have the security if you sign with the union. Otherwise we don't—we have no guarantee. After that he closed up. He settled with us but he closed up the business.

I used to work for Swartz. I used to make gabardine coats at that time. I worked also at Canadian Rubber Company, where I used to make raincoats and so on. But you know, there were some older people working there, in the raincoat business, and they used to put the blame on me for things, but I kept quiet and let it be and I continued to work there. You see, I was on the Joint Board of the International Ladies Garment Workers' Union— I still have my book from when I worked there—and I was one of the original union members then. I worked there because the union had control of the raincoat business.

Later, I went to New York, and even though I was on the Joint Board of the union and working in raincoats, I still didn't get a job in raincoats— they didn't know me there. But I was working. I got a job by somebody I knew from Montreal there. He said, Go over to this shop and you can work. I went to work there but a few people said that I couldn't work in the factory, and I said why? I am a union man. But they wouldn't let me work there. They were afraid I would start to make a strike. They fined me twenty dollars and I say, I can't pay. Anyway, another fellow sent me to another branch of the union where I got a new book for $1.25 and I went into work. And they started again, and I said, I am not in your local. I'm in another local. It was not a good time.

Of course I had learned the Jewish language [Yiddish]. I tried to belong to different cultural organizations. At one place the chairman told me he would teach me to read and write. I said, Yeah, all right. So when he came to read, he said, You know better than I do! I belonged to left-wing organizations, like the UJPO [United Jewish Peoples Order] because all my friends were in the Left. And I am still a member.

When I married and had my children, I couldn't attend too much. I was secretary in the Jewish organization too. I was with Mike Buhey, if you remember him—and with Mrs. Buhey. Also with Alex Gold. I know them all. I used to take part. I had a friend, he was a socialist, and I used to go around with him and we would talk politics most of the time. Of course, we didn't agree on certain things. He's a rich man at present. He was also a pants maker but he got out of the trade and he was—what do you call it— he used to go out on the street, a demonstrator. He made good money. He's all right!

All the bosses then were Jewish. It was very hard. I don't know … they have no pity. They didn't have no pity! They only had pity on themselves! And somebody else was not a human being as them. It was always their selfishness. I even saw a picture this week, on Sunday, with Charlie Chaplin. It shows that this man also didn't have pity on certain women. He went for the rich ones. Then after when they tried him for murder, he complained, he said to the judge, Look, all the governments make wars and they kill thousands of people. They rob the people. They do everything to the people and then they give them a medal. Give me also a medal. I have done the same thing!

That was a very interesting part there that Charlie Chaplin played. The philosophy is good, to show people do wrong and they don't get taken to jail and they get out of it. Yeah! That's what it is.

In the First World War they didn't take me. My friend also, they were supposed to take him in the war but he smokes cigars to show that his heart is weak and they shouldn't take him. In the Second World War I tried to help out a little. I used to go round with my friends and pick up things [*probably scrap metal*], you know, to see that we should win the war against Hitler.

I have two children that are sick—mentally sick. One boy and one girl. The boy, he is living with his family; and my daughter, she's all right. You know children. They've got their own troubles. So I am alone.

Pauline Chudnovsky

Pauline Chudnovsky was born in 1900 in Scitzenitz, near Kiev, in the Ukraine. She came to Montreal in 1921. I had the great pleasure of talking to Pauline in 1974 at the Baycrest home in Toronto, where she was residing.

Pauline Chudnovsky died in 1986.

I CAME HERE TO CANADA in 1921, in April, and the time was a terrible time then—it was a crisis. People were out of work and life was terrible. Why I came here is a lot to tell. We went out of Russia because of the pogroms of the pre-Revolution and because people were very militaristic. A very terrible struggle went on in the country where I was born. So we were young—myself and my husband—and we decided to go first to Romania.

I was born near Kiev, in Russia, in 1900. I am now seventy years old and you know where I am now! [*Baycrest*]. We went through quite a time. It was very unpleasant and yet we were young and we were homesick a little bit and so we were married in Romania—in Kishenev, they called it—and then came to Canada.[30]

I suppose I am getting mixed up and telling you about the circumstances in Canada at that time. The needle trades started to organize. They built an industrial union. The head office was in Spadina Avenue and we had to go to the union every week. There were people there who were gifted to organize unions—very talented people. This was right after the First World War. The First World War, I guess, was in 1914, and then the revolution in Russia in 1917, and the immigrants from all the countries came to Canada, to the United States. People were just travelling to get away from something to get better, but whether they got better is a very big question.

When I came my husband was unable to find a job because both of us were pharmacists from the Old Country. There we worked in one drugstore.

It was a government drugstore. In Russia there were different laws than in Canada. It was very hard for Jewish people to be educated; because they are Jewish it wasn't so easy for them! So we went to look for jobs. In the meanwhile we were married in Romania and I went to a drugstore to work there for a while, and then my husband's brother from the United States thought that we were going to live with him and his family and he sent us affidavits and money to go there. But by the time we reached the border from Romania, the quota was filled and we weren't allowed to go in. So we corresponded with people in Canada. At that time in Montreal, Quebec, there lived an uncle of my husband. He was the editor of a paper and he sent us affidavits to Antwerp to come to Canada.

My oldest son, Ben, was born in Antwerp, Belgium. (Maybe this makes some kind of sense what I am telling you because sometimes I am forgetful and I have to think.) We stayed in Antwerp for five months and we arrived in Montreal. We lived in Montreal for eighteen years. We looked for jobs, but the law is when you emigrate from one country to another you have to go to school again in order to be able to possess the language of the country; otherwise you can't get a job. We didn't know the language here. So, in the meanwhile, time wasn't still and two years later I gave birth to Hymie, our second son.

My husband was looking for jobs. He found a job in a cleaning factory cleaning and dyeing, where they needed a chemist. The factory was a French-Canadian factory—I think the name was, maybe, De Chou? Something like that. And it was a kind of factory where they didn't hire very many Jewish people afterwards. So he worked there for three years as a manager and was fired. My husband didn't think that he was from the *chachabatoni*—the best folks in the world—but he thought that he had a right to be proud of our nationality! So he didn't work at that time because people liked to assimilate to a stage that it is even a shame sometimes. Assimilation is very nice, but they deny themselves—meaning who they are—and my husband wasn't a person to deny himself. Whatever he is, he is, and he thought that whatever a person is born that person is supposed to stay the same nationality. He could possess many languages, but he needs to have dignity, otherwise it isn't nice. I am talking too much!

When we arrived in Montreal we didn't have ten dollars to pay rent for a room—this is said in the very honest language. So we rent a room for ten dollars and we got very beautiful friends there. We had at that time a friend named Myers—Myerovitch. There was a family named Smith that we associated with. We went to a Jewish *shul* with our two boys. Then we had a third son two years later. With three children we start to realize that we can't have any more. At that time it was different—there wasn't those pills with which you could control and plan your family. You had children and they came. So it was very hard.

In Montreal we lived in a big house on Colonial Avenue. This was considered a very poor district because the rent was not too much. We had a relative here and they were a little better off. He was a designer and he made a lot of money and, since they were here in Canada from before us, so they were better off. On Colonial we rented out three rooms. I had one girl, one boy, and a married man for board and room. I cooked for them. I did everything. I cleaned for them and I went to work and I brought my mother-in-law from the Old Country. Actually we brought her here to spend part of the time in the United States with my husband's brother. But she liked me better and decided she wanted to stay with me.

So we had four bedrooms: my mother-in-law was in one and the three boarders; the three children and myself and my husband used to sleep on the floor. This is the real truth! The conditions were horrible.

Prices, you know, were next to nothing. The price of bread was ten cents—five cents for bread that was yesterday's—stale you could get for less. Meat was very reasonable; you could go out with two dollars and buy vegetables and fruit. Now you can go with five dollars and not get as much. I am not now familiar with family life, but my children are telling me that everything is sky-high even though people are having higher and better wages. Technology and science is working day and night and people are more educated so the world is changing. Terrible change!

My routine for the day, with children and boarders, was like this. I got up very early in the morning, but I had a little bit of love—the children start to realize the situation, what is going on. So Ben, the oldest, went to work in a jewellery store. He was very young. He was maybe twelve years old. And Hymie started to sell papers. And Sam went to learn a trade in General Electric, so he didn't make very much, but we wanted him to understand a trade or something. So it was easy. When Ben used to come from the jewellery store on a Friday, he used to hold his wages like this [*Pauline holds her hands out and laughs*] and he would say, Now, Mama! And he used to give it to me.

I got up in the morning. I gave them all breakfast. I send them to school and I made my beds. My husband starts to suffer very much from heart trouble. So the doctor says he can't go to the cleaning business; he should relax for a while. He was diagnosed with angina and then he stayed home. He stayed home and I went to work. He looked after the house a little bit.

So my husband helped me out in the house and the doctor put it this way: like you can't go to the cleaning factory because of his angina, and then he said "coronary." Then we were frightened. So he stayed home. He did a little bit. When I used to come from work, he used to cry because I had to support the family. He used to speak to me in Russian, because when we spoke we always spoke in Russian, and therefore Benny understands every single word. Our children's childhood reminds them what Papa used to say; what Mama used to say; and this and that, and they kibbitz me around. But in one respect we were very fortunate: we were terribly in love. We were so much in love! I don't know—maybe, Seemah, I am mistaken—but I don't see the love today. Although people are talking about love, love, love, I don't see that honest love and devotion from person to person. It's true!

We went to *shul*. We gave the children quite a decent education in Yiddish and also we sent them, of course, to English school. Living in Quebec they learned French as well. Since we were right from Russia, we had gone to Russian schools and worked in a Russian drugstore—so we spoke Russian. My husband knew Hebrew. He was a very educated person. So in our home there were many languages being spoken.

My husband was fired from the cleaning and dyeing shop. I had a very good friend, Adamson, who was the forelady in a factory, and I went in there and they hired me. At that time there were finishers and operators. I knew how to sew. I made everything for my children, little socks and shirts, and whatever they needed. And this helped a little bit for us to get along. They paid me at that time—and this was considered a very good wage—twenty-eight to thirty dollars a week. I worked five days and on Shabbes and Sunday I didn't work. I worked from 9 a.m. to 6 p.m. Of course I went to the Industrial Union and became a member.

We lived in Montreal for eighteen years and then it became impossible. People start talking about going to live in Ontario, in Toronto. We went to a little town, Lindsay, Ontario. There was in the *Star*, in Montreal, an advertisement that they needed a spotter and he should have chemistry, and we decided my husband is going to Lindsay. In order for me and the boys to go there I had to sell my furniture—I didn't have money for the transportation for us. Our oldest son, Ben, was left in Montreal as he had a job and didn't want to change. I took the younger boys, Hy and Sam, and we went after my husband was there for two months. We rented a place from a Mrs. Sender for two years. Then the factory owner died and the place was closed up and so we thought Toronto was closer than Montreal to Lindsay, so we went to Toronto. We wouldn't turn back and go to Montreal. This was around 1939, just before the Second World War, and we rented a flat on Beatrice Street, No. 37.

My husband didn't work all the time. When he worked he worked as a chemist, a good chemist. Before they fired him at the cleaning shop they thought the world of him. When he did work he made good wages. At that time, a person with three children who got forty-five dollars a week, it was considered a lot of money, but it's not today.

In the factory—I don't know why, but today I feel so weak—but when I was working I thought, Why can't I be a little bit sick like other people? Stay away. But I was so strong. It didn't matter how much I worked and what I did. I used to paint some of the rooms in my house. I was strong. So in the factory the boss was like this. He wanted to have production and it was good that I was strong and healthy, because they were driving us like slaves. Not the boss—but the foreman and the manager, the forelady. I always worked in a union shop. We were progressive and not dark-minded people. The Industrial Union was well known all over America and Canada.

In Toronto we worked very hard and didn't come home until it was dark. So when my David [*Pauline's husband*] was home he prepared supper for me and the kids, for the family. We used to go out and, when he thought I had a very horrible day, he bought me an ice cream for after supper for five or three cents—I don't know how much.

[*Pauline says to me at this time, I'll take you upstairs after to the cafeteria so you can have tea with me. Okay? My guest, my young friend!*]

People came to Canada and America because they were lucky if they had a trade. A trade they thought, It's no worry. It's America, Canada, or South America! So when they came in they start to see the trade and that you didn't have to be a full-fledged tailor. If you could make something— sew buttons, make buttonholes, or something—you're already in the trade. So everybody went into the needle trades. Now people are going into different professions. The technology is developed, people understand more, they learn more because they are educated. But in that time it was different. It was like being dead! Sometimes, I think, maybe I was dead and I came out to a new world, because everything is different and what is considered very nice—it is really not. It's not! But they call it moral, they call it … When people go somewhere and they want to make a good impression, they take some kind of drug. Is this healthy? Is it really good? No. But sometimes when you look at the youth you are shivering. They don't want to work. My children started working when they were thirteen, fourteen. They understood the circumstances.

I worked in shirts. Shirts is section work. We don't make a shirt. You make, maybe, the cuffs, the sleeves, or the collars, or the yoke. You don't make a shirt. I made sleeves. I used to sit and work on sleeves. I was so strong, it is unbelievable! You know my weight? It is now ninety-five pounds. It is horrible to understand that. Look, I live here at the Baycrest. I don't do anything. I eat here. I sleep here.

There were Jewish schools here and I was the secretary of the Morris Winchevsky School. Yosel Kleinstein was a chairman—he died last year. We had the YKUF [*Yiddishe Kultur Farbund*].[31] I started to learn Yiddish in Montreal when I lived there so when I came to Toronto, there was a fellow named Binder and that Binder was a *rikhtik* Yiddishist and we were learning Yiddish. There was already grammar. It was a literary Yiddish. So I become accomplished in how to speak and they called me everywhere. You see, I speak the language of Morris Winchevsky;[32] and the others, they speak dialects, you know. It's not their fault. But the Polish people are coming with *their* dialect and the Russians with *their* dialect. So I become accomplished in the grammar, *grammatik,* which wasn't before, not in this country. They spoke jargon, a *fachspracht.* I am not a first-class learned *mensch*, but I am getting along. [*Pauline says something in Yiddish.*] Can't you understand me when I speak to you in Yiddish? [*I tell her,* A bisl. *A little.*] I speak five languages. For my age I think it isn't too bad ... it isn't too bad. Here in this home people speak in Spanish fluently, in French, in Yiddish.

I am only three weeks in this home. They haven't got a place for me. They are building somewhere a home for the aged, so until it will be ready ... I am here.

Bluma Kogan

Bluma Kogan was born in Prostora Gubernya in Russia, around 1900.
The village must have been very small, as I have been unable to locate
it on a map. I met Bluma at the Baycrest Home in 1974 when I went
to talk to Pauline Chudnovsky, and Bluma kindly agreed to talk to
me. Pauline Chudnovsky sat in on the interview and contributed now
and then with her thoughts.

I WAS BORN IN PROSTORA GUBERNYA and my name is Bluma
Kogan there and Bluma Kogan here. That's my father's name and I keep it
all the time.

Conditions in the Old Country for us were not very good. My father
couldn't make a very good living. So we were poor. And my Dad has cousins
over here in Toronto. He made an application to come here and he came
first. This was around 1909. I think it was 1909. We didn't even have money
for the voyage but some of our friends were here already and they were very,
very friendly, so they sent us money for my father to come here. In 1913,
after my father had been here for several years, he made a little bit of money
to send for us to come. We were six children. You want to know them? My
sister Dora, my brother Morris, and myself came here first. I began to
work, my brother began to work, and my sister Dora was too young to
work. Anyhow, we chipped things together. We took a little piece of a very
dirty place to live. And I worked there day and at night after work to make
it livable.

The place we rented was a front place, the front part of the house. It was
large and had a table to eat on, and a stove and a sink with water. We lived
by ourselves. It was off the street, a couple of steps up to the door and you
come in. But it was very, very bad and very poor. There was no bathroom—
it was someplace outside. There were more apartments and more quarters

all the way around—they went this way and this way—and here was the street. [*Bluma motions with her hands.*]

I collected horse manure from the street and bought some lime and made a paste and plugged up holes in the home. It was raining in and so I plugged things up. After that I bought some paper and papered it. And it looked a little bit brighter. In the first room was a great, big, old stove, dirty and not working. Somehow we got rid of it and bought a smaller one that was workable. In the back of that big room, where the stove was, was a closet. It was very dark and very dirty, very roachy and very ratty, and very, very bad! And my father and myself worked there. We plugged up the holes, papered it, put a light in there and it became bright. When people came in a few weeks after, they didn't recognize it. I don't remember how much rent we were paying there. [*Pauline says, Ten dollars was how much at that time.*] It was very cheap because we didn't have any money.

My father became a *shochet* here—do you understand me? And he arranged the rent there. When I came we arranged a different accommodation. I remember that. It was cheap. We bought furniture that was—at that time—a hundred years old. Very inadequate! The light was of particular trouble. There was, what do you call these lights on the ceiling? It wasn't a bulb … [*Sunlight? A skylight? I offer*] Yes, that. It was raining and the rain came in. It rained on me in the bed. Okay. Well, I tried. I tried very hard to plug it up. I did the best I could, with my Dad—we were like that—we co-operated.

By the time I came here I got a toothache which was very, very bad. We came here to some cousins. I was in bed with that toothache. My face got swollen and ten days—ten days—I was in a fever and I was very sick. I got better and I am here!

After I came in 1913, 1914, I looked for work. I looked and I found a place. I don't remember how I found the place. I asked around. We had some cousins here on Delucy Street, east of Yonge, and by that time I was able to read. I was already adapted to the surroundings of Toronto. I said to my cousin, Will you please tell me where a library is? Or where a school is? I want to go to school at night to learn English. She said, Never mind school and never mind library. You go to work!

So I went to work—not because she said, Go to work! I went because I had to go to work anyway. But at night you want to do a little bit something else. Well, okay, I found it myself. I went to night school.

I found a place to work in the needle trades called Rosenthal & Shapiro on Bathurst Street near the lake. I didn't know how to do things but the foreman put me near a lady who was there before me and she gave me work. The first week I made three dollars. At that time it wasn't too bad but it was bad. Even then it was bad. I was with her for about a month or so. When I saw that I was doing well and she made money on me, I told Mr. Ron, the foreman, I want to do work by myself because I can't live on three dollars a week. So he let me do that. The first week I didn't make any more than three dollars, but the second week I already made seven dollars. And on the fourth and fifth week I began to make about twelve dollars; and that was the limit that everybody else made. I was doing ladies' jackets from suits; not the skirts but the jackets. I was doing the lining, sleeves, pockets, and I was doing pretty good work.

I remember it was a large place, about 150 people—operators, cutters, finishers, button-sewers, pressers—they all belonged to the union. After several weeks of working there, the chairlady of my section said, Bluma, you have to belong to the union. At that time I didn't know exactly what union meant but I found out. So I said yes. I would be very proud to belong to a worker's organization, as you call it, a union. I paid in my dues and I got a union book and I have been in the union for years and years.

My days were like this: I got up in the morning and made breakfast for the family—I am the oldest. I suppose this must have been at 7 a.m. because eight o'clock I had to be at work. I had to take the streetcar and go there. Maybe I even got up before seven. My father was preparing lunch for us. I didn't come home for lunch. It was too far to go and come and then the carfare. I took my lunch to the factory and I ate it there. At six o'clock I came back and helped along with my Dad to make the meal and wash the dishes, and wash and iron the clothes, mend the socks, and everything else. And some nights I went to school.

I made a living. That factory was large. It was a big place with many sections and it was a fairly good building. After that job, I got rotten buildings and sweatshops but that first one was in fairly good condition.

The sweatshop was on Spadina Avenue. Do you know Toronto a little bit? You know Spadina? [*Bluma laughs.*] Everybody knows Spadina Avenue! All European countries know Spadina Avenue.

I left the place where I was making jackets because Foreman Ron wanted to reorganize the place. He didn't like the union. And he talked to Mr. Rosenthal and Mr. Shapiro that he would take over the executive part, the manufacturing of the suits (the ladies' suits). He would take it over and he would reorganize it in such a way—he didn't want the union—and then he could just hire the same workers but on his terms. Well, the union stepped in and didn't like that and the union explained to us what the foreman wants to do—why he wants to reorganize. The majority of us didn't accept it and we went out on strike. And we were on strike for six or seven long months! It was a terrible struggle at that time in Toronto. Everybody remembers the clothing factory—I forget the name.[33] Everybody knows that that strike lasted so long.

We lost and the bosses also lost. Somebody went out and poured acid on the goods and on the garments, so a lot of the material got spoiled—burned or spoiled. That took a long time. They couldn't meet their orders. They had to send orders to Montreal, to Winnipeg, or wherever. They couldn't make it because all the goods were burnt. So they got out of business. We lost our strike and they lost too!

I remember I had no shoes! And the bakers were out on strike and I'm a union member. The dairy was on strike. It was bad. It was bad. How do you live? You live from hand to mouth. You don't eat three good meals a day. You don't have shoes. You go with shoes [*she chuckles*] that your feet scrape the pavement!

[*Pauline says, I remember the grocery man used to come and say, you can have some groceries, but we would only take some potatoes and milk.*]

We were in the needle trades, which is not so important. It's a less important thing. But to the coalminers, the steel workers, the automobile workers, the glass workers—they go out on strike, it is different.

This was 1915–16, because in 1916 we lost the strike after six months. All of us got very sick—with colds. I didn't have shoes. We didn't have strike benefit at the time. It was poor. We lost the strike and they lost the business. It was a long struggle. A long big struggle; and labour trouble, union trouble. I didn't understand it very much but I went with the majority, with the workers and with the union. I didn't go with the foreman, even though I didn't understand it very much, but my feeling was with the working class, with the workers.

Well, okay, we lost and we couldn't get other jobs. Some got jobs in a bakery, some in a shoe factory, and some went away from Toronto. And I also went away from Toronto. I went to New York. I worked a while in New York and I got into a hospital, training for a nurse and was there for three years—thirty-six months without stop and I became a registered nurse. I went back and forth but lived in New York. I came back later, much later.

During the strikes, oh, during the strikes! We had so many court cases and so much trouble. I remember, there was a foreman who was on skirts: he worked on skirt toppers—people who were finishing skirts. There were about twelve girls and he was managing them. When we went on strike, he was a scab, and he was doing things that *we* were supposed to do. You know, we called them scabs, strikebreakers. And we had a presser, he was a Lithuanian I think, a big strong guy, and this Neven—that was his name—he took his job, the presser's job. When people go out on strike there are always people who don't like the strike and work as strikebreakers. So this Neven took away his job. So one morning, one Monday morning, the presser came up—that was on Niagara Street—he came up to that place and saw this Neven ironing, pressing, and the press irons at that time were used with coals, live coals. So he took this iron from Neven and gave him a wallop over the head and that guy fell down. He got burnt. He got hurt, both. The ambulance came and took him to the hospital. I think that he was there for about four months. He was near death. We didn't want him to die. No. We didn't! He recovered all right. But there was a big court case after that. We had, I think, during that strike—about fifty-two court cases.

But the strike took so long and everybody has to make a little money. So there were strikebreakers and a few of the girls went back to work. They went back and we didn't like it. So we organized a strategic business. Every one of us—there were twenty or thirty of us—had a place at a corner. And there was one girl—particularly that one girl—we wanted to give her a lesson. She was from the shop on Niagara Street and Bathurst and she lived on Kensington Avenue and Elizabeth Street. It was a long stretch. So we were two at every corner and each one of us gave a sign that she is coming. So to the very end, where she had to turn and go back to her home, we attacked her. We attacked her physically. We hit her. You scab! You strikebreaker! You take away the bread from our mouths? Go home and strike just like us!

[*Pauline says, In Montreal the girls used to work just for lipstick. As long as the boss gave them for lipstick and for powder, they said, It's enough for them. So two girls went over and said to them, Do you understand what you are doing to people? You are taking away the bread, everything. The children are going naked and barefoot.*

And they took those two girls and they beat them up. You know, they made them into union girls afterwards!]

Now to get back to the sweatshop. It was on Spadina in an elevator building; very dirty, unpainted, and we had to go up to the shop where there was no closet—there was washrooms in the hall but no closet for clothes. It was very cramped, very cramped, and sweatshop conditions. I worked there for three years. There were a lot of people. We were about twenty. By that time I had changed my job from jackets to dresses. I worked on dresses, as an operator. There were cutters. The boss was also a cutter. There was a presser or two. There were finishers. We were about twenty operators and so; twenty machines on one side and on the other side. All in one room. We worked seven, eight hours a day. The pay there was much better and much more than at the beginning. We were doing piecework. You got a dollar, $1.50, $1.25 maybe $1.05 to operate a dress—bundles of six, bundles of ten, so on. They made certain that the machines were running *prrrrrr ... prrrrr ...* all the time.

So why did they call it a sweatshop?

[*Pauline interjects: Because of the fact that twenty people worked in one room. This is a sweatshop!*]

Not twenty but about thirty people, you know ... altogether ...

[*Pauline says, Thirty! And there wasn't even a place for to hang up the coat! And probably the light was ...*]

Was very, very poor.

[*Both women talk over one another in Yiddish, recalling the times.*]

[*Pauline says, Sometimes when you have to climb stairs, they didn't have an elevator to go. And the toilet was outside.*]

That was exploitation! They made money, yes. If I operated a dress for a dollar and the boss sold it for twelve dollars, and the rent and the light, the cutting and material, maybe cost him up to six dollars and he gave me a dollar—so he makes five dollars on the dress. So he became rich.

[*Pauline says, You know what they used to call the workers? Little hand,* ot a hant. *When the workers start to work for the boss it is in order that they should have something to eat! But the rest of the big profits go to the bosses.*]

So he is so long a boss that he enlarged his belt! He took in twenty other machines because twenty other people were standing outside and waiting for a job, and he said, If you please, you could come in! You would work for fifty cents an hour. You would work for twenty-five cents an hour. You would work like this. And he made the money.

[*Pauline says, And even if he paid twelve dollars for a dress he could sell it for sixty. At that time getting twelve dollars you could live for a week, you see.*]

The worker made for him for three dollars a day several dresses, and he took twelve dollars a dress ... So they lived from the sweat and the blood of the workers. So here you have it.

We, the Jews, belong to different classes. We belong to the working class and the boss belongs to the capitalist class. He did not come here as a capitalist. He became a cutter and he also became an operator, but little by little his idea was to be in business. So they ...

[*Pauline says,* Shuslugen kapital. *You see they was* shuslugen kapital—
*big capital. So he became a member of the Bank of Montreal or Toronto and
he starts to exploit two hundred people and he takes in two hundred
machines ...*]

[*At this point both women are interrupting one another in their excitement.*]

But Paula, before all this, he came here as a poor man as I was, but then
he saved and they became partners. He took another Jew and that way they
open a shop. Or there were two or three partners.

[*Pauline says, Do you remember the Decklebaum Brothers in Toronto?
They start from nothing and they used to tell the people, the workers, in Yiddish: We are workers like you—*]

That's true!

[*And if you want to work, you want to have money, you have to work day
and night, Pauline says.*]

And he succeeded! That's the way it was. It wasn't because I was a Jew and
he was a Jew. He was a boss and I was a worker. It is the same way with the
Italians and the Greeks. Two classes. Maybe it is hard for you to understand,
but when you are in it, you live it, then that's the way it is.

[*Pauline says, We were in it—that's why she* (referring to me) *comes to
us!*]

It is very true that Mr. Sherman, my boss, maybe in Europe he lived better
than I did. Okay, I grant you that. But he didn't come here with a million dollars or a hundred thousand dollars. He came just as a worker and he
became a cutter in a dress factory. When he accumulated or saved a little
bit of money—the same thing with Mr. Smith or somebody else—they went
into business. My bosses were partners and that's how it developed.

One time there was a strike or there was slack—there was not much
work in the trade and I had to work to make a living—so I went down to
Spadina Avenue to work on caps: men's caps, boys caps. And knowing how
to use a machine, I was pretty good at it. Okay, so I worked there for a few
weeks just before Christmas time and then my place got work again. So I gave
my boss notice that I am leaving and I go back to my old trade, my old boss.
This man wasn't a Jew. He became so infuriated and so mad and he says to
me, How dare you leave me before Christmas? I have shipments to make: so
many here, so many another, all before Christmas. I say, Mr. Boss, you have
to make a shipment. You want to make money on your caps. I'm just an
operator and I have to make some money for myself. I'm just like you. You
want money and I also want money, so I'm leaving.

By this time he was so mad because I opened my mouth. And he said, All you Jews that came here ought to be taken together on a boat and dumped in the middle of the Atlantic Ocean! He was so angry that he was going to hit me, I think. I was standing by the door, holding it, just in case he comes to hit me I would run away. Well, he didn't come to hit me but he was just about to do it. I say, I want my pay. I worked last week and I want my pay. He said, Get out of here. Anyway, I got out and I was afraid to come back for my pay. So I got some friends to come with me and of course he had to give me my pay.

That was Spadina Avenue!

When I am working here I was already old and I got sick. I had a heart attack—right there in Sherman's shop I got a heart attack. And Dr. Bierenbaum was my doctor. He was a medical officer of the union. So he treated me and of course he stopped me from working. He arranged that I get sick benefit—by that time the union had sick benefit—for four months. After that he wouldn't let me go back to work. So I applied for old-age pension.

I just got a letter from my union. I get union retirement funds of seventy dollars every month. It used to be sixty dollars, but they raised it to seventy.

Norman Massey

Norman Massey was a union man and a left-winger. He came to Canada from Poland in October 1929. I interviewed Norman in the summer of 1974. Unfortunately, the electrical outlet in the interview room was not functioning and I failed to recognize this immediately: consequently, his opening statements may perhaps appear terse. His manner was straightforward and to the point, and he was very political in outlook.

WELL, MAYBE I'LL CONDENSE it a little! I left Poland when I was eighteen. I ran away from fascist terror and hopelessness, together with hundreds of thousands of young people, especially young Jewish people from Poland. I was active in the revolutionary youth in Poland and the police were on my trail, just like it happened to tens of thousands of others. I came to Canada. I came the end of October—there was that famous Wall Street Crash—the Depression of 1929—we called it a crisis at that time, not a depression. When it started we felt it immediately everywhere. It was hard to get a job.

I became an upholsterer, although I had no experience in it. The reason why I became an upholsterer is because my younger brother was here already and he was an experienced upholsterer making the frames for the chesterfields, chairs. So he took me into the upholstering section believing that, by learning that trade, I'll make money.

This was in 1929 and the beginning of 1930. So I didn't stay long with this trade for the simple reason that most firms failed and I lost the job. All my friends and colleagues here were active in the cultural centre—Jewish cultural centre—a Jewish cultural institute which was composed mostly of young people; and also I was in the Young Communist League. Most of them were needle trades workers and I followed their footsteps. They were so numerous—the shops—that it was easier to get a job. I got a job in a non-union shop.

Generally the needle trades weren't well organized at all at that time. The International Ladies' Garment Workers was in the process of organizing—progressives played a decisive role at that time—in fact they were about to organize a progressive union, but due to machinations from the office in New York, the leadership went over to the right-wingers. The Amalgamated was already traditionally a well-organized trade [union], although they controlled only 50 percent of the shops here. It was the Amalgamated Clothing Workers of America, to make it precise.

I began working as a pantspresser. This was an unorganized shop, a non-union shop. It wasn't a very big shop, about a hundred people. I worked there and, in the course of two years, I got a few reductions. I couldn't help it. There was no one there to protect me and I needed a job. The boss claimed he can't compete on the market and has to get cheaper labour. Finally, the boss folded up, failed! This happened around 1932.

At that time the clothing workers—men's clothing workers in Montreal, where progressives were excluded since 1926 because of their militancy for the interests of the people—these workers revolted against the Amalgamated bureaucratic leadership and they organized their own union, the Canadian Clothing Workers Union of Canada. That's what they called it. Of course, those that organized the revolt, those who took advantage of the discontent of the people, tried to capitalize on it by getting in touch with various politicians to lead this union. One of them was Maurice Hartt, who was later MP, a Liberal politician. He became the manager of this union. Other politicians were attracted to work behind the scenes. But the people were honest-to-goodness for the interests of their own families. They wanted a higher standard of living. They wanted to make a living, never mind a higher standard.

The progressives got into this union and they assumed leadership in the important locals, especially Local 209, which was the biggest local. It was a Jewish local. Sidney Sarkin became a leader of the cutters in the United Clothing Workers of America. [*Sidney's story appears earlier in the volume.*] Abie Rosenberg was the spokesman of Local 209. And there were numerous other progressives, less well known.

There were traitors in the United Clothing Workers Union—agents from the Amalgamated bureaucracy, who tried to break it up. Because of the fact that the United Clothing Workers Union did not satisfy the people, they did not improve the conditions, these agents succeeded in convincing the majority of tailors to go back to the Amalgamated. It is my personal opinion that it was a mistake to revolt and get out of the Amalgamated. They should have revolted inside and thrown out the leadership and taken over the union. This is my personal opinion. I wrote about it in the *Canadian Jewish Weekly* a few years ago.

Finally we got back, and there was an agreement signed between both factions of both unions that there should be no discrimination against anybody. The left-wingers went back to the union. When they got back it didn't take long: it was 1933, and a strike broke out immediately. That was the understanding that we should go out on strike for better conditions. The workers gained a 10-percent increase. At that time it meant an awful lot because of the Depression years. Gradually they built up confidence towards the union. There was an agreement for two years and we planned to fight for better conditions in general. But, basically, there was no change in the conditions of the needle trades—of the men's clothing workers in Montreal.

The same thing happened in Toronto. A united front was formed around 1937–38 because in these two years the arch-reactionaries in the union were pushed aside by the more liberal elements of the bureaucrats. They approached the progressives who were a force in the union and in the shops to form a united front to fight for the interests of the people. There was a joint leadership—Sidney Sarkin became one of the business agents. The Joint Board and the executives had representation from all groups including the progressives. I was on the executive of Local 209—I mean 277, pardon me— and I was also representing Local 277, a pants-and-vestmakers' local, in the joint board of the Amalgamated.

I also represented, for a number of years, my local in the Trades and Labour Council in Montreal; so did Abie Rosenberg, representing Local 209, and Sidney Sarkin, representing the cutters. There were other progressives who represented their locals. This kept up until the Second World War broke out. And since you are asking me for information, as far as I'm concerned, I lost my job as a vestmaker. There were no vests. People made suits without vests. Being an experienced operator who could handle the machine well, I became a pocketmaker in men's clothing and I'm a pocketmaker up to this moment.

I met my wife—by the way, she passed away about six months ago—I met my wife in many places. In the Industrial Union she was working at a dress shop and she took part in a famous dress strike led by the Industrial Union in 1935, where Joe Gershman was the leader of the union. [*Joe's story appears later in the volume.*] I met her at mass meetings. I attended meetings of all kinds of unions. I was interested in knowing of the conditions and what's taking place. I could say that—but I don't want to praise myself!—I was political dynamite in the needle trades!

It's there I met my wife. She was five years younger than I was. I don't have to give you the reasons why boy meets girl. I also met her in the cultural centre. Her name was Sima Stutman. The Stutman family were progressive. It was a progressive family. Her oldest brother was first active here in the progressive movement and then he went to the United States. He's still there, active in the progressive movement. His name is Eddie Stark. The whole family worked: the father, the sisters. And they were all trade union members. Three of them were members in the Amalgamated Clothing Workers Union, the same union to which I belonged.

Sima, my late wife, was a member of the Industrial Union until we got married and she lost her job and she wasn't looking any more for a job. We lived, I would say, happily; without much comfort, but we were happy. We worked together in the organization, in the Young Communist League. That's how we progressed.

When I came from the Old Country I was living with my sister. She had a house on St. Urbain Street. This house is still standing there. They were no good at that time: heated with stove and coal. And my younger brother was living with her. She was married and had one son who is now a famous doctor psychiatrist. And we lived in a room sleeping with my younger brother in the same single bed. Conditions were tough.

There were no more people living in this house. There was no room practically—there was my sister and my brother-in-law and the child, myself, and my younger brother. There were no more rooms. There was a living room and a bedroom together like ... separated just by a partition. The house had another small backroom—that's where we slept. We didn't live in that living room we slept there.

You will see if you follow the history of the class struggle—as it was in Germany—German bosses hiring fascist gangsters and giving them power in establishing a Hitler regime to destroy their own workers. That's class struggle. I know of cases in the dress industry—not in our industry—where Jewish girls put crosses on their necks to get a job! And they also spoke French—many of them learned French—to speak to the boss to give them a job. And when the boss found out that they were Jewish, they had a slim chance of getting a job because they called them troublemakers, that they may organize a union!

The dress industry wasn't organized yet at that time in the 1930s—in the beginning of the 1930s. Yes—this happened. The class interests are always above the national interests amongst manufacturers, whether they're Jewish or Italian or otherwise. In fact, I know of a case of a shop on St. Lawrence near Mount Royal—I've forgotten the name of the place, it's a big place—and, at the time of the organization of the dressmakers, the boss made anti-Semitic speeches—a Jewish boss—to French girls, telling them he doesn't want to hire Jews: they're troublemakers, they're communists. Yes, that happened. It happened in Canadian Waist and another big firm. I forgot the name. One of them is still in existence. Canadian Waist doesn't exist anymore.

The majority of Jewish immigrants who came were needle workers at home, in the Old Country. Whether they were qualified technicians and mechanics or not, they were needle workers, the majority of them. And when they came, many of them became bosses. They worked themselves up and their relatives were in the needle trades or they had relatives who were in the grocery business and they were linked with the needle industry—just like the Greeks who come here now—most of their relatives get jobs in the needle industry, or the Haitians—they go into the needle industry, the French-speaking people.

Language didn't play a role because the Jewish workers learned English fast. It wasn't the best English. The Jewish Immigrant Aid had classes—evening classes for English. It is remarkable, but I regret it, up until today, why I didn't learn French fluently at that time. Now I understand French and speak a little. It's too hard to learn the language now. It was a crime on the part of the Jewish leaders who did not urge upon the Jewish people to learn both languages. And they could have done it. They learned English and of course, the radio was English. The bosses spoke—many of them—a broken English. And most of them worked on Shabbes, on Saturdays. Very few took Shabbes off. That was in my time. Maybe fifty years before it was different. But we worked Saturdays.

Albert Abramowitz

Albert Abramowitz was born into a religious family in Poland in 1907.
His mother dreamed of his becoming a rabbi. Albert came to Toronto
in 1928. He was a union activist.

I interviewed Albert at his home in Toronto in 1974. He died on
19 March 1989, at the age of eighty-two.

I WAS BORN IN LODZ, POLAND, and when I was about seven or eight months old, my parents moved over to a tailor town about twenty-odd miles from Lodz. This little town is known throughout Poland and throughout the Russian empire because of the nature of its work—it was a tailoring centre. They used to produce most of the clothing for export. So, when I came over, my whole life actually had centred in that little city until I left in 1928.

When I was born, my parents were not labouring people. They had a store, a variety store, and they were very religious and I had a religious upbringing. The usual case with all the Jewish boys in those days, their mothers always had dreams for them: that they should become a rabbi. And some of them did develop into rabbis. That was a great sort of thing, an important thing, in the family. And since I was the youngest—there were eight children—I had a special sort of privileged position in the family. All of them liked me extra. They treated me nicely and mother had extra plans for me.

I was thrown very early into a synagogue choir. My father was a very good singer and he didn't sing for money; but, when the cantor was away from the city, he was asked to officiate and he did the best he could. My brothers sang in the synagogue and when I was about six years of age, they drew me in too. I had by then a soprano voice and, after a little while, I turned into an alto. Then later on, when I was about twelve years, I believe I sang contralto.

It was at about this period that I start into the tailoring industry. When I was about six or seven years old, I lost my mother, and I lost my father when I was about eleven. And so I learned tailoring. I was about thirteen years old when I was already an operator, a tailor. This was in 1919, 1920. Labour conditions in those days were very harsh, very difficult. At least I just couldn't take it! You had to get up in the morning about five o'clock or 5:30 and be on your way to work. Sometimes we worked until twelve, one in the morning: eighteen and twenty hours was the order of the day in those days.

I must have been influenced by some radicals by then: that life doesn't have to be that way; that if you establish a collective sort of group, you can exert pressure and win better working conditions and thus reduce the hours and also raise the wages. That brought me together with a number of people of that kind of thinking. We discussed these things. I believe that I have been together with others in the leadership of establishing a union in this city, Lodz in 1926; that we had established a branch of the—what we called—the *Beglagin Centralle*, Central Body, in Warsaw, which was the centre of all the men's needle trades throughout Poland. We got a charter, although a charter wasn't given to us because we were too radical. But, they had one fellow in the city who belonged to that movement, to the *Bund*, which was a social-democratic sort of organization, and they entrusted him—although he was not a tailor—to sit in on all the negotiations. The rest of us being from Communist, Poale Zionist, and other sorts of socialists in the trade, we were not given that charter. It was given to a man by the name of Ackerman. But this didn't stop us. We felt that it was unjustified to be under the dictates of one man. However, there was no other alternative but to accept it as we did and we established a union.

Then we had a very difficult sort of task. You see, the shops there were not shops identical to the shops that we know here on this continent. Every family, in the kitchen, had a little factory. Either it was the father or the son that was the head of it. And they hired two or three hands and in a sense they were the bosses.

So in organizing six, seven, or eight hundred little places like this, you had to do it with the sons, with sisters and brothers, in every family. So sister and brother sometimes had to fight against each other, sometimes against the father who was the head of the little factory in the kitchen. We knew the difficulty of it. But it was a new generation. There was something in the air: that we are not going to accept and submit ourselves to the life like our ancestors did and do the work. We felt there must be another way out. Life isn't worth living that way. After a short period and a lot of effort, we have organized a union and from twenty hours we went down to ten hours. And that was in 1926!

While we understood the importance of organizing, we also understood that we needed to have better legislation that will protect us, which we couldn't do through the union. But this could be achieved by the many levels of government. We were now a little city and we aimed at striking at city hall. There we had Jewish representatives. It was almost a Jewish little town, mostly 90 percent Jewish, and the non-Jewish population lived around the fringes of it, most of them in the countryside—farmers and so on. But they were all interconnected with the city life because they had the goods, the produce. They brought it in. We were the customers and we had quite a number of stores there. But the Jewish population in the main was concentrated in pants making, vest making, coat making. There were very few shoemakers—just a few. The rest of the city was just plain middle-class people with stores and all the other things, living at home on the backs of what I call labour, because labour was the foundation of everything there. So we have achieved at least that.

At the time I was a Left Poale Zionist. I was thrown into the organization when I was thirteen years of age. I got a drift of political things when I heard one of them speaking about conditions in the land. He said that this is an unjustified thing that the rich get richer and the poor get poorer. What we hear sometimes here. But in those days for us children going out from the *kheder,* from Jewish school, not knowing anything yet having the education that the children have here, a basic education. (Although I think the basic education here is not so basic if you consider that they are not taught Canadian history.) Afterwards, of course, we did not have that formal education altogether; we only got what the *kheder* gave us. Later on, after the independence of Poland, they did introduce public school, but most of the poor children could not go there although it was pressured by the government, like it was compulsory. Those that couldn't go to school had to help—as small as they were, seven, eight, or nine years of age—they had to help their parents with whatever they did, otherwise they would be starving.

In those days Poland did not have a structure of social benefits, reforms, etc. It happened later on and, when it did, there were more social reforms in Poland than in North America (which didn't know anything of the sort—even years later after I came here!). But things kept on improving in Poland. I have been, in the main, influenced by a fellow, his name is Yankel Benkel, and I was thrown into the Left Poale Zionists— and in those days the Left Poale Zionists in Poland were not far away, I would say, from the Jewish

Communist movement in Poland. That helped me a bit to understand what a labour movement is and being there I began to read something that was *treyf*, not kosher, when you went to *kheder*. I took a number of pamphlets. And the more I found something which was very important for me to understand, the more I read. I had such a thirst for it that I was never satisfied with what I learned. I saw there was so much to know and I kept on going after it.

Poland at the time (1926–27) was a semi-fascist country. That was the year when I was about to go into service. I didn't feel I wanted to serve under a fascist state. I would readily give my life in the hands of the country for democracy. For socialism. Yes. But to go into an army which is anti-Semitic, for a government which had anti-Jewish legislation, discrimination; you don't feel that this is the type of government to be maintained. Yet the only way to protest against it was to get away from it. If you could help it. Some couldn't.

Somewhere I had two brothers here in Canada (three in the States). They sent me papers and somehow, one way or another, I came over here in that particular period. But I could have gone—this was in 1928—I had another option. The other option was to go to the Soviet Union, which was already known to me what kind of a state it is. Here came in for me a bit of nostalgia.

I didn't know my oldest brother. He was here in Canada. I had lost my parents and I didn't know too much of parent love since I didn't realize what it meant. When I was about six or seven years old I was an orphan. I had a feeling then that no matter how much economic conditions might be better in the Soviet Union, that here in Canada ... I didn't know exactly what it is like, although some Jewish newspapers described the life here like a paradise. That was in the *Forward,* a so-called socialist paper, which is still in existence right now, unfortunately! So the papers here described life in a way that a worker in my trade or in dresses, or in the cloak industry, could make about $350 a week! The furniture that they discard is much better and nicer than what the manufacturers, the rich ones in Poland, buy when it is new! When you read articles like this—and this is not the main reason that I was aiming to come here—but the consideration for, I thought, a brother which you don't know, who takes the place of a father, a parent (which in a way is imaginary as nobody can take their place), so I wanted to know my brother first and I decided that, regardless of conditions, I'll come over here. I did and I found him in Toronto.

I had another brother at the time in Canada; he's the one that sent me the papers, who lived in Montreal. Somehow communications were mixed up or something happened. He left Montreal for Winnipeg. That was in 1928. When I arrived in Montreal, he wasn't there. But a friend of his was there and the address was known to me. So I took the cab and went down to the friend and stayed there in his place. His name was Izzy Weiner and now he lives in Toronto with his family. I stayed with him for two or three days over the weekend and then I came to Toronto. My brother in Toronto—his name is Hymie Abrams (so the name is changed and also two others in the family). I found a place in their home for the first two or three months. Then I rented a room for myself and I got a little job here. I made seven or eight dollars a week, which was enough just to get along with.

It's a little story by itself, how I got the job. My brother was married to the sister of a son-in-law of one of the biggest clothing manufacturers in Toronto: the Tip Top. When I was there at the son-in-law's office, there was a brother named Harry Tait. My brother asked him whether Cohen can take me up, give me a job? He said, Cohen has no more factory. He is out of it and Dunkelman took over the whole thing—the Tip Top. But Cohen's brother has another factory doing contracting. I'll talk to him. Maybe he will give him a job.

So he spoke to the other fellow and this fellow says, Let him come up on this and this date. I have a job for him. And, in this way, I went up there. It was little work at that particular time—contracting—and I didn't get a job which I should have gotten. He had a factory, a regular factory, K.W. Tailors. They were two partners. It was on Spadina near Grant. He gave me what I learned later on was a girl's job: not that a man couldn't do the job, but because they didn't pay enough and they usually took on a girl to do it.

They gave me that job and I was working on special machines, but they gave me only seven dollars a week, which was very little even in those days when the dollar was a dollar and a penny counted. I didn't make very much in this place at all. I was promoted soon to a pocketmaker, which is more skilled. It's one of the most skilled sections in the trade. I could do it and I did it; but I only got a raise of $2.50 a week! The regulars, the union hands, I found out then, were making $37.50 a week.

I went over to the chairman and told him I want he should take me up to the union. He said, You can go if you want to the union. I won't hold you back. I went up and showed them my union card. I still have it from the Old Country. It is something I hold dear to me because it was a union I helped create. I showed them that and that the dues are all paid up. I asked for admission. The reply from the chairman, who was Moishe Gatla, was that I was not making enough to be taken into the union. You've got to have a regular wage, he said. I said, How can I get a regular wage when you don't protect me and that's the reason why I'm getting $9.50 a week (maybe I got by then eleven dollars)? I said, I came up for your protection and your argument doesn't seem to click at all. I was one of the creators of the union in the Old Country and here is this to verify it. We invited people who came into the city when they had no jobs, to come up and register with us so that we can protect them and protect those that are on the jobs, so that we don't allow any open shops to take advantage of labour. And with you, it is just the opposite. You are sending me back to a place to be exploited, knowing fully well that a girl takes $18.50 for the same job that I am doing!

So the only thing for me remained to make a battle with the union. Now, how can you do this? Well, you always figure that there are some fair-minded people in a shop and I found one. And they gave me his work to do. In the beginning I refused. The boss told me, Either you do it or out you go. You have nobody to protect you. That was true. He asked me to remain and do overtime when the others went home. And this I couldn't refuse or else I wouldn't have the few dollars to maintain myself. I remained. And then the next day, when the others came in, they saw that a number of things have been done in the pockets which, the night before, it was still undone. They asked me whether I did it and I said yes. Why did you do it? I told them. I said, Unless you come with me in the union—I'll go again and I'll appeal to them and I want you to help me get into the union. There's no reason why we can't be friends and why I can't be a union member. I want to pay the same amount that you pay.

And Louis Anders was his name, he helped in that sense because he was an executive member there in the union and he made a big fuss. He could open a mouth, you know! And eventually they decided to take me in. So I became a union member and they asked me to pay ten-dollar initiation fee, which was more than a week's wages. It hurt but that was that and that is how I became a member in this union.

Years later, you know what happened? That shop disappeared almost completely because they had taken out all the union hands from it and it became a separate company, a different group.

I came a year before the Depression. It was the worst times and I didn't get a job. When the Depression started, of course, most of the people suffered but some of them had some jobs but I didn't have anything to hold on to. I was out completely for a year. I was not married at the time. I got married in 1932, four years after I arrived.

In most cases the leadership of the union had surrounded itself with a bunch of favourite people who were looking after their election and to perpetuate their jobs in the union. These were the first ones to get the good jobs. The ordinary person was a second consideration. The left-winger was completely left out if they could help it. So I was considered a radical, too radical for them. And this is the reason why some were given more attention than I was given. I kept on going to the office and asking for a job. I always found that the answer was no.

The relationship between the progressive radicals and the others reflected itself on all the needle trades—whether this was hatmakers, cloakmakers, dressmakers—you had the same identical thing that has taken place. It had its origin in 1919–20. You know, from the early days immigrants came to a land, in either Canada or the United States, to a land which they didn't find any roots. They were just in the air, hoping to make a living establishing themselves; a country that has no social reforms whatsoever that you could lean on during a period of adjustment. If you had a family, well, some families could help, but some couldn't because they couldn't help themselves. In most cases this was the case. So they began to organize *landsmanshaftn*—sick-benefit societies. All this was in order to collectively take care of themselves, so that when they fall sick they should have a certain bit of support by paying in a certain amount.

In 1930 there was discrimination in the union in Toronto. It was not racist discrimination but it was discrimination against the progressive left-wing workers. Most of them were standing up and fighting for the policies against cuts, against the class collaboration policy, against being expelled from their jobs—thrown out from the factories. These people didn't have any other trades. There was always small places popping up so they found jobs. These were non-union. By 1931 the same thing happened also in Montreal. Dissatisfaction with this type of leadership in the union. And a rebellion took place in Montreal and the Amalgamated stopped being in existence for a little while there. A new organization came into being, the Canadian Tailors—that's the way it was called—with the wrong methods: a method of underselling labour to the manufacturers so that the manufacturers deal with them. Consistent left-wingers immediately moved against this one. It is one thing when you fight for better interests and another thing when you go on to destroy the main union because you disagree with the policies. It is bad enough in the old union, but you are becoming a worse appendage to the labour movement that it should be cut out before it grows any bigger! This was in 1931.

What they did was to set themselves up as a dual union against the Amalgamated, sending letters, officially, to each of the manufacturers, telling them that they will supply them the necessary hands, the necessary labour, for lower prices. For instance, say, if a pocketmaker made say fifty dollars (as an example), they would supply him for forty-five or forty. They will make it worthwhile to the manufacturer if he deals and makes agreements with them. This would not include people like myself as we would not agree to this.

We came out very strongly against it and started a fight against them. We weakened them. What was the alternative? The real left-wingers who understood this question of struggle said, We will set up a labour council, a tailors' council here—not a dual union—to organize about nineteen or twenty little shops which the Amalgamated doesn't intend to, not on the basis of lower incomes but on the basis of higher incomes. Using this as a base, we will appear as a delegation to the Amalgamated joint board, telling them that we are ready to rejoin the union without any discrimination against us and we'll bring in—I was the secretary, by the way, of this council—so I had the situation well in my hands and I knew what we were talking about. I knew that there were four or five of the little open shops which we could, in time, also organize, getting them into these folds. We had to have somebody to deal with the manufacturers. A capable man, a business agent.

We had one who had lost his job in the Amalgamated named Label (Louis) Goodis. He was a very honest sort, an intellectual, capable man, understanding the composition of a nation, the composition of classes, knowing exactly what problems we are having. He was a man who could talk and you could respect him even though you might disagree with him. He was respected, even by the clique in the union, and his honesty and his sincerity could not be doubted. This man was not in the best of health. He couldn't find a job in the industry because he had been expelled from the Amalgamated.

At that time, I believe, he was a driver of a truck. We talked to him that he should take the job to become the business agent. We said to him that we would try to pay him as much as we can if it is agreeable to him to organize these places and then we'll try and get into the union this way. We didn't consider this a permanent sort of thing but it was the only way that we could have a strong union so that all of us can benefit since it was difficult to get a raise when the Amalgamated kept down the prices.

He became the business agent and we organized about fourteen shops and we began going back to the union. We did not find them very receptive.

They wanted to deal with us individually so that they can pick who is going into the union and who is not going into the union. They were afraid of losing their jobs because we had, at that particular time, honest and sincere and capable people who could really strengthen the union, who could improve their conditions and create a state of affairs so as to be an example to other trade unions.

However, at that particular time we had, what is known as, a president that was a racketeer. His name was Bigenits something ... never mind his name ... when you have a person like this who tried to use all his means to keep us out! But there were other people sitting on the joint board. I remember when I appeared as an individual (after we agreed we'll appear individually). But that brings me back to a certain state which is a famous chapter in the men's clothing industry in Toronto, which was well heard of in many countries: the Shiffer & Hillman strike.

Remember I said at the beginning that I was about a year out of work, that I had a little job here and there? Then the chairman of that shop, the late Hymie Wolkovsky from Shiffer & Hillman, saw me—he was a *landsman* of mine from the same little city in the Old Country. So he came over to me and said, Why do we have an agreement with the firm? I am going to switch the union because it has struck not against the boss but against us. I said, Why should the union strike against you? He told me that in the paper *Der Kampf* [*The Struggle, now called* Vochenblatt] had published a number of articles calling names—a spade a spade, as they say in English—which gave a very clear, candid description of this president of the Joint Board, this Bigenits— much to his dislike, you know, and he saw great danger that this paper comes into the union or gets into the factories, and he put a ban on *Der Kampf*, because people for the first time started to read and just sat up and thought: is this the man who is leading the Amalgamated? But he didn't just stop at the ban.

A big number of left-wingers were thrown out because they collected a few cents for the sustaining fund for that paper. I was told by a man—he's in his eighties now and I was a young chap in my twenties—that a man with a family is going to be thrown out by this Bigenits, this racketeer president, for the simple reason that he was collecting from us for the *Kampf*, the paper, ten, fifteen cent pieces!

We decided in the shop not to allow conditions like this. Either a democratic union or the union is nothing. So, this same man says also to me that one person was intimidated by them and has left the shop. He happened to be their head pocketmaker. He tells me, You're a pocketmaker, and

I said yes. He said, Well, you could take his place if you think that we are right. And I told him, I think that you are right, that the union has no right to deal the way that they did deal on the strike.

You see, to my knowledge, I found out at that particular time that the joint board minutes that's supposed to go around to the seven or eight locals—whatever we had then—to be approved, didn't reach more than two or three locals. So the rest of them had not yet dealt with it. And this president called a strike, which made me really rebel. I said, What if a president thinks he is sufficient enough to take action disregarding the majority in the union? This should not be tolerated and some battle must be put against it. If you can't do anything else but to do it this way, right or wrong, I said, then there's no other way, obviously, under the circumstances. And I said, Yes, I'll join you.

I went up and worked there and this got me involved. I was nearly stabbed to death because of that by one racketeer that they had here from Montreal. He was with a knife after me. Then they brought down some gangsters from Chicago, to beat us up, intimidate us, and take away our rights! Some of us, including me, was one of them! I was marked for that. This was, you should remember, 1931.

A man who was a progressive man—he is now travelling with the Left Poale Zionists—became a manufacturer and then became a manager and fell back politically. He was a member of the joint board and was representing the dressmakers' local. His name is—he is still alive—Sam Shulman. He saw me. He made his business to see me! He said, I heard that somebody—and he told me the name, he said it was Moishe Gatly—who said that I am the one to be shot. Take good care of yourself!

It was all related ... well, a few days later, they had the gangsters here. It was quite a battle. On the way to work one day—the date of the day I don't remember; I never made it my business to remember but it was quite a number of years ago and it is very vivid in my mind ... so on the way to work one day, the sidewalks, both sidewalks, are filled with people. The police, mounted police and otherwise, were there. The strike lasted for eleven weeks. And it was a "battle royale," what you would call it. A real battle! And I said to the committeemen with whom I went to work, that it's too dangerous; we don't know, someone can be moving with knives between them. Because they already are using strong-arm men and gangsters, so I said, We better make a diagonal sort of pass.

There are still tracks there from the streetcars. We used to go up and down there. It was right in the middle of the tracks that all of a sudden, not far from the building on our left hand, the building at the corner of Adler and Spadina, I see Jack—I'll remind myself about his second name—I see Jack, that he drops. I was just talking to him! So I extend my both hands just to keep everybody, anybody, just away from me.

The moment I did that the policeman already was holding somebody and was twisting his hand behind his back while I helped Jack up from the ground. He was bleeding—he had knocked out a few teeth. And the policeman held the man which I had never seen before. And I saw people rushing from both sides. If the policemen weren't there—not just one alone, but policemen—that gangster would have been dead at that moment that he hit Jack. He was fortunate to have himself arrested by that policeman.

There were another few goons in a car that the caretaker brought down. We had a living witness—who refused later to say anything (because they promised him a job in the same factory if he will not be a witness)—so he refused to point out from what car and who brought the goon down. So we knew who brought him because the witness told us. But he pleaded with us to not be a witness because he needs the piece of bread!

It didn't do us any justice, you know, because we could have gotten in most of the leadership and put them behind bars where they belonged rather than be leaders in the union and endanger the lives of honest people with an attempt to kill.

So what the police found out is this: that the gangster, together with a number of others, came about half past six in the morning from Chicago to Toronto and made their lodgings in the Royal York Hotel. At half past seven they made them for union members … perhaps that makes them legal gangsters!

The man was arrested and got sentenced for quite a while. I don't know if it was years or months but they got him out, I believe, before his time because someone paid enough money to get him out. But he was arrested and the story was known. The papers wrote about it.

That same week I happened to come home from night school. A brother to the landlady of mine happened to see me on College Street in front of a restaurant and told me that a man my size, who lives next door to my sister, was grabbed and they yelled that he is Abramowitz and they tried to pull him into a car. He said the men were big, the size of some detectives in the city. But they were not detectives. They were some of the gangsters intending to take him for a ride, never to see Toronto again. But that man kept on yelling so loud … you know he is still alive, that man! In fact I saw him on Father's Day! Well, he kept on yelling: I'm not Abramowitz! I'm not

Abramowitz! Then the neighbours verified this man is not Abramowitz, that he does not live in this house. So they let him go.

When I heard this, I telephoned home to my new place on Euclid Avenue and I called my landsmen there and asked if anybody was asking for me. They said that two tall men were asking and the landlady downstairs—who didn't know my name as I lived upstairs with a couple—she says that there is a man here lives with a couple but we don't know his name at all. However, I made sure not to be in that house and for a number of weeks I slept in my brother's place. Then I had friendly protection from a number of people who went with me and saw me back to the house at all times during that period.

The strike finally ended by the union giving a great wage cut to Shiffer & Hillman, to the bosses of that place, sufficient enough to break the agreement that they had with the people in the shop. And then they made a lockout of all the people.

During this period when we were still working, there was a man, a *landsman* of mine, Sam Peyzman, who told me that they were willing to pay me as much money as I want and give me the best shop in the city if I leave the place. They thought that I am instrumental in maintaining the shop because you have to have the pockets. Without pockets you can't produce any further, you know. All other workers they have and they figure that, if I'll leave, no one in the city will dare defy them anymore. So I sent them back a message. And he came. Sam Peyzman came. He knew I wouldn't be afraid of him. And as I came out from the factory he came across the street. He said, Hello, Albert, and I said, Hello, Sam. What are you doing here? You're going to talk against me? No, he said, I have a message from the union. Okay, let's talk, I said.

They are willing to give you money, he said. They are willing to give you the best job if this is the reason why you did go up [against the union]. I said, Sam, this is not the reason why I did go up. I would rather starve to death and not be involved in such a struggle of life and death if this struggle were not justified. You may not know me since I was a child because you were here a long time already. I know you by name and I know your relationship in regards to the family. My way of seeing things is this: as long as a union is interested in improving the conditions of labour, their existence is justified. The moment they begin playing the game against labour, a union like this either has to be reformed or, if you can't reform it, you've got to replace it with something else. There is no other way about it and I am not doing this for money, believe me. I need every penny that I could put my hands on. But

I will not take it—no matter how much money they will offer me—or the best job in the city; and I know what it means to make a good livelihood. I will not accept it. And this was the end of it.

I remained without a job—suffered the consequences until we stepped into the union and I was not allowed to run for a certain period for office, and Label Goodis could not run altogether. And Blugerman had the same fate. [*Blugerman's story appears later in the volume.*] He couldn't run for office, and Hellenofsky, Hymie Wolcovsky, myself. We couldn't run for office for one, two, three years. So actually it was a question of discriminating against us from the point of view that they were afraid of losing their own positions.

These were all Jewish people. The leadership in the union was Jewish. The owners of factories were Jewish and the workers were Jewish. To see reality the way it is we must approach this from the class point of view. A nation contains in the main two classes which have diverse interests in the economy of the land. Those—the manufacturers—their aim by putting up a factory is not to supply jobs for the people because the people have to make a living! Their aim is an investment to make profit. The higher the profits the better the business is for them. In order to achieve this they have to keep down, give—or at least aim to give—as little as they can to the workers. Make them work longer hours if they can help it. So, that will yield a higher profit. Because at all times ... and this has no national frontiers, you think that because you have the same origin that is why all these class interests disappear? Not at all. This is not the dominant factor. Birth is not the dominant factor. It is the money and the exploitation and the existence of the two classes that is in every nation that are the dominant factors.

On the one hand you have people who want to have a better living, shorter hours, better fringe benefits, which run contrary to the aims and purposes of the manufacturer who wants longer hours, lower wages, no fringe benefits whatsoever. And politically that same thing and the same line runs parallel: legislation to benefit the rich, legislation to put the burden of taxes and many other things on the poor so that they get away with it. Before you get a raise, they raise the price of the garment you make. If they get a tax to pay they shift it over to the articles. So that is what you have here. It's not funny! It is realistically looking at it and finding out what happens in the labour movement now.

[*Before his wife, Lil, came in to be interviewed too, and by way of an introduction, Albert talked about his marriage. The following is an excerpt from his remarks.*]

I got married in 1932. Now that was a bad year. If you'll listen to my wife, she'll tell you shortly a story like this, that we discussed this question: she had to have a room. I had to have a room. Both of us paid too much for the two rooms. And she says, If you don't have money and you love me, you would pay for me. If I had the money and I love you, I'll pay for the room of yours. Let's take one room and get married at least, and it will cost us cheaper this way. If you suffer, we'll suffer together but it will be a different suffering.

She convinced me and we decided to get married and this is the basis on which we got together.

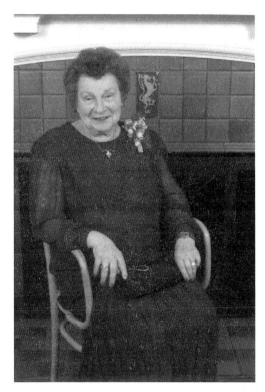

Rose Kaplan

Ben Kaplan

Rose Gordon, far right, with parents and siblings in Koznitze

Rose Gordon

Rose Gordon as a young woman in Vancouver

Harry Ullman

Harry and Nina
Ullman

Murial Grad

Shaya Kirman

Fanny Osipov

Abe and Rose Smith

Rose Smith

Sidney Sarkin, seated and in civilian clothes

Sidney Sarkin

Rabbi in Vilkomer

Pauline Chudnovsky

*Lily and Albert
Abramowitz*

Annie and Max
Dolgoy

Abe and Sylvia Klein

Zaida Moishe Klein

Jennie Litvac

Masha Goldkind

Bertha Guberman

Postcard showing a factory in, probably, Lodz, Poland

Lil Abramowitz

I interviewed Lil Abramowitz after talking to her husband, Albert, at their home in Toronto in 1974. Lil was born 25 May 1907, in what is now Austria but was then Poland. For 123 years, Poland had been partitioned by its imperialist neighbours: Russia, Prussia (then Germany), and Austria, finally regaining its independence in 1918. This event was followed by six wars, fought concurrently, by Poland between 1918 and 1921, before a reborn Poland emerged.

Lil Abramowitz came to Canada on 21 October 1928. She passed away on 17 January 2003. She was ninety-six.

I CAME FROM POLAND. I'm born in Austria, but during the whole mishmash of the wars and all that, Poland took over the last bit of the war that they had in 1921, and they chased out the Russians, the Bolsheviks at the time. Poland took over and that is when I started my schooling. I had my public school during the war and in between.

I left to come to Canada … oh, that's a big story! I didn't want to come to Canada. I wanted to go to Paris. That's why, when I was in high school, I took French instead of English, because some of my girlfriends' sisters were dress designers in Paris and they wrote such romantic letters about Paris and all that. So all of us kids decided that we will all go to Paris and kill the English and take the French course! Greek mythology was a compulsory thing, Latin was something you had to do. But you had a choice with one of the other languages. We chose French.

My mother and my younger sister, one of twins, didn't want me to go to Paris. According to my mother, I was too young. I was under twenty and I would be all alone there. She decided that if I come here to Canada—there were two brothers, an older sister—they would sort of look after me. But it wasn't so. I came to Canada and I was on my own. My first job here was as a saleslady in a dress store. I worked many hours: from nine to midnight. As a matter of fact, he [*pointing to Albert*] used to wait for me to pick me up and take me home.

They started to pay me eight dollars. The first week I got eight dollars and then they gave me ten dollars and in a few weeks time I got fifteen dollars. I made more money there because the dresses, let's say, were priced ten dollars a dress. If I sold a dress for fifteen dollars, then half of the five-dollar commission I had to divide with my bosses. Oh, I made more, the highest maybe was nineteen or twenty dollars, depending on the week and if I worked that late. The store was closed on Saturday. Friday I finished at six. The stores were closed until the next day after the Sabbath was finished; and then I used to go in.

During all that time I went to Harbord Collegiate for one year. I don't know whether Al told you how we met.

I'll have to go back a little. I came here 21 October 1928. I don't know why we lived on that particular street. I didn't like that street where my brother lived because I had already lived in Lemberg, Galicia, a big city, in posh places, and my friends also did so. This was such a gloomy and dark street. Albert took me along to look the place over—what he's going to build soon. And I thought, I sort of felt ... I don't know what it was; whether it was my upbringing, the environment I was in over there ... I had a very beautiful environment, social environment, of course, and the home I came from ... those things. My mother was a very religious woman. A rabbi's daughter. I was brought up without a father because he was killed, he was shot and died of the wounds a few weeks later. This was in 1918 on 11 November, just the day that the First World War stopped ... I believe that was the day.

This was at the time our oldest brother, Velvel, came home—he was in the war. One son was lost already. Velvel was in Vienna or Budapest at the time. However, pogroms started and the Kerenskys—and what other names they also had then—were fighting before the Bolsheviks came. It was terrible there. People were killed and there were a lot of homeless children. My father died just two weeks after my brother came home. It took my brother two weeks to come home from Budapest! He was travelling on the top of the trains and had to dodge the wires—a lot of soldiers were killed that way.

When my brothers left and came to Canada in 1920, I was young. I didn't have anything to do in a small town. My public school was finished. Public school in the Old Country is finished when you are twelve years. My mother made me an old maid before my time because she put me into school younger. I was supposed to be six or seven years when they started school. Because of the war she put me in when I was younger than six. So I was even younger than I should have been when I finished public school.

First of all, at home, they put me into a tailoring place. When my brother left home he said that if I will learn a trade he will be able to bring me here to Canada. So when I went there to the tailoring place, I was one child and they made me look after another child. I don't know what it was but, until I had my own children, I couldn't look at a child. It was such a dirty thing. I wasn't used to that. So that's what made me leave. I was three months there and I couldn't stay. I used to come home every day crying that I'm not learning anything; and, as far as learning sewing, well, I was already very good at embroidering. I did an awful lot of embroidery while in school and my mother was teaching me too. However, I ran away from this tailoring place and took my chances and went out on my own. I was around ten years old or so. And I start to save money to go to Lemberg. I sort of went away without my mother's permission and I went to Lemberg in Galicia on my own. I left home and nobody knew

While this went on, a lot of people, families, had gone away before the war—we were the only family that was left in the city. So they came back with their children. It's a big story.

What happened was, we were trying to go from the city; and it was too late and the children were packed in a wagon to go. We met with a fire and turned back. Some of the children were already dead. Coming back, fortunately, I was one of them that was alive!

However, when I saw there was nothing else in this small town and to become—they called it a *shnayderke*—how would you say that in English?—seamstress?—this wasn't my idea. I wanted to go through with what I was always expected to do. My parents were university graduates and they always wanted their children to go through that and I didn't see that I would be able to do that. High school? There was no high school in our town. So I found a friend who visited our town. She was a housekeeper in a rich family's place. She said, If you come to Lemberg, I can keep you, *nu*, until you find a job. But I was not too small. I was very developed but I was short. Not too tall now as you see, but I was a chubby little thing. Apparently I looked very young. Well, I fixed that up! I used to dress like an old maid later on and I got a job. However, it was impossible for me to get into school because I didn't have anything. Now the people from this small town, when they go to bigger cities, you're not supposed to take any milk, butter, all these things. You were not supposed to take things into the city. It was smuggling. But there was this young fellow, he did that, he smuggled, and he offered to pay my fare if I carried a pail of butter and cheese and all that stuff. Dairy things. Of course, I did that and he paid my fare. I went through. He was caught but I wasn't! I took his pail and took my pail. And shoved it through and nobody even bothered me. Once on the other side, he just paid a small fine and they let him through. It was just, you know, sort of the police who made a few dollars from taking a few pounds of butter.

Well, I came to this girl. It happened to be this young man's cousin. When I came there, the people she worked for were very religious people. And they wouldn't tolerate me there. I used to hear then talk. Oh, if they only knew I was there! So I slept under her bed. They left in the morning for business and I went out to look for a job. I had worked three months at the tailor's place at home, so I thought that I know something and I will be able to look for a job as a girl that can sew. I came in several places and they started to make fun of me. Once they made remarks about my mother's breast and another told me I need a bottle! They were very rude—the boys and girls that were working there. At least that is what I thought: that they were rude.

I didn't understand union procedures. I didn't understand anything of that sort. They were organized union people and here comes in a thing, she wants to work and take away their bread! So I decided the only job I could get through my friend was a job like she has, to look after children, a family. This I didn't intend to do. This I did not intend to do!

I saw somehow an ad in the paper after four weeks sleeping under the bed. What I had taken with me from home was a huge onion and a great big bread. My mother used to bake bread every Friday to last the whole week: black rye, good bread, we don't have that bread here. I wish I had. I took a whole big onion and also a piece of sugar. (They had sugar little pieces, not the small little chunks that we have here.) And that was all I had.

I lived on that for four weeks in Lemburg. I had left a note for my mother not to look for me. When I'll be settled I'll write to her. And if I won't be settled she should not expect me to come home to that small town. I slept under the bed and lived for four weeks. Only once in a while the girl gave me a glass of milk; she took it from her own mouth and shared it with me. She was very nice, the kid. She was also a young girl who came from a different town and had nothing to do, so she took up looking after somebody else's children.

However, I looked in the paper. It was a Saturday and I was just sitting with her and talking and we found a paper lying there. I looked at the papers every day, but this was an old paper, and I didn't realize that a lawyer was looking for a girl who can speak so many languages and which were all the languages that I spoke—it didn't ask for French but the Slavic languages and German and all those—and they needed someone to be his helper. So I went. So this girl, my friend, says to me, Lookit, you didn't make out [get a job] in the shop, you want to make out in a lawyer's office? You must be crazy! I says to her, I'll take a chance.

I went in and dressed up like an old maid who wore their hair like this, and something like that, and here they had it like that. I had something of a picture in my mind, how they took it around and made a bun like that—the same! I took some red paper and put a lot of lipstick on and she fixed me up—this girl, she was a big-city girl. She knew already how to put something here on my cheeks, also from red-coloured paper. I had a new dress—what would you call it here? A flannel dress, with lots of flowers and it was the latest style, the best dress my mother made me then. It was new. It was very much in style in Lemburg. It was too long for me! I never wore it because she made it a little too long. Being my age I wore my dresses like I was supposed to, way up. But being an older girl I had to wear my dress below my knees. And this was just right and she gave me a jacket she owned and I looked just the part.

But when I came into the office they were sitting about four, five girls there ahead of me and I was looking: Mmm, all these dressed up ladies with hats, manicured fingers. I was the fifth in line. The four ladies went away. And I heard the girl on the other side saying, We'll let you know. Nice meeting you. And hope to see you soon, and so on. Then I get up to go away. Those four ladies didn't make it. How in the heck in heaven's name have I got a chance! As I get up to go, the girl calls me back. What is your name? I said my name is Miss Sobol. She said, Would you please come in? Mr. Masengel will see you now. I came in and he asks me how old I am and I told him I'm eighteen and he looked at me and he said I would like to see your—we have to have a certificate going from one town to another.

This was very easy for me. I got a guy who worked in one of those places that was called community council and he was a good friend of the family. This certificate—I couldn't live there without it—and so when I was leaving home, I said to him, Mr. So-and-so, how about giving me a working card that make me, oh maybe eighteen, nineteen? You can even put down thirty. At that time I was twelve years old. So he gave me a card then that said, I believe, seventeen.

But Mr. Masengel wanted my birth certificate. I told him, I'm eighteen. I think I have the card here. It's a year old already, so it says here that I am seventeen. He said, I'd like to see your birth certificate. So I said, I'll have to write my mother to send it to me.

In the meantime he hired me. I made fifty zlotys a month. When I heard he hired me I looked at myself. I came home and looked in the mirror and said to my friend, Saba, I got the job at the lawyer's office. She looked at me and said, Really!

He knew. He told me later on he knew that I was not that age, but he knew that I needed a job because he interviewed me. I told him the story. I wanted to … my mother wanted me to be a seamstress and I hated it and I ran away from home. And here I am alone, a stranger. I told him exactly the way I lived. I'm telling you the truth, I need a job, otherwise I'll probably throw myself under the tramline, under the streetcar, because I don't want to go back to that small town.

He had a brother in that small town, also a lawyer, but he didn't tell me. I used to know that guy very well. I used to work for another lawyer (his daughter was my girlfriend), and I worked for him during school holidays when I was that small and the chairs were too low for me to sit at the desk, so they had a special leather cushion made for me to sit on to reach the desk. And I worked there during the school holidays for this lawyer doing all sort of paper work that was necessary.

So I told this lawyer about that experience and he told me that this guy is also his brother. I said to him that I never worked with such a huge, big man. I was always afraid of him. He was a very nice guy and I worked there until 1927, until my sister left for Canada.

This was in 1920. So this year I worked through and the next year I signed up in high school. And I finished high school and after high school I was with mother, who insisted I come home and I insisted I go to Paris. And because I wasn't eighteen years yet, she can do anything with me she wanted. So I stayed home a year. Going back and forth, working, until finally my brother wrote me a letter saying that it's not so terrible, you'll come over here. It's just too bad you didn't learn the English language. You should have taken English instead of French. In this case you better start learning Jewish so you will be able to communicate with ease with the immediate family because I couldn't speak Jewish either! It was Polish, Ukranian, Russian, German, Hungarian—all those languages that were spoken in those days.

So I took a course in Yiddish and apparently learned very fast because I knew Hebrew well. And the ABCs are the same. The only thing is that Yiddish hasn't got so many vowels. Hebrew has no vowels but they have little dots, so it was easy and this is actually what brought me here, because I couldn't go to Paris. I had no money. You have to have money. I thought my mother would help me. She had land. She could have sold a piece of land to send me. But she wouldn't! So here I paid for half of the ship's ticket with my own money. I had enough money saved up from the work because he increased my income from the fifty, seventy-five, eighty, eighty-five, one hundred, and I made over a hundred already. Over two hundred zlotys before I came to Canada. I invested my money and doubled it and when I came here I had a few dollars. I invested here and it went *kaput*. I lost it.

And so I came here, it was 21 October 1928. As I said, we lived on Yarsa Street and I didn't like it. Meantime I enlisted in the Catholic school. I didn't want to go to the other school, which was close, because I thought we lived closer to the other side. And my brother lived with these people who had a house on Brunswick already. They were supposed to move but he was supposed to stay with the new landlords. However, he arranged to move with them so I knew that we were going to move to Brunswick and I looked around that Sunday afternoon with my younger brother who came from Buffalo. I said I want to go to this school—King Edward. And Monday night I went there and enlisted and came in the same classroom as my husband and that's when we met. It was public school and I was just taking English to know a few words.

I had trouble getting a job from the factories here, too. I couldn't sew on the machines. It just didn't work with me. I didn't like it. Now I like it, but I couldn't imagine myself spending a whole lifetime in a factory like I saw the girls here. So I was looking for something else. I was going around to the ship agencies because I saw an advertisement that they needed interpreters. And I was very good at it. Every language I knew that they wanted except English. I remember one guy, Schlachter was his name. He had a studio, he was a photographer, and he was the nicest guy, and he gently received me and he asked, What kind of languages do you speak? I told him of all the languages and he said, You're hired. How about English? And I said, That's the only one I don't speak. Well, he said, that's the most important one that I need. The books you'll have to carry out in English. Whatever you do, the talking as well as the writing you will have to do in English. So he said, Come back in six months, I think you'll make it. I told him I'm in night school.

Meantime I got a little book, you know, self-teaching stuff: How do you do? What can I do for you? I saw these signs, "Girls wanted for sales girls," and this sort of attracted me. I went into a bookstore at Spadina and I bought that book there, and it said: How do you do? What can I do for you? Will you please be seated? I'm busy with a customer. And all that language I learned and I went in and this guy, Mr. Rosenbaum, had an ad and I went in and told him, and I spoke already in English to him, How do you do, sir? And he said, Yes, what can I do for you? And I said. I'm looking for a *jawb,* and that I saw your *ayad,* and I stretched it so, because I wasn't so fluent; so I made sure that the pronounciation comes out right. He said, What can you do? Did you ever work in a dress store? Oh yes, I said, I worked in a dress store long before I came to Canada. I worked for several years. I was very experienced but, as you see, I'm only a few months in Canada. My English is not so good.

Of course I didn't speak long sentences like that, but I said to him that I think I can make it, given the *cha-a-ance.* He said to me, If you want eight dollars a week you can stay until you learn a little bit more English. He asked, Can you sew? I said, Oh yes, I can sew. He taught me how to make certain alterations. I could sew on a treadle machine, but I couldn't sew on an electric machine. So he gave me a treadle machine, and said forget the electric machine. He taught me how to make alterations and I figured out the dress and the customers, etc., and I made a lot of money for him.

I worked there until about three months or six months after we were married. Then by that time I gave up public school. In second year night school I met a teacher there. In his class I was. I was pretty good already in English and he started to talk to me on the way home. He took me home. He asked, What are you doing here. I said I just want to learn the language. He said, You'll never learn the language from here reading from the *Telegram* articles, from the *Star* articles. What are you doing with this rubbish? You know more than that. I can see that. We had a talk and he said, Here, why don't you go in tomorrow and enlist at Harbord Collegiate? They were just building it—it was just new at the time. So I went and enlisted and I took night courses. When I started again I got very chummy with teachers, they were very nice to me, and I asked one day, what am I going to derive from this? If you want to go to the university, have you got credits? He said why don't you go and show it to the dean of the university? I said I was there; that's the first thing I did, I showed the dean what I had done and he said I was too young—if I was twenty-five they would accept me, but at the age of eighteen to twenty I am too young, and that I have to have a certificate from high school. In the meantime I can wait until I'll be that old and I have to do something. So he asked what can I do, a trade of some sort that I can be independent? I'm independent as far as the store was concerned, but that's not enough. He said, Nobody makes enough, and he told me his pay and how much he makes and it was not much more than I did. He suggested that I go to Tech. I said, Could I take dress designing at Tech, because that is what I really wanted to do. He said, Of course. That's a good profession and taking Tech dress designing with your English, you know, is enough. Then there's a course in English you can take too.

So that's where I landed and how I got my degree, and in 1932 I got into a shop as a dress designer, a small shop where they sold dresses for $1.35 to the Yonge Street stores. Then they started me on blouses. They made four to five dozen blouses a day. I made one blouse in three days. That's how good I wasn't in sewing! My brother-in-law actually helped me get into this shop because they, he and my sister, had a stand in this building, and they asked the boss if he would take in somebody that is not experienced yet in the trade but needs a chance to get the practice.

I had never worked on an electric sewing machine, and I asked my husband how to adjust. He said just put your foot slowly on the treadle; don't put both feet like you put it on this machine, just put it a bit. Well, I put a seam on there and put my two big feet on the treadle and right through the fingers sewed the machine! He saw that; but I just took a handkerchief out and wound it around my finger and then I remembered what Al, my husband, said—just slowly—and I made that seam already.

The boss came over the day after that when I had finished the blouse and he said, Look, Lil, I don't think you can sew yet or make a living from that. You'll never make a living from that. But I know that you are a good sewer. Come out with me and do some drawings for me.

He took me to stores and I did the drawings for dresses that he designed— because he had to design them. So this I'll will pay you, ten dollars a week, and the rest you can do making samples. If it takes you three days to make a sample, I don't mind. and I'll give you ten dollars a week and then we will be able to examine the dresses because I think you know what the dress is. (I needed to know how to make a dress from start to finish.) But a dress took me a whole week and not thirty dresses a day. So he gave me that chance and gave me ten dollars a week to do that. Then I joined the union, but I didn't need to join because I was not an operator. But having a husband who was an experienced trade union guy, who had fought for it tooth and nail—at that particular time it was the Industrial Union, a new union—and he said, You are not going to work in a non-union shop. It was a non-union shop! My wife is not going to work in such a shop. I said, But the boss doesn't want me to belong to the union because I am not an operator. I'm just taking bundles to distribute among the girls and for this the boss needed me because nobody else could speak the languages—Ukrainian, Polish, Czech, you name! There were all sorts of nationalities. And I was good at it because I knew how the dress had to be completed. I knew what was wrong and all that stuff. And in between I sort of shoved in a sample which took me a few days to make but a sample maker didn't make it like I did. His sample was just like the dresses what the other girls made. My sample was a sample where every stitch was just so.

However, Albert insisted that I go and join the union. I went in and that's when I met Gershman and other union leaders and I actually talked to Chik, who was my neighbour, a very nice man. I told him I wanted to join the union and he wanted to know where I worked and I told him, Good. Good. We need you to organize the shop. I didn't know the first thing about what it meant and I was ashamed to ask. When I came home and said I was asked to organize the shop, and I said, What is there to do?

Albert tells me what it needs to organize a shop, the workers, and tells me what to say to them to join a union to make more money. I made ten dollars a week and they made fifteen to seventeen dollars, but they used to turn out thirty dresses a day. There was a couple there who used to turn out seventy-five dresses a day! They were just shoving the seams, the speed at which they went! Oh boy! I looked at them and I didn't see the needle going up and down! That's how it went.

I started to get together with some of the girls and talk about the union— the Ukrainian girls, the Polish. I said you can make more, thirty to forty dollars a week in a union shop, instead of going home with seventeen dollars. I did everything that Albert told me to do. I succeeded and sure enough they made me a chairlady, the shop chairlady! [*Albert interrupts to say, "You did a swell job for the union," and Lil rocks with laughter.*]

I come home and I say, What is a shop chairman? What am I supposed to do? And he tells me I am supposed to chair the meetings, go after them to join the union, see that they pay their dues, look out for something wrong which I should report right away—oy, that was something!

I became the shop chairlady and the boss found out and he didn't like me very much. But he was a very nice person, he was socialistically minded. His name was Mr. Sam Fox, the late Mr. Fox. The whole family was progressive. He said, You want to be in the union, all right. It will cost you dues and

I'm not going to pay it. I said, okay. I don't want you to pay for it. You won't lose anything. And he said no. Not much, only I'll have to pay ten to fifteen dollars more on the week. However, the shop was well organized and even I got a raise of five dollars a week. The shop made him raise me too. I kept on doing that. Meantime I got more experience. I already made ten dresses a day. Unfortunately he was a very, very nice guy and, just because he went broke, the shop closed.

I went and looked for a job and came to a shop which had a very expensive line and I came in that shop and I saw them—they were working men and women there—and a very young lady was a sample maker there. I came in as a sample maker. I told the boss my experiences. I gave him references and he phoned in while I was sitting there and was told that he was getting in a good girl. So I started there at twenty-five dollars a week, doing samples, and that shop was a union shop but they never had union meetings, they never had anything. The union sort of fixed it up that I go into that shop to organize it. I did. And the workers started to pay their union dues. Also on dresses, we took a dollar, dresses made from chiffon and velvet and those very, very hard to work on. A dress like that needs to take at least two hours of work—two hours for a dollar—and I asked them that they should ask for $2.50 for a dress like that, and on other dresses $1.50— like the ordinary, cotton dresses that is sold for the housedress. But the high-class dresses were twenty-five cents for the cheapest dress, and up. So I called for a meeting with the group and they decided that this is the condition, and we put this to the boss and he said, this little communist, this little thing; she is going to be my ruination. But why does she have to be so good in her work!? This must have been in March 1935. And that was my experience at that time.

Albert and I were married in 1932 and lived in one room and shared expenses. He wasn't working for a whole year. When our son, David, came my husband was earning already sixty dollars a week and we had a flat of one room, a bedroom, and a kitchen. Then he earned a little bit more and we moved to three rooms so David had his own room.

The war [World War II] broke out and, as they say in Polish or Ukrainian, "while half of the world was crying, the other half was having a good time." My husband made more money from making uniforms and we were able to save up to buy our first home back in 1942. So we decided to increase our family because, while living in an upstairs flat, it was impossible to increase the family. Within three years time we had two children—David was seven years old when our second one was born, and three years later the youngest boy. From then on Albert didn't want me going to work. I wanted to go back, but he said, Let's raise our own children. I stayed home and raised the family and I hope I made a good job of it.

Max Dolgoy

Max Dolgoy was born in 1900 in Dagda, Latvia. His father had left the Old Country in 1904 and came to Toronto. Max arrived in Canada a number of years later, in 1913, along with an older brother and a sister. They all went to Winnipeg. In 1931, Max moved to Toronto as president of the Industrial Union of Needle Trades Workers.

Max spoke to me in 1974 at his home while his wife, Annie, was busy in the kitchen. Max Dolgoy's sisters Nina Dolgoy Ullman and Bertha Dolgoy Guberman, also have stories in this volume. Max died sometime in his eighties.

I CAME TO CANADA in 1913. We were three children—my older brother, Louis, and an older sister, Annie, and myself—who came together. We are a family of six children. Three were left with mother. My father just managed to bring three of us over in order to help bring the rest of the family from Russia, where we lived in poverty.

In 1904, during the Russo–Japanese War, my father left for Canada, leaving mother with the six children without any earnings whatever. We had to live from day to day. At times we had no bread to eat. Until I came to Canada, I haven't slept in a bed. The three boys used to be put to bed by pulling chairs together. No covers, no bedding. The three sisters, until then the older ones, used to be on the stove. A stove over there used to be made of brick. They used to sleep on that. The entire house was just one floor. The windows were sagging to the ground and there was no foundation. I can remember that myself, and all the family, as soon as we were on our feet and able, we had to go out and earn as much as possible. One brother went in a store, my younger brother. I was arranged to work for two years to be trained as a *kamashen-makher* on shoes; that was the upper parts of the shoes. We had to pay ten dollars to the boss for learning the trade. I was nine years [old]. My older brother worked in a cellar, which was practically unbearable. He was a tinsmith. My older two sisters—one was working, she was helping out in men's shirts and clothing. My younger sister was trained as a dressmaker and, as of today, she still is one of the best dressmakers in the city of Toronto! A custom tailor. Now this was the life.

I remember my grandmother; in fact, I have a picture of my mother's mother yet. And my father's mother was blind. In those years she had cataracts. They had no cure for it and she was blind—totally. But she loved all the children. She used to knit socks for us—blind—and gloves, and whatnot. And we lived like one family on my father's side. I don't know what more ...? There's lots that I can tell you. It's more in my memory today than at any other time.

I remember when we had to travel. The date was the end of the year, sometime in November, five days crossing the Baltic Sea. The boat was more underwater than on top of the water. Sometimes we were under the water! Well, after five days travelling, we landed in Glasgow, Scotland, and we had to wait there. Finally, we have arrived in Canada in December 1913. We had no money to show for to carry us through from Saint John to Winnipeg. And the three of us were put into detention, and we were kept there. It was horrible. There were rats. There were people in the detention who were waiting there: either to arrange for landing or to be deported back.

The immigration people told us that they were going to wire my father as to our arrival and that he will have to send money in order to be able to bring us through to Winnipeg. My father received no such information and luckily there was one man with us, on the boat, who went on to Winnipeg and through him my father got to know where we were! He had to go to the Jewish Immigrant Aid and finally, when the Immigrant Aid reached us, we were loaded with food. I came to Winnipeg with a sack of bread on my shoulder. That's how much food they gave us to come, to get to Winnipeg. And that was our arrival.

We came to Winnipeg. In the olden days it was a city just being built with hardly any paved streets. We were in a home where we only had one room. We were five of us. My father and his brother—he was a shoemaker—and the three of us. And my sister slept with an older-aged lady on a couch here in Canada when we came. My brother and I also slept on a couch. I remember that it was at the end of the room. And the weather in those years was forty below zero and our bed was frozen to the wall. This was in Canada.

And my father and his brother slept in one bed. That is our family: always on the rough, always hard.

My father was officially a Torontonian when he arrived here, but *landsleit*—people from our hometown—they were like our own family. The reason how I came to be chosen, one of the younger boys, to come here was because the family that was here, their mother had raised me. According to my mother's story I was a *zibelah*—I was born in the seventh month and they didn't expect me to live. And it was the mother in this family who made it possible for me to live through all this period and I'm still on my feet! And so there was our family and friends, *landsleit*. That meant quite a lot, you know. We used to eat and sleep together and so on and so on, and that's why my father landed in Winnipeg in order to be with these people; and help was received through them.

There were five brothers. They were known as the Gelfand brothers. They were dairy people in those years. They were farming, and they bought farms, and so on. It was during that period.

Now, I don't know what else you would want me to cover as far as our arrival. I know that, during the First World War, my brother worked in a tinsmith shop. I was working in a leather shop: fancy leather goods. I spent my time with a firm by the name of J.D. MacKay. I was practically the only workingman. He and his wife used to work, myself, and a couple other helpers. I was well received, you know, and did quite a bit of work.

I got into the needle trades a little before the Winnipeg General Strike, which was in 1919. When I came here I was only thirteen years old, and didn't know about any movements whatsoever. I belonged to the Left movement and we had campaigns to organize the working people.

I will tell you how it happened. We got together here in the olden days, a long time ago, and we organized clubs for the immigrants who used to come. We had a club: a young boys' and girls' club. In those years there was no radios, of course, and no televisions; and we used to have reading circles, and we used to have discussions. We used to have picnics. Then, during the First World War, I was involved with the organization known as the Western Alliance for the War Sufferers. I still have the picture of the president and all the higher-ups of the organization. In fact, Lewis Hyman—I think in the middle of the 1920s or 1930s—he was mayor of the city of Winnipeg; and he was the president of that organization. I was very active in that field, collecting money. Each one would have a street to cover and every Sunday we used to go out and collect the contributions that were for the Jewish Sufferers, the pogromized people in those years, you know, in Europe. And that's how I became involved in the labour movement. We started to organize in the needle trades, and I was one of those that acted as secretary in the first place in the cloakmakers union.

I got into the needle trades because I was involved in helping them to organize. During the Winnipeg General Strike, I lost my place where I was working on leather goods and I had to pick up something in order to make a living. I was already married and I—no, no. I'm sorry. I wasn't married. I had to go in to learn a trade and two of my friends were in the trade and I was taken into a cloak shop to work on ladies coats. And that's how I got involved. Through that I started to work in the needle trades and became involved in that only. (On the side, I used to also work, a little later on, helping out in a restaurant business: working at banquets, and so on, in the weekends.)

I was first a charter member of the International Ladies Garment Workers' Union in 1923, and when the split took place throughout the American continent from New York down,[34] I was one of the ones that helped to organize the left-wing union in the needle trades. We had one council. The Furriers in 1926 had a strike, and from then on they remained with the Industrial Union. The cloakmakers, we succeeded in organizing some shops. We had a number of shops organized. We even had a strike.

I remember especially one incident where I happened to be at the head of it, and it was the Freed & Freed Sport Shop. We had a strike there where a skirmish developed and police came around with the wagon to arrest the disturbers, and so on. And I went over to the policeman and said to him, You've seen who started it. It was one of the manufacturers. The boss himself raised his hand on one of the workers. Why did you pick up the worker and not the boss? He said, I'm sorry. And he took the boss along too. He took him along and that helped to settle the strike at that time. The boss almost had a heart attack because he was the one who called the police! Now that gives you a picture of what it was like.

Now during the Winnipeg General Strike, no other than a man named A.J. Enders—if I remember his name correctly—was the chief lawyer to sentence the leadership of that strike. A.J. Enders happened to come down to that place, to that shop of Freed & Freed, to find out what's going on and who is at the head of it.

And I remember the officer came over to me, and said to me, You know who is over there? I said, Yes, I do. He says to me, You know I want to help as much as I can. So if you could give me your name and address, I can tell him who you are and who you represent, and so on. And I said, By all means.

Here's my name and here's my address. I have nothing to fear and you can hand it over to him. And the officer thanked me for it—because the police still remembered the Winnipeg General Strike, that we were on the picket lines together with them!

Now there is a lot that can be said about the needle trades. J.B. Salsburg[35]—who is now a deserter as far as the left-wing movement, and the trade union movement especially, is concerned!—happened to come from Toronto, and he happened to be with me. He was the one that officially assigned me as a paid officer and the head of the Winnipeg organization. It's needless to say that I was at that time already a married man with two children and that, as far as wages were concerned, it was practically nil. My wife worked all the time in the needle trades. She didn't work in the needle trades in Winnipeg but she was working in Toronto for one firm for thirty years until she retired.

Now in 1931, at one of our conventions in Toronto, I was elected president of the Industrial Union of Needle Trades Workers in Canada. And I stayed on in the Dressmakers' Union at that time. I have gone through quite a lot of experiences there! Finally, when we dissolved in 1936, the Industrial Unions and our Dressmakers' Union joined again fully the International Ladies Garment Workers' Union, I happened to act as chairman of the joint board in Toronto. During the Second World War I was a full-time officer in the Dressmakers' Union in Toronto.

Well, in those years, in the needle trades, the majority were Jewish working people and so were the bosses. The odd one, I remember, wasn't, and there was Melvin Van Kemp, who had a cloak shop, but they didn't last very long. I happened to work there on upper shoes. They used to have upper shoes—spats. And I happened to work as a cutter on spats for that company for a couple seasons. And it was taken over in the main by Jewish manufacturers. The only one that I remember, Jacob & Crawley, was one. He was no Yiddisher—Crawley—but he was more *Yidn* than Jacob!

I left Winnipeg and came to Toronto in 1931. I just want to record that my coming to Toronto as a president of the Industrial Trade Unions didn't mean that I travelled on a big train. I travelled on the freight. There was no money for fare. And my family, my wife and the two children—the younger one, Lenny, wasn't five years old yet—and my sister had to help us with twenty-five dollars in order to bring them in Toronto. My wife landed in one of the summer camps, the left-wing camp at Rich Hill, with a family she worked for to cover the mere upkeep of the children. Even then the camp expected a little more money out of me to cover their stay. That's how we arrived and settled in Toronto.

When we finished the season at the camp, my wife happened to be with a family here in Toronto. He lost his wife, his name is Dordek—he's well known in Toronto as a furrier—and he had three children. My wife had to take care of the house and the three children and our own children—that made five.

We came here in the Hungry Thirties—that was an impossibility! I wasn't a paid president. I had to go and look for work and I knocked around from door to door and I couldn't find a day's work anywhere. We were on relief at $2.50 a week—a $2.50 allowance for food for an entire family! My wife and I, we did everything possible to earn a living. My wife worked for three dollars a week in a shop here, on blouses, I think. I worked as a cutter on slippers on College near Dufferin and I earned, I think, about seven dollars a week. Rent was twelve dollars a month on a flat that wasn't heated. When I moved in, I found out that the landlord didn't have money to pay for gas, and the gas was shut off. And that was on Dundas near Crawford—somewheres around there.

There's a lot I can state as far as union activities are concerned. At the time I came to Toronto, the shops here were in bad shape: operators were getting twenty-five cents for operating [working on] a dress. Twenty-five cents! Six cents for pressing, and there was contracting and what not. And when we stepped in to organize these people with strikes, and so on, it took a lot of effort and energy.

But it was done. And out of those years we succeeded in getting much today. We have people who come into the trade now who enjoy benefits. We had no sick benefits; we have it today. It was through my time, when I was in office, that this was accomplished, and through the management of Hymie Langer, who was at that time head man (he passed away already since then) that we have the retirement funds, which we started at fifty and sixty dollars, and we are now receiving seventy dollars a week.

Now people who are in the industry today as newcomers don't know what we went through in our time in order to achieve this: all these struggles during strikes, with police and horses on the sidewalks. We had to wrestle with all this in order to achieve organization, to get recognition, to have to go to court, with arrests and so on. There are people here today that served jail terms for one thing only: for organizing and helping people to at least receive a minimum of earnings—a minimum of earnings!

Now this was in those days. In 1928 I retired. I retired because my health failed on me. It was doctor's orders: better to leave than to remain! I was given a plaque honouring me for loyalty and devotion to the union—even under this present leadership I received that. I had a clear record. I served no distinct political view in the union. To me, every workingman in the shop was a workingman, no matter what race or what opinion or what political opinion he had. I served him. I pleaded with all of them: your place in the shop is to see that you share, you help one another, and you don't exploit one another. And this was really the case, because under the piecework system, where you settle each garment separately, there are certain times when people have the choice to get a garment which pays better, and there were times when some people made good money and some had none.

Now these are the things I have fought bitterly to make sure that every workingman and -woman received their equal "division of work," which we used to call it. We used to have a shop committee who used to divide work, but the committees used to get the cream and the others used to get the leftovers. Now these things are still going down in the shops today: the control of the people over their elected officers is very, very meagre today. I haven't been in the office for a long time, you know, but I am still in contact, at times, with people. I talk to them and they meet me and greet me, and they tell me that those were the days—they were different times, there was more friendship and so on. And that's about what I can cover of that time.

So many Jewish people went into the needle trades not because of a question of language. The immigrants who came in those days came from the *shtetl*, the village. They were not working people. Some already had a little knowledge of the needle trades and they came here and either they opened a little contracting shop or they had to go into a shop. They had no choice. They couldn't go into business because they didn't have no means for going into business. To become businessmen they had to work up a little sum of money. There is a whole history as far as the needle trades are concerned where, on the American continent, an operator had to carry his own machine on his shoulders, you know, to be employed. That was his means; otherwise the boss wouldn't even hire him because he had no machine of his own. (Now there are books written about these histories on the American continent.)

So, little by little, you see, in groups ... for instance, I was offered, more than once, by working people who had earned a few dollars, you know, to get together, to start a shop. That's how a lot of them started in. And they became really wealthy during the war.

During the Second World War there was a chance, because there was a price control, and this thing and that thing, and a difficulty in getting work. A union officer couldn't give a working card; it had to be approved by the government employment bureau. And some manufacturers had no people to work with because some of them got together; they left the shops and they got a little thing of their own going; or they opened up a little shop and took out the work from the shop into their homes. Most of the biggest manufacturers today, I've known as people I have worked with in the shop as operators.

The question of exploitation has one answer whether it is Jew, Gentile, or whoever he is. The Jewish manufacturer happened to be a workingman himself; he knew all the loopholes and every angle: how to get around; how to play; who to play up for and who to play up against; and play up one against the other and so on. And sometimes they're throwing a little bribe, you know, and one thing and another, which is, unfortunately, how they succeeded. Some of them failed because of that. Some of them failed, you know. There's no difficulty also in understanding why Jewish bosses treated their Jewish workers the way they did. In the end it is the dollar. It's the thing that talks. It doesn't matter who you are. You're in business to make a dollar. You don't produce dresses because somebody goes around naked! You produce dresses because you are selling it and you've got to make your profit as a result of your investment.

Well, here is something that happened, just for an instance. We used to come to the president of the Dress Association and tell him: this manufacturer isn't living up to the standards of payments, or that one is not dealing in the right way with settlements; and he said [*Max bangs the table*], You get me that guy. I'll go with you—because why should I pay and the other one shouldn't? And he was right, that Mr. Green. I still admire that man. He knew very little. He was American-born, and his father was a designer; and his father started the business. He passed away. The sons took over—two brothers. But they still left a fortune here in Toronto in manufacturing. And that's how things were at that time.

There are very few shops now, you know. Mainly it's all imports: from Thailand, from Japan, from all over. There are very few of them that still carry on manufacturing. It's mainly the more expensive garments now that are produced here.

I just want to tell you, I was in the needle trades for over fifty years!

James (Jimmy) Blugerman

Jimmy Blugerman was born in a shtetl *not far from Kherson, in the Ukraine. He came to Canada in March of 1908, and I interviewed Jimmy in 1974. He was eighty-seven years old and very sharp. He had much to talk about and remember, not all of which is in the account presented here. Jimmy was over one hundred years old when he died.*

I WAS BORN on 22 June 1887, in the Ukraine, on the river Dnieper, in a small village close to a bigger city called Kherson. At that time, Kherson was the capital city of one of the provinces, or as we called it in the Ukraine, the capital of the *grubernya*, that is, the province. Around the city of Kherson there was, at the time of my birth, a Jewish colony with about one hundred families spread on the farmland, raising vegetables, wheat, chickens, cows, horses, and so on and so forth.

Now in that colony near Kherson were two families by the names of — we called them pioneers on lands, *kolonitse* we call them in the Ukraine. There was one family, quite a large family, by the name of Blugerman; and another family that eventually migrated to Canada, and will be mentioned as we go along, by the name of Chaikoff. Now these two families, with their children and grandchildren, lived quite peacefully surrounded by villages after villages along the Dnieper River where today, in the Soviet Union, is the big power station near Prostroy, which supplies the entire area with electricity and power.

Looking back to the childhood in that area of life, we used to have to import a rabbi into the colonies to teach us children and youngsters the Jewish language, and to teach us the prayer in preparation for the thirteenth confirmation—the bar mitzvah. So while the entire Jewish colony spoke

Ukrainian and Russian—because it was the Russian schools at the time which predominantly taught those who managed to attend—it was the rabbis, who were imported, who helped teach the Jewish children. As a matter of fact, the grandfathers and fathers of this Jewish area in the neighbourhood of Kherson were mostly well educated in the Russian language, in the Jewish religion, and knew the history of the Jewish people, even going back to the days of Egypt and Palestine and so on.

We children grew up in that atmosphere until the age of ten and twelve, knowing practically the elements of three languages. It happened that my mother, being very educated in Jewish religion, had a very strong ambition to raise us five boys and two girls in higher education; and so she utilized an uncle of ours who managed to live in the big city of Odessa, which wasn't too far away from where we were born and raised—a ferry boat would make it from our Kherson to Odessa within seven or eight hours, you see. And so, having an uncle in Odessa, my mother made a trip there and made arrangements with the assistant to this uncle, to move the family to Odessa. It was there that I remember attending a public school.

There were very few public schools at the time, and that takes me to the period of being twelve or thirteen years of age. I managed to finish public school. My father was a shoemaker. We lived in a neighbourhood where he was making a living by making or doing alterations of shoes. Some more Blugermans and Chaikoffs joined us in time in Odessa, and it was after graduating public school that I entered a technical school in Odessa. It was just like our technical school in the city of Toronto. In their case, in the afternoons, we were taught workshops: there were carpenters, cabinetmakers, and mechanical trades. By the time I and hundreds of other Jewish boys, and Russian boys, had graduated, we had practically the education of our high school plus being able to build tables, chairs, fixtures, etc., etc., so we were ready, so to speak, to take employment in small shops.

Now it was at the end of the high school period that some of the teachers in that technical school (which we called Trud, meaning labour, work) were revolutionary-minded and somehow engaged in the underground revolutionary movement at the time of 1902 to 1904, or 1905. We were invited by these teachers to their place or to the park. We understood that it was to be a secret assembly! We knew already that there were spies that would watch the underground movement, and such days as celebrating May Day was introduced to us in the parks and suburbs of the city of Odessa. It was in 1905 then when, under the pressure of general strikes on the railroads and the steel works and there were mass demonstrations of thousands and thousands of students which took place in the city, that we learned the same thing was happening in other cities throughout Russia and the Ukraine. It carried the revolution against the Tsarist oppression.[36]

I remember that the most revolutionary upsurge happened after 1904, when we lost the war against the Japanese and the soldiers were coming back with their tales about surrendering a good portion in the Far East like Vladivostok, and so on and so forth. Now apparently, and it is clear today, that it was under the pressure of that revolutionary movement that the Tsar, advised by his advisors in Petrograd, issued a proclamation in October 1905, granting the people a constitution by promising to allow property owners to elect members to the parliament, or Duma, as we called it in Russia. Freedom of the press and freedom of assembly. And it spread like wildfire throughout the entire country.

This proclamation, appearing on street corners in the city, encouraged the students and the workers, and every radical-minded and liberal-minded person, particularly the educated younger generation, you see. It affected the workers in various factories and mills around in the suburbs of the city of Odessa. And what caused a terrific upsurge was the revolt of the navy boats near the Port of Odessa, the battleship *Potemkin*, where the sailors revolted after finding worms and rotten food; and when they arrested the captains and generals. It was on the third day after the proclamation of this here manifesto of freedom, so to speak, that the generals of the fleet recaptured the *Potemkin* and a number of sailors were shot and put on small boats, which arrived in Odessa where tens of tens of thousands of workers and students congregated, you see. The entire city appeared to be paralyzed because the people wanted to pay tribute and honour to the dead sailors of the *Potemkin*. This created a terrific upsurge and there were demonstrations throughout the city.

This celebration, however, was short-lived. Street-corner meetings by student speakers and the Red Flag waving came to a halt when the order went out to the Cossaks to disperse the people, and thousands were arrested and locked in jails. Simultaneously came the promotion of, now we call them, fascists, but we knew them as the patriots of the Tsarist government and the Tsar Nicolai Romanov [Nicholas II], and were called the Black Hundred, or *Chyonaya Sotnya* in Russian. Now the *Chyonaya Sotnya* spread throughout the Russian country, in the Ukraine, and after the Cossaks began to shoot the demonstrators and arrest them in the hundreds, the *Chyonaya Sotnya* organized a pogrom in the Jewish neighbourhood in the city of Odessa within two weeks of the Proclamation. An absolute terror, you see, a cloud of terror then came into being over the skies of the city of Odessa and its suburbs. Hundreds and hundreds of Jewish men and women and children were murdered in front of us, as we the students at the university had organized a self-defence as soon as the pogroms began. *Somorborona*, they called it, and I happened to be with a cousin of mine, who had already graduated from university, who had participated in the organization of these groups. It is a mystery to me, even to this day, from where those revolvers and arms were procured in such a short time that were in the basements of the two universities, in the centre of Odessa, to arm dozens and dozens of groups led by elderly students and revolutionary leaders into the neighbourhoods, where for three or four days the massacre of the Jews were carried on day and night. You could see broken windows from homes, the beddings and things thrown from the second or third floors: in some places there were such big buildings! Then, when the shooting stopped, we went to the Jewish cemetery at the end of the city neighbourhood and we have seen hundred of our people murdered, you see, and I never forget that sight!

When the revolution was suppressed, then, through the arrests and blood and killing—not only in Odessa but in every city: Kiev, Krakow, Moscow, Leningrad, all over the place—we were informed about the undergrounds, the secret groups we have met, and we knew what was going on throughout the country.

After the outburst of the 1905 Revolution was drowned in blood and terror, and after the fascist activities of the Black Hundred, a terrific reaction developed among the youth in 1906 and 1907. We had very bad periods throughout the country during those two years [following the] defeat of this revolution. A pessimism kind of developed—as we can detect even now in our days, when we read that some people commit suicide, some people take refuge in drugs—and the youth began to lead a degrading life of depression and loss of faith in humanity. There was a writer, I think by the name of Vashavashev, who wrote a big book about that period of depression amongst the revolutionaries and the students' generation. The defeat was terrible.

Mother, naturally, like all mothers would be worried, was concerned about her two sons—the elder two of five children—who are so actively engaged in these secret meetings in the self-defence movement and in spreading leaflets throughout the night. She knew that one of these days the boys will be arrested and sent to Siberia or elsewhere. She happened to have one of her six brothers—a Chaikoff—who had left a long time ago, who had deserted the army.[37] His name was Hyman Chaikoff, and he had managed to find his way into London. There he married a Jewish girl who had grown up in London, and they had a few children, British-born. He knew there was a possibility to migrate to Canada without any hardship or qualifications. He happened to be a cabinetmaker, and he did know a few people who had preceded him. And so he managed to establish himself in Toronto with his wife and children. And, being a cabinetmaker, he found a job in a cabinet-making factory in the east end, somewhere around Queen Street and Logan Avenue, and worked there for a long time.

He was instrumental in purchasing two tickets—at the time, permits were not necessary as long as you had a ticket to get on a boat. The CPR, the White Star Line, and the Baltic-American Line were transporting at the time thousands of immigrants from Europe. These transportations were promoted by the shipping companies, the mining, and other private enterprises in Canada. While they promised jobs, it was hard to find a job at that time.

We are coming now to the time of 1908, when finally letters came from Uncle Chaikoff, who lived in a small little beautiful home at 52 Kensington Avenue, with flowers in the front and in the back. And it was Uncle Chaikoff who, to oblige his sister (ha, ha!)—my mother, that is—and to save the two youngsters from jail, managed to send the tickets. Now having the tickets was not sufficient yet, because we couldn't get no passports. However, in the city of Odessa there were at that time, in 1908, some Jews with long frocks and white stockings—Hassidim we used to call them—from Berdichev, and they were there running around looking for people to smuggle across the border. It was an open secret amongst the Jews in the city of Odessa in 1908, in the spring, that all you needed was between ten and twenty-five rubles to get across the border. And so, my name is Yasha Blugerman, I tell them, and there is my brother. We were well provided, you see [*chuckles*], with that kind of money by the rest of the family in Odessa, and so we got across.

The Blugermans and Chaikoffs cleaned their savings and sent the two fellows to Canada. We got to Berdichev and through good contacts, were taken to a place (I think it was called Grieu) that was the border town near Bialystok.[38] We were directed where to go and what to do. And, on a farm not far from the river where we were to cross, we waited two days for a big hay wagon, and about twenty-five Jewish people—families and singles—were taken across the river. The whole procedure took a half an hour to cross this narrow bridge where the Russian soldier was counting heads and the Prussian soldier was counting heads as well. All we had between the two of us was fifty rubles. We still managed to get to Antwerpen [Antwerp], where we used the tickets on the Baltic-American Line to come to Canada, to the city of Quebec and finally to Toronto and to that beautiful little street of Kensington Avenue and St. Andrew and watch the streetcar circulating!

On arrival in Toronto, my brother and I were well looked after by Uncle Hyman Chaikoff, and for a few weeks we were welcome guests and nobody thought anything about looking for a job. We couldn't speak a word of English. My uncle was working steady, and the auntie was busy with her children and cooking anyways. Bread and milk and meat was five cents, ten cents, and fifteen cents; and a basket of tomatoes, that we were so proud of having, cost us, for a double basket, only twenty-five cents. So there was no problem at that time when a fellow was working steady and is a foreman in a cabinet factory. So we were well taken care of.

Having been born in 1887 in June, and arriving in the spring of 1908 ... let's see how old ... I was twenty-three about that time. My uncle started to look for something for us to do. I picked up cabinetmaking at the technical school. My older brother, Joe, was half a mechanic when he finished at the technical school in Odessa. However, uncle found me a friend of his, a tailor, a Max Persutsky at Church and Dundas Street, who agreed to teach me the tailoring trade. Uncle bought me an old bicycle for eight dollars so that I could travel from Kensington to Church Street, to the tailor store.

My first job was to use the bicycle and deliver things. Mr. Max Persutsky, the tailor, gave me a few weeks of lessons on how to underpress garments that he was making to order. In other words, he was teaching me the beginnings of the tailoring business by becoming a seam presser, an underpresser with a hand iron. In the factory, uncle told his friend that I can work free for two months, without any payment, as long as I learn to do something. I realized that I could already be an underpresser and I suggested that to uncle, that maybe if he has a friend who works in the T. Eaton Co. in the men's clothing or the ladies!

At the tailor store I worked nine hours a day as an underpresser. We started at 8 a.m. and worked until 6 p.m. My uncle did find a friend who worked in the men's department of T. Eaton Co., and he spoke to the foreman, a Mr. Allan who happened to be a Canadian, who gave me the job. He told me through an interpreter that the minimum wage of the T. Eaton Co. in 1908 is six dollars a week for an apprentice. And so it was eight hours a day but people did work longer. I worked there for nine months and became an overpresser.

At the end of a year I had a girlfriend already who was an immigrant from the Old Country, who went through almost the same experience of the revolutionary days of 1904–5, by the name of Gerty Soren. She was an operator in the ladies department in Eatons and she was working on piece-work. I got engaged to this girl and we decided that at the end of the first year after arrival, in 1909, we would get married. You see, Eaton's was paying married people a minimum of nine dollars a week. Within the year or less, she was making eleven dollars a week working nine hours a day, so that between the two of us, we decided that we can be quite prosperous on twenty dollars. So I told Uncle Chaikoff that we plan to get married and we are going to get a raise immediately. So he made a wedding party in his house.

He invited almost twenty-five people of all the relatives and friends: the Chaikoffs, Blugermans, Sorens, and others. He bought two barrels of beer—at that time it was twenty-five dollars a barrel—and we had two barrels with all the herring, tomatoes, and black bread we could eat! And a lot of *vursht*, salami! We had a big party and everybody was eating and drinking and congratulating and singing. And so the wedding was done!

My wife-to-be lived at Dundas and Huron, in a corner house with a Jewish family, paying four dollars a week rent for a room with kitchen privileges. She spoke to the landlord to see if he would change the single bed into a double and how much would he charge for a couple. He said seven dollars a week. And so I took my two suitcases and we carried it, with the help of everybody, and moved into my wife's flat and we were happy ever after: for about a year, when she had to quit her job, expecting to be a mother. And that was the end of the story about Eaton's employment of her where she was making skirts, you see. That's the way we started the family life.

In Toronto, contrary to their policy perhaps in Vancouver or elsewhere, Eaton's did employ Jewish people. As a matter of fact, from 1908 to 1912, 75 percent of their employees in the men's and ladies' departments were Jews, predominantly from Poland. And in the ladies' department there was a Jew who was the foreman. The only trouble Eaton's got into with the Jews was in 1912, when most of us at the time had already been very active in the trade unions, like the United Garment Workers of America and the Ladies Garment Workers. The Canadian locals were affiliated with the American Federation of Labour (AFL). When there was a strike for a regular eight-hour day and wage increase, it caused T. Eaton Co. to take a prejudiced attitude toward the many Jews who were unionists and fighters. Perhaps that had an affect on the anti-Semitism, if there was any, but we at the time never experienced it.

I worked in the T. Eaton Co. for perhaps a year and a half, maybe two, and then it was 1914. I left and found better jobs, more money, in organized private shops like W.O. Johnsons Men's Clothing, and Lyons Men's Clothing, and a few others that were organized by the United Garment Workers of America, an AFL affiliate. In those shops, you see, which were unionized, they were paying more wages than Eaton's because the strike in 1912 was not successful for the working class and the strikers. At Eaton's we were getting, say, nine dollars. Well, in the other shops you could easily get fifteen or eighteen dollars a week as a presser. And in proportion it would apply to the operators and tailors and finishers.

It was in 1914 when we, the needle trades workers, the men's tailors, members of the locals of the United Garment Workers of America [UGWA], were involved in a split that took place in the national unions. It happened in New York, Chicago, and all on account of the 1914 Convention of the UGWA, which took place in Nashville, Tennessee—way far in the south— where the delegates, the Jewish delegates, some thirty to forty of them at the convention, under the pretext that their locals had not paid up the full per capita tax to the general office, were excluded from attending. But this was only a technical excuse by the leaders of the general office—from the president down—to exclude these delegates, mostly Jewish, of the cutter's locals and the tailor's locals of Chicago and New York. They were progressive, you see; more aggressive in preventing the collaboration with manufacturers and in demanding shorter hours and better pay.

When the delegates were discriminated against at that convention they held a conference in a hotel in the same city and decided to form a dual union: an independent dual union, and they called it the Amalgamated Clothing Workers of America (ACWA). The ACWA were refused affiliation by the AFL, who was backing the bureaucrats of the UGWA and therefore campaigning against the dual union as an illegal, so to speak, illegitimate union.

Now in Toronto and in Montreal we had quite a sprinkling of immigrants that had brought with them, from 1908 to 1914, the tradition and spirit of revolutionary class-consciousness. We then were the leaders in these two cities to oppose the bureaucrats of the UGWA and form unions affiliated with unions like the Amalgamated. We managed to overtake shops like the Tip Top, W.O. Johnsons, and others. Of course, it necessitated strikes here and there. We had a hard struggle with the manufacturers here in Toronto, and even a much harder struggle in Montreal with the Jewish manufacturers who were opposing the dual union because they sensed that the dual union represented a more aggressive rank-and-file union. And so we managed through strikes and negotiations to organize the most important shops in the clothing industry in the city of Toronto and this was followed by Montreal.

I conducted a number of strikes. Well, I'll tell you. I had a strike in 1918 against the Tip Top. It just happened that the pressing section walked out on them because they wouldn't give them a raise or something. So I was business agent. I came in to see Dunkleman and Cohen, two bosses (Cohen is dead now), to negotiate the reinstatement of the pressers. I couldn't make no head nor tail of it. So I took the whole shop out—almost seventy-five people! So I had a strike for a few weeks. They managed to get a few scabs, but I conducted the strike. We had to be tough sometimes, you know, to prevent scabs from entering, and ... off the record, you know what I mean ... it's okay to use violence in the interest of the people. In other words, I justify a revolution, but I don't justify a counter-revolution. Ha! Ha! I had quite a few strikes and most of them I won.

At that time there was no strike pay. The union had no treasury. As a matter of fact, I was getting thirty-five dollars a week as a business agent at the time and that was a high wage, you know, and yet there wasn't enough money. And so for the first time the wife went to work and she was making forty to fifty dollars a week. However, we didn't have too many bad strikes.

It was in 1918 that the first big convention of the Amalgamated Clothing Workers took place in Baltimore; and Toronto was strongly represented by myself and a half dozen other delegates representing already hundreds and hundreds of members of the ACWA. Between Montreal and Toronto we had a strong delegation at that first convention and it was there that the first general officers and executive was established, and from then on the Amalgamated began to flourish through campaigns and strikes and to overtake the position of the United Garment Workers.

From 1908 on, for the next twenty years, there was no question of religion which had any influence or effect on our trade union movement whatsoever. As a matter of fact, as far as Ontario was concerned, nobody could work on Sundays because there was a law. Until recently when they have broadened out and have changed the Lord's Day Act, you see, in Ontario, and even in Toronto, that was known as Toronto the Good because of so many churches of all denominations, there was no work on Sundays permitted legally. If there were only small shops, or somebody working, well it was on the q.t. But I don't know whether this question of religion has any influence in Quebec. In Quebec, perhaps due to the domination of French-speaking workers in the manufacturing industry, needle trades, dresses, or what have you—perhaps there the Jewish experienced discrimination on the basis of religion. But we didn't have it in Toronto in the industry.

A lot of our immigrants in my days, for at least twenty years before the First World War and after, they drifted into the needle trades because hundreds and hundreds of them from Poland and the Ukraine happened to be good tailors from home. It was the young generation of students—you know what I mean?—like myself—who were far away from the needle trades. We were far away from being religious. So we would learn any trade.

Now the influence in Toronto and Montreal for a lot of Jews was such and it worked out this way: because dozens of manufacturers, foremen, and important tailors, designers and so on, happened to be Jews, they would bring in Jewish immigrants to work. It was through contacts and relatives, or youngsters who were under protection of someone, who were taken into the trade. In fact, you take today: Shiffer & Hillman for instance, at that time, was a 90-percent Jewish factory as far as workers are concerned. So were Tip Top, W.O. Johnsons and other big custom tailors and ready-to-wear. All these trades; and the furriers, as a matter of fact; and the capmakers—they were all in the hands of predominantly Jewish manufacturers. And the Jews would patronize immigrants because of their position in the synagogues or societies. You see, there was a very large movement of Sick Benefit Societies of organized Russian Jews, Litvishe Jews, Polish Jews, and so on. It is for that reason that Spadina, King Street, Queen Street, and all these neighbourhoods were flooded with needle trades with predominantly Jewish manufacturers and Jewish help.

It is only now, the last twenty-five years, with the influence of immigrants after the Hitler war, that has stopped the incoming of Jewish immigrants who are tailors. It stopped the interest also! In the last twenty-five years you wouldn't find any father or mother in the Jewish community who is trying to put their children into the needle trades or work in it, period! Ninety percent of our children are going in for higher education: university and then they become professionals. You see, you must remember and consider that particular period of time when the Jews were flocking to Canada.

I came as a cabinetmaker but I didn't go into that trade. Why? Because you see it is the contact of the *landsmanshaftnn*—you know what I mean? There was—you have the Kensington Avenue, Elizabeth Street, the Chestnut Street, College Street—these were the aristocratic streets that were the main streets of our Jewish community at the time. Most of the people were in small or large businesses in the needle trades, capmakers, furriers, cloakmakers, dressmakers, skirtmakers, men's clothing. You see the point? And it was for that reason that all immigrants of those twenty-five or thirty years predominantly produced in these occupations. Everybody who comes, he brings a *landsman* into the shop, he teaches him to do this, that or the other thing, and so he develops. And the other point is that at that time you didn't have to learn for long a trade because there was the development of technology and production. Instead of the tailor making the whole garment by himself, it was split up in the division of labour: the pocketmaker, the sleeve-maker, the lining maker, the underpresser, the finisher. It takes ten or twelve people to make one garment. And there's the designer, the cutter. You get it? So you see, the technology and development of the know-how is split up; and it was that reason that for the last twenty-five years Jews began gradually to disappear from the needle trades occupation. Newcomers of my age, from my period, are too old. We are retired and on pensions—dismissed! They are supposed to be retired at sixty-five years. There is nobody to retire now in the needle trades because there is no young generation of Jews left. Thirty years ago you couldn't get a Jewish youngster to teach him in the needle trades. They wouldn't go to Spadina Avenue. So what happened? The invasion of new immigrants began after the Hitler war. Gradually the Ukrainians, the Italians, the Portuguese, and about a dozen different nationalities from all over the globe who are coming here, are inspired and organized by the Ontario government or other governments, because the old ethnic groups here have become too influential politically. They have a great influence on loosening up the immigration laws and they bring in, by the thousands, immigrants of various nationalities who are being given the preference, because they were brought in by the invitation and financial assistance of the provincial government, and they are getting jobs without speaking a word of English. You take a walk down to Shiffer & Hillman, a Jewish-controlled manufacturing enterprise, that 99 percent was Jews, and today you couldn't find 10 percent Jews from top to bottom. I was at some of these factories today. I could hardly find a Jew to talk to. They are simply not in the trade today.

I remained in the needle trades. I was the first business agent of the Amalgamated from 1915 to 1929. Between 1920 and 1929 there was a development in the trade union movement, especially in the needle trades, when the progressive socialists led the Amalgamated and the Ladies International Garment Workers—the Capmakers and the Furriers Union—and we organized through strikes and struggles in the US and in Canada, and we established the eight-hour workday, with extra pay for overtime and with a minimum standard wage. That is what we accomplished.

There were unfortunate developments that went against the best interests of the working class, and it is for that reason that a split between the Left and the Right took place. As a result, of course, the progressive leadership was eliminated, not constitutionally, but they were expelled under any pretext. In the States they introduced the employment of goons: armed goons. The Joint Board of the Amalgamated had engaged and paid for goons! I wrote articles in the paper that we had organized here: first *Der Kampf* [*The Struggle*], and then the *Vochenblatt*.[39] I was the President of the Kampf Publishing Association and at the same time I was a member of the union and working as shop chairman in a big shop, the Habolin Co. In the article in the *Volkenblatt* I wrote accusing the General Office of the Union for permitting the hiring and using of strong-arm methods in the locals of New York; and of beating up and using violence to subdue the criticism. Consequently I was tried by a special commission sent by the General Office of the ACWA and was charged with slandering the leadship of the ACWA: slandering and accusing them of gangsterism, etc.! In other words, of being a destroyer of the union. And when they asked me: Brother Blugerman (that's what they called me as I was still a member at the time), Brother Blugerman, would you retract the statements you have been writing in your paper (they called it God knows what!), retract it officially, and we perhaps would then withdraw the charge of slander, etc.

And I got up and I told them, the bureaucrats of the Toronto organization, I said, Gentlemen! Well, I'm in the habit, I told them, to call the meeting "gentlemen," and I said, Gentlemen, you local officers and you from the general office—the judges—I don't withdraw a single word that I have been writing in that paper for the last few years. I accuse you of using terror and gangsterism to subdue left-wing critics and fighters, the pioneers who built the Amalgamated and every other progressive union in Canada and the States, and I don't withdraw. I plead guilty, and I don't take anything back. Goodbye! And I walked out.

I was immediately expelled from the organization and instructions were given to the local officers to go to the shop where I worked and tell the boss that they cannot employ me; that I have to be fired. And the boss came over to me and he said, Blugerman, you know damn well that I'm 100 percent with you—he was a small boss—but I don't want them to take off the workers. He said, I have to leave you. I says, You don't have to leave me. I quit!

I was forced to walk out in the presence of the business agent and the joint board president. So I walked out. The fellows there, about twenty of them, said, What happened? What happened?

Do you know, these people went out on strike against the union for taking me off, and another twenty-five left-wingers off in other shops? We were all taken off the jobs because a lot of them were selling the papers in the factories: *Der Kampf* and the *Vochenblatt!* So twenty-five of us were deprived of a livelihood at the time, which was 1928–29.

It was a bad time. I never regretted to take that position, you understand. And as a matter of fact, I was one of the best mechanics in the trade. As soon as some of the small shops discovered that Blugerman was thrown out by the union, they gave me a job, you hear? And I was making more money in an open shop for the next ten to fifteen years! So they did me a favour. You see the point? But most of our people lost their jobs. This is what took place. It is hard to believe, but that's just what happened.

The funniest part was that I was away from the union 1928 to 1929, and I worked in every shop (everybody wanted me to work in smaller places, that they ran) to make more money than I was making. The union scale, for the best presser in the union at the time, was forty dollars a week and if he was very good, so, he would make fifty or sixty dollars. Now I worked in a small shop for ten to fifteen years and I was making $110 and $120: two dollars per garment. I was making $150 on average a week and they were good enough, you hear, they were good enough to pay me twenty dollars off the table, because they had to take off income tax, you get it? (Is that going in the record? Well anyway, I don't care! But the funniest part of it is that they can't do you nothing after twenty years anyways!)

Okay. So look. I was making good money. What would happen fifteen or eighteen years ago was this: a manufacturer had a union shop and needed a presser in a bad way. They had four people and they needed five. And the union didn't have a presser to give them. You see, the contract with the manufacturer and the union is this: the union gets the preference for hiring employees from members of the union. However, if the union, within forty-eight hours, two days, cannot supply the help, whether it's an operator or a presser, then the manufacturer has a right to advertise in the newspapers and employ any first comer. So the boss applied to the union for a presser and waited a week and was nothing there. Well, he didn't advertise in the paper. He phoned me to the house. He says, Blugerman, I have wanted you for so long and now I've got the chance. Would you like to come and work for me? It was Izzy Feldman of Feldman Bros. & Weiss, a union shop, a Jewish manufacturing outfit; and he says, Blugerman, I have a right to give you a job. You want to take it? I says, I'm working but I'll be there next Monday. Well, I came next Monday and I stayed for a few years!

For a year or two they didn't want to take me in the union and I worked there with the union book. You understand—they didn't have somebody. So

I am out of the union since 1929, but I went back. It took them a few years before I had a chance to be taken in. When I was taken in, for two years the executive of the Presser's Local didn't want to call me to a meeting and they, *moykl toyes* (I don't need their favours! I can do without them!)—they didn't want the Jews! They didn't want me to start trouble in the unions. However, the people in the shop insisted. We want Blugerman in the union! He's not a scab! And do you know? They forced the union to take me in. So they took me in the union until I decided to retire.

When my first wife began to have babies—and we had three daughters and a son—so for the first fifteen years she didn't go to work. When my three daughters and son had to go into Harvard, my wages were not enough. So my wife went back to work. She was an excellent skirtmaker and dressmaker, and temporarily she went back into the trade for a couple of years. She joined the Industrial Union of the Dressmakers' Union.

However, it was unfortunate that my first wife, a real comrade, you know, she developed cancer thirty-six years ago. We were already grandparents. All the children were living in flats. No one having a home yet. We were just the two of us. She developed cancer and died thirty-six years ago and I became at fifty-four, fifty-five years, a grandfather and baby-sitter. I was still either working or being a salesman.

Within a year and a half I met a girl who was not married. She is twenty-seven years younger than I am. And the first thing I did was introduce her to my grandchildren. She was so crazy about them: she used to take them to the zoo, and so on and so forth. Finally, I used to take her out, and I says to her, How would you like to marry a grandfather? She was silly enough to say yes! I took her out for quite a few months to make up her mind. However, she was silly to decide to marry this guy thirty-four years ago and again we had three daughters and one son. The baby got married, three years ago, and works in a bank and helps her husband to be a lawyer. The middle one is married and lives in Vancouver and that's the girl I want you to see someday when you get back. And the oldest of the second marriage graduated from [the University of] Toronto and [the University of] Waterloo as a social worker. He intends to go back and get his Ph.D. My wife wants him to get married because she wants to have grandchildren! I told her that if she'll have as much patience as her husband, she'd be a grandmother with God's help.

And now that's the story of my involvement with the trade union movement. Then, of course, I got involved with organizing the Labour League. But that's another story!

Samuel Nemetz

Samuel Nemetz was born in the Ukraine, in the city of Yekachinyoslav, in 1890. He arrived in Saint John, New Brunswick, in 1910, on the run from the Russian Army, which had posted him to Siberia. Samuel settled in Montreal, where I interviewed him at the Young Men's Hebrew Association in the summer of 1974. He was eighty-four years old.

MY NAME IS SAM OR SAMUEL—which way you want, short is Sam. And Nemetz. You know how to spell it? I can tell you that I didn't have no intention to go away to America. No. I was a fighter there in Dnepropetrovsk, in the Ukraine, at that time. Dnepropetrovsk is a city in the Ukraine. At that time it was Yekachinyoslav and today it is Dnepropetrovsk. Four years ago I went to visit but I could not get in there because there was no immigration. I was in Moscow, Kiev, and other cities, but there I couldn't go. But I have a niece and nephews still living there. So they came to see me. I was in Zaparosh, today it is Zaporizhya—that was two hours away. You got to go by train or bus, or you can go by boat. When I came there to Zaparosh my niece and nephews were already waiting for me there in a big car. I arrived by plane from Kiev.

I had the intention to be in the army, as I have told you, so I didn't want to go away. The police watched me and it was three months before they took me in the army. Until you are twenty years old, everybody is called to the army there. I made an outfit to go there. I used to go to the army barracks. I went there many times to eat. There were huge crowds there. Lots of Jewish people and Ukrainians there. A lot of Russians. And there's this officer picks out where to send everybody every day. The last party they picked up I was there. The officer comes out and I was sure—I was strong—and he wanted to send me to Siberia. I wanted to go into Russia, do anything, go anywhere. I wanted to go! But Siberia I didn't want!

They didn't tell my mother. She used to have a chicken store with live chickens in the market. I came over there—she liked me very much—and I came to my mother. She looked at me in the eye and she said, Are you crying? Something like that. She notices. Mothers can notice quicker. I wasn't happy to go there.

So my mother says to my stepfather, Harry, stay with the business here. And she went over to an agent. She made arrangements for me. She comes over and she says, Tonight you are leaving for America! I was twenty years old at the time. I had a girlfriend there!

Don't tell anybody, my mother says. This is a secret. I took a taxi. (I don't know if we had taxis there at that time—I think I took a taxi.) And it brought me to the station. My stepfather said he wants to see me leave. People were spying. People dressed in civilian clothes are watching—who is leaving—and they are suspicious about things. So my stepfather wants to make sure I go away all right. I went in the station and bought a ticket to somewhere past Warsaw.

I got on the train and it was full of youngsters there. I could speak Russian. They were drinking, singing, and drinking. I don't know what gave me that idea but I mixed up with them. I drink with them all the time. The army must have been looking for me already the next day when I didn't come in. I was travelling already. They must have looked for me. But I don't know what gave me that idea to mix with the youngsters.

I travelled almost two or three days. I got on the train Monday and it was Thursday when I came to Warsaw. There I had to change the train to go to eastern Germany, to a place of the name Bendeen. [*I was unable to find a record of this place.*]

When I stopped in Warsaw I had to wait from morning until later in the afternoon, about four o'clock. It was raining. The weather was miserable there. I walked around. I had time to walk around in Warsaw. As I walk around a gendarme, a guard, he sees that I don't wear the clothes that the Polish, Jewish people, used to wear. No hat. You see I was there like an American or English. The guard says, Stop. Who are you, and this and this, and where are you going? I'm going this way, I say. What are you coming here for? I said, I don't know.

They had given me a passport for somebody else—for a barber. I've never been a barber. If they ask me to make him a shave, I would do something and he would get me right away. And the gendarme would make an investigation. I said to myself, Oh my goodness, they're going to get me and I didn't sleep. I was afraid at night they were going to wake me up and ask, Who are you? What's your name? And I might forget. I was so frightened.

Something hit me again; something in my mind. I had Russian rubles, silver rubles in my pocket. I take out two silver rubles and give him in his hand and he takes it. That was good. And he let me go.

That saved my life. Then I didn't go no more in the street. I hid myself. If anybody was there, I would go and hide. I was watching myself. I had to stay all day there. When I came to Bendeen—that was Friday four o'clock, like Shabbes—I come to the hotel. My mother gave me some meat there, some chicken—a barbecued chicken, something like that. But I didn't eat it. I had no time. I didn't want to eat nothing. What I want is sleep. I was so restless. I didn't sleep because I was sleeping with one eye open all the time. I used to go with the boys on the train, drinking, drinking. But the further the train went there was less and less boys there. It was dangerous too because they divided into different directions afterwards. But from Dnepropetrovsk there was a lot of boys on the train and I enjoyed myself with them.

So when I came to Bendeen I was tired. I go in a hotel. I try and undress myself. Who wants to eat when I want to go to bed and rest. There's a knock at the door. I say, What's the matter? You can't stay here, they said. Tonight there's going to be detectives coming to look around in the hotel ... anyway, we'll take you somewhere else. It's dangerous at night. I said, I'm tired. They said, Dress yourself and we'll put you in another place, and they took me to another place. This was on a Friday. We came to a one-story house, with nothing, the floor is of mud. I opened the door. I go in there. There's a light? No, no light. It's Friday, the Sabbath, you are not supposed to put the light. So there's only a little candle. And there on the floor I see, I don't know how many, nine, ten people. I said, Where do I go? He said, Step in. Go inside with the others.

I don't know. Girls or boys or men? Or what are in there. I'm tired. I go on the floor to lay down to rest. I undress somehow ... I don't, I don't take off my underwear! ... I just lay down about ten minutes. I get attacked from an army—you know—bugs! Why the others are sleeping and they don't both them and why did they attack me? I'm a new person with fresh blood. They attacked me like hell. No matter how tired I was, I want to sleep, but I couldn't. So I got up and took a chair. I sit down by the door there. I was sitting all night. No sleep.

In the morning they took me to the man that is supposed to take me over the border. That was Saturday already. Everything was arranged from that agent in Dnepropetrovsk. He arranged everything. I didn't have anything with me—just an address in Montreal from my uncle. I had some money there but nothing; no other papers. (I had some papers, which I had to throw it out. You see, by mistake I had kept it and somebody saw the papers. At the time I was like half crazy for the excitement of going from home. And this man said, What are you doing with this? Tear it up. Throw it out, he said. Oh, if they get you, you would get arrested right away.) So on the train when I was going, I tear it up and throw it out the window.

In the morning then they brought me in a house. It was Saturday. A man was there with a big beard, a Jewish man with a hat, and he was smoking on Shabbes! I am not religious, but a man with a beard should smoke on Saturday? I brought a lot of cigarettes. My sister used to work by cigarettes in a big, big factory and they gave me a lot of cigarettes when I left. But I didn't want to smoke.

The Jewish man with the beard and hat is telling me, Tonight we're going to take you over the border to Missel (or something like that) by the German border there. The arrangement is like this: Today at two o'clock there's going to be two officers, two soldiers, Russians, that are going to bring you over the border into Germany. That was the plan they made up. Tonight, the officer in charge, the guard, will go with his wife to the baths; every Saturday night he goes with his wife to the baths. So when he goes away to the baths and they are changing the guard (they wouldn't change it immediately, about fifteen minutes or a half hour), then between this time we'll have to go through there and that is the plan, see?

At two o'clock he comes in. Knock on the door. It's Russkies with rifles on their back. Like hunters they are, very strong boys with three stripes. (That's how they make their money there. They only have three months on the service and if they are caught they would get in trouble. But still they want to make a little money and so they didn't care. That was the way.) I put away my cigarettes. So during the day we were drinking with the two military boys. I speak Russian, he speaks Russian. We drink. He shakes my hand. He's from the government, but never mind, he's still taking on a bribe. Then he stays there an hour or less. I can't remember. He goes away and he has to come at night when it is getting dark. At twilight, he'll come and he'll bring me over the border.

Five o'clock. It was five o'clock. He came. No. Five o'clock and he didn't come! The son of that Jewish man with the beard (the old man didn't come), came and took me over the border. I took my valise, whatever I can in my little valise, and I was just going there to a little house just near the border.

He says, You see the border there and it's just fifteen minutes to run over. Come on now, we got to go.

It was raining. It was wet. From far I can see from the German side a boy is going on a bike with a light in the front to show his way. So he speaks to him in Polish, or whatever. I don't understand what he asked him. He says, Now, come on, run. Come. Go quick. In ten or fifteen minutes I was over.

He brought me in there. This is a big house from the Jewish agency that they have for the immigrants there. He brought me in there; but before he did he said, Lend me a dollar or two. I don't know what he wants and when is he going to give me back? I wouldn't see him any more. What shall I do with him? He says, I have to buy something. I forgot to take some change. I'll give it to you back. I gave it to him, anyway. I'll never see him again.

They brought me inside the house there. I can't remember if they gave me something to eat or not. I have to stay until tomorrow and then take the train to go to Antwerp. So I have to undress everything. They take your clothes and put it in an oven there to disinfect it. The next morning it was like this! [Sam indicates his clothes had shrunk.] I don't know what they did to my derby hat. Everything was small. But I had to dress. What could I do? I got to go to the train. They must have looked on me—the Germans know their ways to dress—and must have said, What kind of a person is that going there? What kind of clothes he's wearing?

I had to go from there, cut through Germany to Antwerp. I had money. I see there the boy who works on the train. I want to buy something to eat. Nothing to eat, only chocolate. I want a piece of bread. Give me a bagel or something. There's nothing. You got to eat bread! If I could eat this, the chocolate, I know that I would. But I couldn't. I would give it up, throw up. I would get sick. So I didn't buy this.

So it continues all the way, till how many hours it takes, until I came to Antwerp. I came there and I changed to another train. The same story. Candy. Cake. No cake even. Only chocolate. There was also a connection with the Jewish agency there for the Jewish immigrants. Marvellous the way it worked, you know! I came in Antwerp. It was already cold. It was raining. The agency took me there. I had something to eat. I remember it was applesauce—that I liked! I ate it with bread. Nothing else I could bear to take. They took me to a barracks and I went to sleep. No heat, nothing there. That's how I had to stay there until the boat left. I waited two weeks maybe for that. But I slept. I couldn't help myself. This was in October or maybe November already. Anyways, it was a couple of weeks there in Antwerp until the ship came. In the meantime I was eating. I eat a little because I couldn't digest too much.

And I still have the barbecued chicken inside there in my valise! I got it out in Antwerp and when I opened it, it was all colours: green, blue, yellow and all kinds! (My mother wanted to support me with a meal; that I should have something in my pocket, you see. But I didn't open it until later as I had no time, and on the train also I didn't open it and it became all colours!)

So a couple of weeks I stayed there and then went on the boat. And I stayed two weeks on the boat. It was a boat that carries cattle to Europe and passengers back. The name of the boat was *Montezuma*. I remember that name. You can't imagine what kind of cabin it was. They spread on the floor the stuff from the cattle—you know what I mean?—and the smell is so strong that you can't stay there, never mind sleep there. I used to go outside on the boat all the time. I couldn't stay inside. I couldn't eat or do anything. I was always on the boat on the top deck, in the front. I was staying there just like a dog, waiting there. It took fifteen days and we come to Saint John, New Brunswick, in Canada. We had Christmas or New Year's, I wouldn't remember—one of those, and they gave me an orange. It was too much! My head didn't work at that time. There was too much excitement. I went through too many excitements. That was my first journey. I never travelled even to the country in the Old Country. That was my first journey and if the police had got me there, you know in the Old Country, what I would get? And I wouldn't be here now!

From Saint John I took a train. I had a paper but when I came here I had no money, not even twenty-five dollars. That is what an immigrant must have in order to let you into Canada. I didn't even have that. If I would be smart, I would go with other people, they can give me twenty-five dollars and I go down here and out of there and I would give them back. But I didn't have the money and I didn't tell nobody. I was afraid. I wasn't smart enough. When I came to the immigration, they asked me, How much money you got? I think I had ten dollars. So they passed other people and I was arrested for to be sending me back or something.

I had people here, my married sister—her husband disappeared and went to America and never came back and left her here with a baby! She came with the baby. And there was another sister, also got married once they came here legally, who had a baby and she came also to take me. But they don't consider those kinds of people. You got to have somebody else that works who you can depend upon. My uncle they didn't accept either. All the lawyers tried all kinds of ways to get me out of there—out of the immigration. I was still there in Saint John. They didn't let me in. The Jewish agency, I think the Immigrant Society here, tried all the ways but lost.

They finally give me to my sister who was working for SemiReady making pants. She was working in a shop. She was a good worker. SemiReady was a big factory, a clothing factory here in Montreal. She was working and she made money, so her application the immigration accepted, otherwise they might send me back to Antwerp. That's what they did at that time.

I stayed with my sister all the time. When I came here they had *landsmen*—you know what *landsman, landsvolk* is?—from the same city. So they knew my sisters; and the landsman had a daughter here, who was married. A mother has an eye. And she, the married daughter, had something, an idea! I was a boy of twenty and she had a girl of sixteen, seventeen. Sixteen, I think. Anyway I used to come to their home. The first couple of days she undertook to find a job for me. My sister couldn't find me a job as she was busy; she was working.

The *landsman* was working for himself making one of the nicest pants you can make by yourself. Cutting for himself. He was an expert. I was nothing. I just know how to sew on the machine. I don't know how to put together a garment. I made the tops of shoes. The top of the shoes they give it to the factory and they make shoes. They make the bottoms. All kinds of nice shoes, big ones, small one with buttonholes, all kinds of fancy ones.

So that *landsman*, that woman, she found me a job. I got to go in a shop, a small shop which was not a union shop. There was no union anyway at that time. Maybe with the garment workers … but no, the United Garment Workers were not here at that time. I don't think so. Anyway, we didn't organize then because there was nothing. We had it for three or six months and then in the next three to six months the conditions were bad, it is the wintertime, things were slow and you have no union already. Every six months you had to organize new, again. At the time it was that way.

Anyway, this woman she finds me a job on Cultus Street, I think. I remember it was an old shop. I came there and they introduce me. It was a father and son. They were contractors; they got work from somebody else. They gave me the job. I was glad that they accepted me and they got to teach me how to make things so that they have the benefit of me. I could sew, make a seam, make it straight—that I can do. And I was quick too. And another thing— there were a lot of parts over there in the garment to stitch.

I worked there for nothing. I don't know for how long. I worked from 7 a.m. to 7 p.m. And on Sundays. We didn't work Saturdays. Some shops they worked Saturday evenings too. They started to pay me two dollars, three dollars a week. I don't remember what they gave me there but whatever they give to me I accepted it. Then a neighbour of mine used to work at Levinson's at that time. It was a big shop. He took me there. I knew a little bit something by then. It was section work. You know what I mean? That time it was week work, never mind piecework. They didn't have piecework then. It was week work and you worked on pieces but got paid for the week. You had to work many hours for that couple of dollars for the week.

There was another man by the name of Charlesky, I remember the name, and he went to America, to the States. He is not alive any longer! So he was a neighbour to where I stayed there with my sister. And the women would talk together and say that my sister had a brother here from Russia, and he was this and this, and he knows how to sew on the machine, that he is working already in a shop, he also worked in a contractor's shop, a bigger shop, Levinsons … and all this about me. So this Charlesky took me in there and he already gives me a salary, a bigger salary, seven, eight dollars for a week, you know, until I got more and more raises.

I used to go on demonstrations in Russia there, at that time, in 1903. They started in 1901, 1902, 1903. In 1905 was already the big demonstration in Moscow when the priests went there to ask for bread and they gave them bullets. But we had a demonstration in Dnepropetrovsk. There were all kinds of revolutionary demonstrations where there used to be holdups, and there used to be expropriations there, where they take away your things. I used to work as a learner in the shoe-tops trade. I used to have to go and carry, go and buy material for the shoes, and bring it here and there.

So I used to go on the street and I saw everything. If I would be in a shop I wouldn't see that. I used to take an interest. If I came another hour or two hours later—it was nothing. The boss don't know. The boss, he had a leather factory, a leather store where the shoemaker used to come to him and buy the leather. And I used to go and take it to them. They had the measurement there and we used to have the patterns and cut it and make it for them. So I had to bring this, go for that, take the ready one there. So I used to be on the streets. My boss told me to go buy cotton, go buy linen there—he didn't have no time—and I used to be the manager for that.

In the meantime I had time to be in the streets and see everything. Demonstrations there, the police, then the expropriations. There was a big wagon, you know, with the money inside, and Cossacks here—two, three of them with rifles there in the front and a couple there in the back. You see? And the people in the streets still got the money!

There were demonstrations and funerals. People used to be killed in the streets and so there were a lot of funerals. Every couple of weeks there used to be funerals and they used to play [*Sam hums a tune*]. The military band used to go and play there. And then it was demonstrations with the Red Flag. I wanted to see the results, what would happen there, so I used to stay a little far away and from far I used to see the police. In a park that we used to have, the police were there with their horses to disperse the people. Sometimes it was amusing. Sometimes I enjoyed it.

One time when I went on the street for my boss, I come near the city hall, and there are girls and the fire department. I come and I see there that something is the matter. There is a barricade. They put a lot of things there, just facing the city hall, and the militia are there, the soldiers, people. You can't pass in the street, there is no thoroughfare—you can't get through. It is blocked and the tramways can't go through too. (We had tramways at that time, nicer than here in Montreal. It was called Fransuska—a Belgian-French concession. They were electric trams. Here we used to have the horses. But in 1905 there we had tramways already.)

Anyway, I said to myself, Let me see what is happening. I went in a little house there. I went upstairs and I sit down. What is going to be there? What is it? Why are the people standing there? What is ...? All of a sudden I hear: *ruskayeetas!* That means they are telling the people: *spread* [disperse]— *if not, we're going to shoot!* In a minute I hear a shot and people are falling on the ground. And the soldiers run away and the people spread and I see a woman there, a Jewish woman, nice, maybe about twenty years, nicely built—they took her. There was people living around those houses there, like here, some big houses, three four stories high—and they took her there in one of the houses. There was a lot of people killed there that day!

When I went back to the Old Country to visit my niece, you know, I couldn't go to Dnepropetrovsk. I didn't have no paper for there. They don't want you in there and other places. Maybe, for other reasons, I don't know.

I met my wife in Toronto through my *landsman,* the woman from my city in the Old Country. My wife used to work in a big shop and she worked by pants, something like that. I used to come there on Saturday or Sunday. They invited me to come and visit. They gave me tea. She used to go with other boys. She used to go to the dancing halls; it used to be an auditorium hall somewhere on Ontario. Now it is out of existence. And she went to other places, like the Colonial Hall, this and that. And when I used to come there, she wasn't there. I used to talk with the old people, her father and mother. They treated me nicely, talking. Then she used to come later on and little by little by little, my wife got interested in me. I take her out. Show her here and there. And that's how we got involved. I couldn't speak English. I couldn't dance. She speaks English a little and Jewish too, of course. And she goes around with boys that speak English perfect, who goes dressed nicely. Her mother tells her, Mary—they used to call her Mary—I want you to go with Sam, with this one. I don't know what kind of people those others are—but his family I know. Mary didn't want it. But the mother insisted and she got it.

So I used to take her out and go to the park, to a show sometimes, to a movie. Gradually she got acquainted with me. Then she says, You know what? I learn you to dance by my house, not in the dancing place. Then in her house she used to learn me how to dance.

I used to go to meetings—I was in the union. I got involved in the union. I was shop chairman and I already knew the trade and was somebody in the shop. They put me to work, to organize the Amalgamated. I was busy with meetings, with the executive and the joint board, and this and that I'm busy. My wife wants to go dancing. I go dancing. After meetings I would go pick her up. I take her home—nothing else. She dance with somebody else sometimes. I take her home. I was the man. I got her at last. That's how, little by little, we get acquainted and we get used to each other.

We got married. I was twenty-four years—around that. She stopped working. It was a shame to work if a woman got married. We moved into a room with my sister. In the back of their home was a parlour. I don't remember where the house was … near a church, I think. We lived with my sister but not for long. In the one house there was my sister, her husband, their three children, and I and my wife. Then my wife and I moved in to a place on Dorchester Street. It doesn't exist any more. We had seven children after we married.

Sylvia Grafstein Klein

❧

Sylvia Grafstein Klein, born 1903 in Voshnitz, Poland, near Lodz, is the mother of a long-time dear friend of mine. In the summer of 1974 I visited her at the home of her oldest daughter, Molly, for this interview. We sat in the backyard and, after a light lunch, Sylvia relaxed enough to begin her story.

Sylvia was a kind and gentle woman who spent her life looking after her husband, Abie, and raising her five children, including a set of twins. Sylvia died in 1982, when her apron caught fire while she was taking baking out of her oven in her apartment in Toronto.

I'M MRS. SYLVIA GRAFSTEIN KLEIN. I came from Poland. I am here forty-nine years. And I came to my uncle Moishe Graftstein in Toronto.

It's a big story why I left Poland. I was nine months old when my mother passed away. I didn't know my mother. I had never seen her. She was twenty-one and my grandfather brought me up. My grandfather, he was a *shoichet* and a *moyhel*. He used to cry and I would say to him, Why you crying, Zaida? And he would say, God took away my adored daughter of twenty-one years but He gave me another daughter. You are growing like a flower in the garden. And one time he went upstairs to the attic and there was a big trunk, like a cedar chest, and he brought down my mother's clothes: long, velvet dress and wine-coloured. I was about five years old at that time. There were those hats with the feathers. And he put me on a chair—he had a cupboard with mirrors—and he says, When you get married, you're going to wear your mother's clothes to the *khupa*, the wedding canopy!

My grandfather passed away and then my grandmother and I was left with one of my uncles. He was single. So he called my father. My father was a rabbi in a different city and he says to him, You have to take Sylvia home until I get married.

I went to my father, who was already married again. I was afraid of him. So he says I will have to go back to my uncle. Finally my uncle got married and he took me back. His wife didn't treat me nice. She used to hit me.

Before my mother passed away (Jewish people, they say a prayer) and she says to my Uncle Moishe, who was sixteen years old at the time, Moishelle, go bring me the medicine but give me my child, put her in my arms. So he put me on her arms and she said the prayer and she says to him—in Yiddish—I don't think you'll see me alive when you come back. When he came back, my mother has passed on, passed away. I was still in my mother's arms. She told my uncle, When you go to America (they called Canada "America" then), remember and bring my child wherever you'll be, take her with you.

I had a cousin, a Grafstein, an elderly lady, who wrote to my uncle Moishe Grafstein here in Canada to say that if you want your sister's daughter alive, you better send for her. So he sent for me, in my mother's name, as his young sister.

When I arrived in Toronto I went to night school where I met my dear comrade, Abie Klein. My uncle, I had an older uncle, Yarmi Graftstein (a *shoichet*). He introduced him to me and he said in Yiddish, You know, Sylvie, this boy is from Ostravske, not far from our city in the Old Country, and he is a very nice man. And he would like to see you, to go out with you. And I said, All right. And Abie asked me if he could take me out. I said, You can phone me. I gave him my phone number and he phoned me, and he took me out to a show.

I was seventeen at the time. He kept calling me. My Uncle Moishe was against this because Abie was a leftie. Abie asked to marry me and I said okay, in Polish. He said, Do you like me? And I said, I like. He said, I like you too. You know, we're both foreigners?

He called me and he said, I'll take you out to the show. My uncle answered the phone and said to Abie—in Jewish—Who are you? And Abie told him. My uncle said, What do you want? And Abie says, I want to talk with Sylvia. I want to take her to the show. Uncle says, No, you're not going to take her out. She's not going to marry you. I want her to marry a rich boy. However, Uncle called me to the phone and I said, Yes? Abie said, I want to take you to the show, and I said, I'll go with you.

And my uncle threw me out from the house. He told me to move out. I said, Why? And he said, You're such a good-looking girl. Why should you marry a greener [an immigrant]? I said, I'm also a greener. I said, I really like him. He said, Well, I've got rich boys for you. I said, I don't want a rich boy, I want a workingman. He said, You'll have nothing. Well, I says, I will have to do whatever is best for me. I like him because he seems to be my type although I come from a rich family. (You see, I came from a background of rich families in Europe.)

My uncle told me to get out. So I went to sleep at my cousin's. And the next day my cousin phoned him that I was sick. I wasn't sick, but she says to me, Sylvia, you haven't got a trade; what are you going to do? I says, I'll go out and work. We'll go out and look for a job.

She took me to a place where they made purses. I start to make purses— I spoilt them. The man said to me, What did you do in Europe? Well, I said, I didn't do; I was with my grandparents. He said, You come back some other day.

My cousin couldn't have me in her room because her brother and sister-in-law didn't want us sleeping four in one room. So she called my Uncle Moishe, told him I have a fever, and he says, Tell her I'm going to pick her up right away. He came and picked me up and said, What's wrong with you? I says, I don't know. I don't feel so good. He says, Okay, you can come back but you're not going to marry Abie. I said, I am going to marry him. It came Friday night, Abie phoned me and I says, Yes, you can come over.

I had another uncle, Melech Grafstein, he was also against the marriage because Abie's a communist. And I said, Uncle, what is a communist? What does it mean, a "communist"? I didn't know. I came from a background of orthodox religion. To me, I said to my uncle, a communist is a working-man. (You see, to me that was my idea.) He said, Yes, he is a workingman, but he is a *linke*. So I said, what does it mean a *"linke"*? I didn't know. So I found out a *linke* is a left-winger!

We got married and my Uncle Melech says, *Nu*, I can't do nothing! There are nice boys, also some rich boys. And I says, I don't want a good-looker. And he says, Why? And I say, I want to be the better-looking one. I want to be the good-looking one. He says to me, in Yiddish, Girl like you—you're six-teen. You've got such beautiful long, curly hair. (I used to have. They called me in Europe, the *shikse*—the *shiksin* means, the Gentile.) He says, Why did you say you don't want no rich boys? I want to marry a working fellow, I said. He said, You won't have nothing by him. I said, I don't care; as long as he likes me. A rich boy won't like me; he'll go with other girls.

So we got married and Abe made the wedding. He was already in the nee-dle trades. He made the wedding at his sister-in-law's. My uncles didn't want to come to the wedding but the day of the wedding, they changed their mind.

They all came: my Uncle Melech and my Uncle Moishe and the *shoichet*, the older one, Yarmi Grafstein, who had introduced me to Abie and who wanted me to marry him, because he said, He'll be a good man. He'll treat you good. And this uncle knows what a kind family he comes from. (Abie used to come to the city where I was born, which was not far from Ostravske where he came from.) So we got married.

When I got married I moved to College Street. I had two rooms, then, when Molly was born. It was very cold. We moved into [Abie's] uncle's house on the same street. And we lived there six, seven months. It was very cold. Molly got sick and we had to move out.

Shapes, Abie's uncle, lived in that house and an aunt and three children and Abie and I and Molly. So we moved out to Cecil Street—39 Cecil Street. During all this time Abie was a pocketmaker. He was a good workingman.

He used to tell me how hard it was when he came here to Canada. Mind you, he came a year before me. He was living at his sister's place. He made very little. He had to pay her for room and board. And for washing his shirts, his underwear. But he saved money and paid her for the ticket (she had bought his ticket to Canada). And when we got engaged he gave my Uncle Moishe three hundred dollars. He said to me, Sylvia, I am going to buy you a diamond ring for this occasion. I said, No, Abie. You're a workingman. I don't want no diamond ring. He says, You come from such a rich background. Your uncle's wife wears beautiful diamonds, necklaces. She wears beautiful jewels like a queen. I said, I am not a queen and you are a workingman; and I am a workingman's wife. I don't want no diamond. Well, he said, it doesn't look nice.

One Saturday, he says to me, Let's go down to Uncle Moishe's store—he had it downtown. And he said, Uncle Moishe, I want to buy Sylvia a diamond ring and she doesn't want it. And my uncle said to me, Why don't you want it? And I said, He's a workingman and I want to save that money for a home; we'll have a family. So he gave my uncle a cheque for three hundred dollars. He went down to Credit Jewellers on Yonge and he bought me the ring, which I still got. And I cherished this ring. It's going to be for Molly. She's the oldest.

So from that street we moved into 39 Cecil Street. Abie was making a bit more than eight dollars, but we couldn't afford a home, you know. Then I had my son, my oldest son—the second child. The landlady from the house said, Mrs. Klein, I like you should have nine children. I like you just the same as my own children. You're nice and clean and you're a good woman, but you have to move out. You need a yard for your own children. So we moved into a cottage, 79 Nassau Street. We moved in there. I had to wash the toilet outside. The toilet was outside. Abie got sick and had to go to the hospital. He was run down, he lost a lot of weight. Thank God, my twins came along in

Nassau Street. They were born before he left for the hospital. Because it was very cold, you know, he got a cold and was run down. He worked very hard, eight hours a day. It was a struggle.

I used to go to work at eight o'clock in the morning. I worked in a toy factory—General Toy—and I worked in a baker shop and also a canvas shop on Denison. Abie didn't work at that time. He didn't have a job. So he looked after the kids. Sometimes he was out on strike. He brought home very little money; must have been from the union. I'll tell you, my dear, I wasn't out much yet in the world then. I was mostly in the house. But I felt it … I felt the weight. He used to be out most of the time, most of the time in the union. They used to want to break the strike and he … he had to watch them. He was a good pocketmaker; the best pocketmaker. He made pockets for uniforms for the soldiers who rode on horses in the Second World War. We ate very, very little. I used to go hungry many times with my children. I used to say, Oy, Abie, I'm hungry, I could eat something. Well there wasn't very much to eat. We couldn't afford it. Yes, I was a good cook. It's not nice to say what I cooked. The *Polishe* will understand. I made *bobe kasha* and potatoes, soup and potatoes. I remember I bought two pounds of Shabbes candles for twenty-four cents. And when I came home from the butcher, he gave me bones, I didn't ask him. And I said Abie, I have a penny, one cent change. He said, you keep, put it—I had a broken cup—put it in the cup, save up, you're a good saver. He used to say, From twenty-five cents you can make two dollars! That's what he always told me. I used to bake my own cookies. I used to sew for the kids by hand. I used to wash clothes on the washboard.

My Abie was a good father, he was a good provider; he worked very hard. But most of his time he spent with the union and also with the UJPO [*United Jewish Peoples' Order, a fraternal organization*], but the union … oh yes, all the time for fifty years. He was always in the union. He was active in the union. He was in the *Ordn* [*meaning the UJPO*]. I never saw him much—very little. I was most of the time with the children. I'll tell you something, maybe I was wrong. I used to say to him, Abie, we're both young—I was nineteen when I was married—I don't want no luxury. He says, Why not? You come from a well-off family. I say, Forget about that. I don't look where I come from. We are both married. We've got a family. So he used to say in Jewish, What do you want? I says, How about giving a little more life to each other, to be at home?

He used to go away in the morning to the shop because he had to make a living and then from the shop he'd phone me, Sylvia, I have a union meeting.

I'll be home late. I know you're going to worry. So I said, Abie, how about having supper? He says, I'll go have a cup of coffee with a doughnut. I know you make a good supper. I'll wait for it. The kids went to sleep. They couldn't stay up!

Abie went in the morning to work; the kids didn't see him. He came home, they didn't see him. They were sleeping. And that kind of hurt me. It wasn't much of a family life or togetherness, you know. Even then it was a different world from now. I know now it's different, but even then, the woman wanted a man to be home. Maybe I was wrong, he was too much and too deep into the organization, and he had heartaches the last time.

The *Ordn*, they wanted to send him to Russia. They gave Shek. (I hope they hear this! Is somebody going to hear this interview—nobody?) They gave it to Shaya Shek and when they saw him at bowling, so Abie says, Shek, heard you going to Russia. So Shek answered him in a sarcastic way, in Jewish, What's the matter, don't you like it? Abie says, Why not? But he was disappointed. I says, Abie, they promised you? He said. Yes. And then they send Shek to Russia? I says.

There were a lot of disappointments in the *Ordn*. When Abie was in the organization, in the UJPO, collecting money for the paper, the *Vochenblatt*, for the *Freiheit* [*another Yiddish paper*], others were looking for houses in my neighbourhood. Wherever they saw a little house, they bought it for nothing. And when he came home from the meetings he was very upset and I'd say, Abie, why are you so upset? Look at your face. You look like somebody would pour hot borscht on you! I say, sit down and eat. I can't eat now, he says. I am going to lie down a little bit, okay? He says, Wake me up. I didn't have the nerve to wake him. He came home, he was very tired. I felt sorry for him. When he woke up, he said, Why didn't you wake me up? I said, It's okay, you're tired. I said, Sit down and eat. He said, You're mad at me. I said, Abie, Eat first. I made for him a *forsh piz*, appetizers, and something sweet. Nothing from the can. I didn't know that there was such canned things, because I wasn't used to them. And I said, Yes Abie, I'm a little bit mad. Tell me why, he says. It was like a joke. I says, I'll tell you why. You gave so much life and my youth and your youth. (He was five years older.) So it kind of hurt me, you know. I said, Look, this woman is going out with her husband, this one is going out with his wife, and I said in a joke, what's she got that I haven't got? It was a joke. I used to *kibbitz* with him. And he looked at me and he says—in Jewish—he says, Come on put your shoes on and we'll go out for a cup of coffee.

Molly Klein Goldsman

Molly Goldsman was born in 1925. I talked to her in the summer of 1974 in the backyard of her home in Toronto, where she still resides. Molly is the daughter of Sylvia and Abie Klein. She generously agreed to share a memory or two of life in the early days when she lived with her parents.

YOU REMEMBER THE POVERTY but you really didn't know you were in it because everybody else that you lived with had the same problem. I know I didn't see very much of my father because he was always ... if he wasn't working, he was on strike; if he wasn't striking, he was picketing for better working and living conditions; and frankly speaking, whenever I meet people now who are a little bit ashamed of their background, I'm not ashamed to say to them that I am very proud of the fact that my father took a stand. At least he did something! Oh yes. My father was very active in the union.

Up until the time he was old enough to know different he was a religious man. But when he was in a position to see what was happening, to see the poverty, he became a rebel and he wanted to do something about it. First of all, his father was very religious and to such an extent, where to learn was a big thing, especially for the orthodox. But I guess my father's background was not a cultured one but somehow he rose above it. His sisters and brothers were not at all like him. He wanted to learn. He was self-taught. When it came to political history, no one would know anymore than he did. And he would predict things that would happen. And they did happen many years later. And we would remember, Gee, if we had only listened to Pa. He knew what he was talking about!

Politics and the situation, the human situation, was always present. He would come home from work. He would *try* to tell us what was going on. But when you are young you really don't absorb it all.

It wasn't until later on, when everything that people like him had fought for was denigrated by a new influx of immigrants after the Second World War—people would be hired for a lower wage and the people like my father were sort of out in the cold. And, of course, these people were getting older too. If it were not for the fact that my father happened to be a friend of the boss (this was at Tip Top Tailors), who was a big philanthropic man in the city, and they sort of had an understanding—he liked my father because he was bright and he could talk to him—my father would have been out of work a long time before he finally did retire.

My father was a bit of a rabble-rouser. He tried to tell the people that things were not right, that the new immigrants were not getting enough money and that they shouldn't work for so cheap, that sort of thing.

Here's an incident from those hard-working days. My father brought home from work tickets, piecework tickets: every time you did a job, they would tear a ticket off the garment. He would turn these tickets in at a certain time during the week, and this is how the payroll was made up. So, of course, the faster you worked, the more money you made. But one night we were all asleep and my father came barging into the bedroom—I think all the children slept in one room—he was looking for his week's worth of tickets from sewing pockets—he was a pocketmaker. He couldn't find them. No one could find them. One of the younger children had flushed them down the toilet!

This meant no week's wages. No money. No food. What can I tell you?

Rose Esterson

*I talked to Rose Esterson in a seniors' nursing home in Montreal in
1974. Rose was born in 1897 in Kiev, in the Ukraine. She came to
Canada in 1925. Rose was a fighter for workers' rights. She was very
proud of her union card, which she pulled out of her bedside drawer
for me to see.*

I AM FROM RUSSIA, from the Ukraine. Like you have the province of
Quebec, I am from the province of Kiev. I lived there from the end of the First
World War, 1914 war, for seven years. I left there because the *burgrich* is killed
my father, killed my brother, killed everybody. This was during the Kiev
Pogroms [1919–20] and these *burgrich* belonged to the rich families, they
were a little bit well off, and it was these people doing the killing. That is
why I left Russia and went to Poland, and I was there from 1921 to 1925. I was
twenty-eight years old and my husband was thirty when he died in Poland
of a heart attack. The Bolsheviks had beaten him!

I come here in 1925 and then it begins a very, very bad time for me. I
used to go to work for one dollar a week or $1.50 a week and I am supposed
to support my three children, three daughters, and pay rent, and pay gas, and
pay light, and pay other things. I lived in a house with my mother. The rent
was twenty-two dollars a month. Five of us: my mother, myself, and my
three daughters lived in one room and I rent out the rest of the rooms—I
rent for five dollars a month. My mother looked after the children and I
went to work. My children are raised without a father and without a mother
because I am always away in the factories and my children were small children. I never got married again.

During the Depression it was so bad! People used to stand here in the
corner for sandwiches, you know. But I didn't stand for sandwiches. The

Jewish Federation used to make lunches then and we all used to go to help. I told her, Thank you, Mrs. Box. I have already. I'll support myself by myself. I didn't take anything, nothing for nothing, I didn't take their charity. I looked after myself. Then in 1939 comes Hitler's war.

I didn't get into the needle trades until I came to Canada because I was not in the trades at home in the Old Country. At home I was sitting reading books and having a good time. But here I started to work in 1925. I worked in dresses, in different operations. A person, you know, is supposed to make a living. So I went there myself. I used to go to a shop and the boss used to tell me, Miss, come in tomorrow and I'll see what I can do with you. And I would say to him that I am a married woman, not a Miss, and I got to eat and make a living. Sometimes the boss used to say, Miss, take your seat and go. I wouldn't give you a chair at the dinner! So I told him, Excuse me, if I have a behind, I have a chair! I don't want your seat.

Everybody knows that I'm a big fighter. Not to fight with somebody but to fight for my rights!

My children went to high school and to business college. I never sent my children into the shops. No. Because at this time the bosses have no respect for a person. You see, at the time, three or four people used to come from overseas and make a little bit of a shop, a little factory, and the workers used to slave from seven in the morning to ten at night, and got paid fifty cents for two dresses, can you believe? Once I worked for this boss who says to me that I should go the next day and have a dinner in a [charity] kitchen for twenty-five cents. I said, Why should I go there? He said, Mrs. Esterson, I gave them a donation of twenty-five dollars, so you can go and eat there with your children. I told him, If you didn't pay me twenty cents for two dresses I wouldn't need to go eat in that kitchen. But you give twenty-five-dollar donation and it says on the wall: Mr. So-and-so give twenty-five dollars donation. I wouldn't go there to eat!

I told you I worked on different parts of the garment in the clothing trade, on dresses; I worked in mens' clothing too—anywhere I worked. In 1939 came up Hitler's war and at the time they start to organize the union. The French girls, the Ukrainian girls were afraid to go to the union. I took the girls to the meetings and I took union books. Some days later my boss comes out from his office and he says, Whoever has a union card cannot work in my place! I opened my purse—because, honest to God, I made the damage, you know—so I opened my purse and I said, Here, Jack, here is my union book, send me home. He started laughing and went in his office. The girls teased me. I say, Don't tease me. I made the damage and I take the damage!

After, we organized the union and we were striking for six months. Six months! And I used to tell him, Mr. Shane—he was the manager in the Ladies Garment Workers' Union—please send me to work, I have three small children to feed. He used to give me six dollars a week from the union. I wouldn't say no. Anyway, he told me no. You will go to the same boss after, and the boss will tell you, Welcome home! So you don't want go to another shop! I didn't want to go to a non-union shop. What could I do? I listened to him.

After six months my boss settled. In the meantime he had scabs working. You know, one time I took one in the head: someone threw a rock at me and I threw it back and it hit a car. Anyway, we settled and I went in with my shopping bag and the boss come over—and it is the truth, just like Mr. Shane said—And the boss says, Welcome home! Here's your machine, here is your box, and here is your seat!

After, my boss brought me dresses not from the union—because a dress has to have your name, like for instance, your name is Such-and-such. So I took the tickets and I go in the union and I show it to the organizer and the business agent and say, Look, that's a scab ticket he gave to me! After that, when anything was no good in the shop or someone complained, the business agent would come in and say, Is Mrs. Esterson here? No? Well, I wouldn't talk with you then. I believe only Mrs. Esterson.

I am telling you the truth. That is what I am telling my grandson and what I am telling you. I am getting a pension now from the fashion industry of seventy-five dollars a month. I worked there a long time.

I want to tell you that before the strike I used to work in a shop and one time, when you are supposed to be in at seven in the morning and if you come in five minutes past seven, the boss took off fifteen minutes of your salary for himself. So, you know what I used to do? You wouldn't believe me. I used to come in maybe a little early and I would run to the window and sit at the window; and when the boss told me, Why you didn't go to the machine? I would say, That's my time. When I see 7:15 then I go to work.

I'm a fighter! I'm telling you, I'm a big fighter for my rights—and not a fighter with the people. Once, when I was in the hospital and I'm sick, and my daughter comes over and there's a Christian woman with a cross is crying, God. God. Don't take away my mother! Don't take away my mother! And my daughter held on to me.

And once, when I went to the shop, there was a lady, a German lady—she was here from before the war years—and she was supposed to go to work—her husband was sick and she had boys who need to eat. And she is sitting near me and the boss gives her about seventy-five dresses in one bundle—that was the style—and she put this bundle by the machine here. I said, What's your name? She said, Miller. I said, Mrs. Miller, put the bundle on the table. She don't want. I say, Mrs. Miller, put the bundle on the table. She told me, I don't want to put the bundle on the table because I am not an operator and you will go and tell the boss because I'm a German and the Germans killed the Jews, you will tell the boss … I said, I wouldn't tell the boss nothing.

I took the dresses and I took the pants and I told her that is the seams, that is the crotch, and that is the collar, the lapels, that is the back, the skirt, everything. She looked at me. I said to her, That's not your fault. And the Jewish people is not all good and the Germans is not all bad. You have to not say that all the people are the same. I and you are not the same. And after that whenever she made some preserve, whatever she used to make, she used to bring me. When I was in the hospital—for six months—she used to come every day to visit me.

Now I want to show you my union card. I was on the executive, on the joint board. Maybe the big shots had money, you know, but not me. But when I see that something is not right, I fight! I fight for the workers. Once a business agent come over to my shop—he used to come to make the prices—and he used to bring a Coca-Cola with an ice cream. And I'm sitting there, but I wouldn't start with him! Once he was calling, Mrs. Esterson, here's for you a Coca-Cola! I said, Don't give me any bottle, because I will give it to you in the head!

Other times there was a woman who used to come over in the morning and she took the best work and put it in her box. I took out the work from the box and go to the boss and told him, I don't care. Everybody can do dresses. Give everybody the bad dresses and give me too. That I used to take to the [union] board and make a claim. I never worked for a non-union shop once I was in the union. If I worked as a scab I would not have my cheque every month from the union.

Joshua (Joe) Gershman

❦

Joshua Gershman was born in 1903 in Sokolov, in the Ukraine. He told me his story while sitting at his desk at the Vochenblatt/Outlook *office in Toronto, with the butt of a cigar stuck in his mouth. He was editor of both newspapers (the Yiddish and English editions, respectively) for many years, and felt that my inability to speak and read Yiddish would be a drawback in researching Jewish immigrants who came to Canada from the Old Country.*

Joe, as he was called, led a checkered life, constantly involved in—and always on the forefront of—trade unions, the Communist Party (in the US and Canada), and cultural organizations. Through it all, he always found an expression for his love of the written and spoken word, and was a well-respected orator. He was well known in the Jewish communities of Vancouver, Winnipeg, Toronto, and Montreal, among other centres.

Joshua Gershman died in 1988 in Toronto.

THE FIRST THING I REMEMBER is when I was a kid, together with my brother, we were so disturbed because we saw two little kittens running and so we picked them up, we brought them into the house, and put them in the oven. You know, in the Old Country, the kind of ovens that they used to make? Well we tried to save these kittens and look what happened! I'll never forget that. My mother was away at the time and when she came back home she found the dead kittens.

I was born in 1903 in the Ukraine in a small town called Sokolov, not far from the city of Vilkomir. My father left our town for Canada in 1912, prior to the First World War. He was a merchant. My mother was a seamstress. This is how we tried to make a living. I started to work while I was still going to school at the age of eleven. I went to a Yiddish school, and I worked in order to help keep up the family. We were four sisters and two brothers. When I was fourteen, I left my hometown and went to a bigger city called Novograd Volinsk. In Yiddish they called it Zvihil. There I went to study in the yeshiva, a Jewish theological seminary. And I was in the seminary till the day of the October Revolution.

While I was in the yeshiva, though it was a very orthodox institution, I did have connections with revolutionary young people, and I went into the revolutionary movement straight from the yeshiva. This I did, not only because we came from a very poor family but a family with honour, you know, we were *yekes*—this means we were nice pedigree, but because one of my mother's brothers was a leader of the social democrats in Tsarist Russia and while I was in the city of Zvihil, I was staying with my grandfather, and where my uncle was also, naturally, living. He was a bachelor at the time and he kept on feeding me revolutionary pamphlets and other material. He taught me Russian. I didn't take up Russian while in school, and at the yeshiva they didn't teach Russian. And even in our own small town when I went to a more modern kind of Hebrew school—they didn't call it *kheyder* at that time They called it Beis Asafar. But there too they didn't teach you Russian, so my uncle used to teach me. He had a sweetheart, a very good-looking girl, who also taught me Russian when I was a youngster yet.

I lived there through the [First World] war and through the Kerensky Revolution.[40] Then, when the October Revolution came, I went back to my hometown. We had a very fine group of revolutionary youngsters. We organized a Jewish library, a Jewish drama group, and a play theatre in the worst of days. Then the Poles occupied part of the Ukraine. They marched as far as Kiev and so we became a part of the Poles.

At the time—this was after the war—representatives of the Joint Distribution Committee from the United States of America, and mainly from the larger cities of Canada, used to come to Europe to help connect families who were lost during the war. Since we were under the Polish regime and had to be underground anyways because of our politics, I decided to leave my hometown and go to the city of Rovno (it is in the same *gubernya*, the same province). My uncle lived already in Rovno because he was a social democrat and did not agree with the Bolsheviks, but he remained a socialist, naturally.

I was there for a short period of time, and while there I met a representative of the Joint Distribution Committee (JDC). They used to come in uniform, like military men. So I got in touch with one of the gentlemen who came from the United States, with connections also in Canada, and he suggested to me that he will try and find out about my father who lived in Winnipeg. The family agreed that I should go to Warsaw, and from Warsaw try to get some information about my father and, maybe, go to Canada. The family was in great poverty, but this had to be done because we hadn't heard from my father since the war. When I came to Warsaw, there I got myself a job with the JDC, working mainly in the passport department.

At the time there were many thousands of refugees from all over Russia and from the Ukraine who came to Warsaw. When the Polish army withdrew from the Ukraine, the refugees came from there as well and were like homeless people. In order for them to travel to the US and Canada, they had to have passports. So I had been working in this department with the approval of the Polish government. The passports that the JDC issued had the approval of the Polish government and were honoured by the Canadian and American governments. I myself, though I'm Ukrainian-born, came to Canada on a Polish passport because I didn't have any papers with me when I came to Warsaw. It was the same situation for thousands and thousands of Jews.

Meanwhile, I was communicating with Winnipeg but couldn't get any information about my father. However, I decided to go to Winnipeg. I had to wait for over a year before I could get permission to go to Canada. My oldest sister came from Sokolov (my hometown) to Warsaw to say goodbye to me before I left for Canada. Thousands of people who had passports issued by the JDC were accepted by the CPR [Canadian Pacific Railway] and so we came by CPR boat. We arrived in Antwerpen [Antwerp] in Belgium. The Canadian government refused to recognize these passports and we spent two months living on the boat! We sent cables to the JDC in America and to other institutions. We made a big issue of it because there were several others stranded in Antwerp and many of them didn't want to wait that long. So they got other governments, like Latin America, who recognized these passports and they went to Argentina, Brazil, and other countries. I had no interest in going anywhere else because my father was in Canada. So I waited and, finally, we did get permission to leave. After nearly two months we were taken to a hotel in Antwerp. (Canadian Pacific had to pay for it because they were responsible for us from the time we left Warsaw.) It was a very big thing! This situation roused the Jewish community and they protested, amongst other things.

I arrived in Canada in December 1921, in the city of Winnipeg, which was my first hometown in Canada. There was lots of snow. I arrived to find out

my father had died three weeks before, of cancer. He was a poor businessman in Canada as well. He was a farmer for a time. Before he got sick, and
during the time he was sick, he started to sell part of his property: the farm,
the horses, and whatever else. His lawyer was Old Man Saul Cherniak, we
called him Alter Cherniak, in Winnipeg, who never got paid in cash, who
never got guarantees in English. It was all written in Yiddish, by certain people: you sign here and it's similar to IOUs. Something like that.

I immediately wrote home to my mother to tell her what had happened
with my father. She said I should go back since my father was dead and we
have no interest in Canada, and so on.

My sisters and other family members all belonged to the revolutionary
movement. My mother, though she was not a revolutionary in the general
sense, she was connected with the movements which were created as a result
of the October Revolution. She was chairlady of the Committee of the Poor—
they called themselves COMBAT—in our town. This included both Jews
and non-Jews.

So my family did not want to come to Canada, and I agreed with them
that I should return. I had to stay in Winnipeg long enough to settle my
father's so-called estate and after that I'll go home. But in the meanwhile
you have to make a living.

I did not have any immediate relatives in Winnipeg. There were some far-
distant ones, some of them even with the same name; but a lot of *landsleit*,
self-help groups of people from one's hometown, lived in Winnipeg. Father
was not a religious Jew. He was a secular Jew and he was called an *epicuresh*
in the Old Country because, in those days, to go to *shul* only on Rosh
Hashanah and Yom Kippur was very bad. And that is all he did in regard to
his religion in Sokolov. He did it [*went to synagogue*] for my mother and for
his mother—my *bubba*—and for my grandfather. But in Winnipeg he did
belong to a synagogue. The rabbi of the synagogue today is a very prominent
rabbi, Rabbi Kahanovitch, he knew that as a youngster I went to yeshiva.

So all the *landsleit*, the people from the same hometown, got together.
"What are we going to do for this *yosim*, this orphan, who has come to
Canada in this situation?" The "situation" was that a big crisis was happen-
ing at that time—an economic crisis. So the rabbi wanted me to become a
teacher in Talmud Torah and I didn't want that. I said, If I'm to do anything,
I would like to learn a trade.

So there was one amongst the *landsleit* who was a partner in the largest
firm of fur dressing and dyeing—Bleese & Koerner. His name was Koerner,
and both partners said they wanted me to come in and work for them and

they'll teach me the trade. I started to work for them at eight dollars a week. They treated me very nicely and they taught me the trade, everything, all the various crafts. There is a flasher who flashes the skin. Then there are stretchers and dyers and others. I learned everything, you see, the whole thing, all the operations. And so I started with them.

They raised my wages up to eighteen dollars a week. We worked eight hours a day and we also worked Saturdays till twelve o'clock. But I immediately (and I did go to night school to learn English), I immediately got very interested in the cultural work, that is, in Jewish cultural activities. At the time, the centre of the Jewish workers was the Liberty Temple. It was called Frei's Temple. In those years there were many big fights between the Left and the Right. I joined the Temple. Naturally I was with the Left. I immediately got very active and when I started to work in the shop, I started to be interested in the trade union movement. Together with some other friends of mine, that's what I did. These were young people in Winnipeg, some of them were later important trade union leaders like Meyer Klieg, who up till recently was one of the organizers of the International Fur & Leather Workers Union. Then there was Pearl Wedrow. She died only a year ago. She was one of those who, together with me, organized the Fur Workers' Union in the city of Winnipeg. My shop did not belong to the union, and in the Liberty Temple the fight between the Left and the Right was going on till we won a majority in the old Workmen's Circle and we took over the Liberty Temple. Simultaneously I was active in the trade union field and also, naturally, working with the Communist Party, which I joined in 1923 and which was much closer and more efficient than nowadays.

This is the way I was dragged in because I was too active everywhere and the settlement of my father's estate dragged on even longer. So I kept on writing home that I must come back; but meantime I was involved and became important, particularly since I joined the Party, which made the decision that I have to stay here.

In this way, in 1925 and then in 1926, we organized the first general strike of the fur workers in the city of Winnipeg and though my shop was not involved, because it was not a union shop, the bosses were very, very nice to me. Their factory depended on the work that they were getting from the fur manufacturers because the raw furs were worked out in Bleese & Koerner and then they went to the manufacturers. So the manufacturers, because they were involved in the strike, insisted that Bleese & Koerner should fire me; otherwise they are not going to give them work. So my bosses called me in and in a very nice way they talked to me and said: this and this is the situation; we don't want to let you go, not only because you are a good worker (I had learned the trade) but because you are ours, we like you.

You see, I was in love with a daughter of one of the bosses and he thought that we were going to get married! (It's a long story, but that's beside the point.) So I told them, I agree with you. I'll quit. So they asked: What are you going to do? I said: I have a mind to leave Winnipeg anyway, so I'll go to Toronto. The only thing I wanted was for them to give me a letter of recommendation to some kind of a firm of fur dressers in Toronto. So not only did they give me this letter of recommendation and reference to a shop here in Toronto, a German shop, one of the best in the fur dressing and dyeing business, but also they paid my fare to Toronto! We were like a family.

As I have mentioned, I was involved in various activities, particularly in the trade union movement and also in the Jewish cultural field. There were two groups in the cultural field: the Peretz Shule [a school] in Winnipeg, which was led by the right-wing Poale Zionists and other social democrats. They had a *Yiddishe Culture Gesellshaft* and we organized a Jewish Workers' *Farbund*—an *Arbeiter Culture Farbund*—and I was the general secretary of the *Farbund*, and the president was the principal of the Sholem Aleichem School (this was first called the Frei Temple Shule). So I severed activities in Winnipeg.

The factory where I worked in Winnipeg employed mainly Ukrainians. They worked for very low wages. It was a very dirty kind of work, dressing and dyeing furs. It stinks. It is raw fur. The raw hides of different animals are brought in, particularly the skunk. You see, skunk is a very, very fine fur. It is like sable. When you process it and produce it nicely, you can dye the white strips to the same blackness as the rest of the fur and then it becomes a very valuable fur. But it stinks terribly. It is skunk. Skunk comes with fat, and so you have to process it and dye it and you are always dirty.

There were quite a number of Jews working there in the shop besides myself. Our own shop wasn't too exciting, but when we got involved with the union we had the bosses against us. The police in those days in Winnipeg were not too bad. I was arrested eleven times during a particular strike! There was a danger that I'd be deported because I wasn't yet a Canadian citizen. But, in those years, we had some good connections with the chief of police, a man who used to take something on the side. There were a few labour aldermen at the time, Bloomberg and others, who had been working in our favour and when the trial did come, I was found not guilty. As a result, there was no record and that's why I was saved from the reputation. But on the picket line there were daily fights with scabs and police.

Not all the police, but a great number of them, were favourable. I remember a guy who lives here in the city of Toronto. He must have come here about thirty-five years ago. He is still a furrier and he still works in a shop. Back in those days in Winnipeg, he was a scab. Scabs used to be brought to work in cars, protected by police, detectives, and others; but we used to beat them up. Once I was arrested by a cop because I was in a big fight that took place in a shop. The scab was also caught as he was fighting too. He was arrested for disturbing the peace. The cop knew me very well and I knew him too. In those days I used to smoke a pipe. So I said, Officer, allow me to fill my pipe. I want to smoke. He said, Go ahead. He knew what he was doing and what I had asked. I didn't fill my pipe. While he was holding this scab, holding both of us, you see, waiting for the Black Maria, the police wagon, to come, I gave it to this boy. He was bleeding like a pig. The police was holding him and I was beating him up.

That's what happened in Winnipeg. Oh, many, many battles took place. That strike was lost. He was a Jewish scab, by the way, and he's still here today, a grandfather already. Anyways, let us leave Winnipeg. There are many stories about that city.

When I came to Toronto in 1926 and was working at Snauffer's, at one time a Winnipeg manufacturer came to this same shop and saw me. It didn't take two days and I was fired. When I was fired I decided to go to New York—without citizenship papers, nothing. This was 1926. I worked there for six months, for Altmans, one of the biggest firms on Fifth Avenue. They had a small little fur-cleaning department and I sold them the idea that I know how to clean fur, which I knew, and that is what I had been doing. But then I got the idea that I want to become a citizen. So I went back to Canada and applied and I got my papers in 1927.

In those days it was very difficult to get a transfer from the Communist Party in Canada to the party somewhere else. So when I got my citizenship papers, I discussed this with the secretary of the party and other leaders and they said, Nothing doing. You are not going to get a transfer.

At the time, the *Freiheit*, today it is called the *Morning Freiheit*, a Yiddish newspaper in New York, was very closely connected with us in Canada and we used to work together. They needed a manager for their office in Philadelphia. The general manager of the *Freiheit* happened to be in Toronto at that time, a Mr. Saltzman, to take up problems on how to increase the circulation of the paper in Canada, and so on. He insisted that I should go to Philadelphia. I told him okay. We'll speak to the party. If the party will give me a transfer, I'll go. I was not married at this time.

I married very late. The party agreed to give me a transfer and I went to work there.

You want to know why so many Jews—60 percent of them—were in the needle trades? The basic reason was because the manufacturers were, in the majority, Jews. In the last two years this is changing. The majority now are Greek, the manufacturers are Greek. But once upon a time, in Toronto for instance, 99 percent were Jewish. Today the majority of workers are Greek because the bosses are Greek and they are taking in their *landsleit* just the way the Jewish manufacturers used to take in *landsleit*. This you should know: first of all, quite a number of Jewish people that came to Canada, particularly after the First World War, and some even before that, were tailors in the Old Country. Quite a number of them. And even if they weren't tailors, this was the easiest way to get a job, particularly in the heavy economic crisis that existed immediately after the war.

When I came, the times were terrible. You couldn't get a job for no money. So the *landsleit* used to take you in. Now you read Sholem Asch, in one of his books, *Uncle Moses*, it gives you a good picture. People who came here, some didn't even have relatives, they were brought here by *landsmenshaftn*, who helped them: they advanced money for tickets for the boats, and generally gave assistance the first few weeks here. In this way they came into the industry as well.

I must tell you that very few of them came to Canada with money. It had to do with a certain … I don't know what you would call it, whether a trend or a characteristic. I don't want to use the term "characteristic" because this is, in my opinion, politically wrong; but it is not only limited to Jewish people. Quite characteristically, the first immigrants who came to this country did not want to work all their lives for somebody else. They wanted to be on their own. And in the needle trades it is the easiest way. If you know the trade, as soon as you get yourself two machines, you can yourself become a small contractor. You take out work from bigger manufacturers and, in this way, you gradually work yourself up to three machines, four machines. And even before they started the little factories, they had these sweatshops where they used to have a machine in the bedroom or the kitchen, rather than work in a shop for someone else. Many of these people, for instance in Toronto and Montreal (and I know quite a few of them), started out as workers who had been very militant workers, as members of the executive of the union; and they were fighting for increases in wages, etc. All excellent. But at the same time as they were in private discussions, they would say to themselves: I am not going to stay in the shop very long! I'm not going to work with the lousy boss! I can be a better boss than him and treat my workers better than he does!

This is the kind of talk that went on. And this is the way it developed, you see. There are some manufacturers here—take the boss of the big Tip Top Company, hmm—what's his name?—he started with two machines in his kitchen. He was a nobody and he worked himself up into one of the biggest clothing manufacturers in Canada. You couldn't do that—you can't open a tool factory, could you? Or you can't run a pulp and paper industry in this way! So naturally, in the needle trades it is very easy to become a boss, and because of that, people came to the trade and in great numbers they came. *Landsmanshaftn* mainly. Then many of those who came had uncles and brothers and grandfathers, who had already been with manufacturing and took them in and gave them jobs. This is the way it developed.

The clothing industry in Canada had a very small percentage of non-Jews as owners; but that was a time when it was very small. Canada didn't even have eight million people—less than eight million. But with the growth of the population when the industry became important, became independent, and you could actually live on what you sold in Canada, never mind exporting, this has been developed mainly by Jewish manufacturers.

There is the question of exploitation of Jews by Jews—this is very easy to explain. It is a class question. That is where it comes in. Many of our younger people, even now, don't want to understand this: that everything grows out of class interests, class position. You know that the manufacturers in Montreal were in the majority in the dress industry where we had a big strike, as I mentioned, and after we lost the strike, we had hundreds and hundreds of people on our hands that couldn't get jobs. They were mainly Jewish people—because the Jewish manufacturers didn't want to take them back. So many of the Jewish girls—and this is a fact, I have written about it in *Der Kampf* in those days—many of the Jewish girls in order to get a job had to put on a cross! Yes, we have comrades in our movement, girls who could have never got back into certain shops. They had been working in the trade for five to eight years already, were very good workers, but they couldn't go back into the big shops; none of our Jewish girls. But the smaller shops, some who were not even involved in the strike, wouldn't take the Jewish girls and so they had to wear crosses in order to get a job.

The children of immigrant workers in Canada are not in the same kind of professions as their parents were, and as some still are. They are teachers, they are lawyers, doctors, and journalists. A great number are professionals. And the same thing happened, maybe even to a larger extent, among the

Jewish people, because education with the Jews was always on a higher level—the urge for education, that is—than with others. It came as a result of the Old Country when—and this is true for all the oppressed peoples—when people are oppressed, they have to fight harder for survival, and in order to survive they have to possess more faculties, in every sense of the word, in order to be able to make it.

You are thinking of the French Canadians now. The Quiet Revolution started in the last twenty-five years. It takes a long time. Three hundred years of oppression for them. But don't forget the Jewish people did not have cardinals in the Catholic church over them. It has a lot to do with that. And they didn't have a bourgeoisie, the kind that played a very important role to keep the French-Canadian workers and farmers down. There is even another difference there too. To be an oppressed nation like the French Canadians in Canada is not the same as to be oppressed under Tsarism like the Jews in Russia.

One might say that education was important for the Jewish people, but the fact is, my dear girl, the overwhelming majority of Russian Jews and Polish Jews, up to the Second World War—the first-generation Jews, those that were born in the nineteenth century yet—they weren't educated people. They knew how to *doven*, to pray, but they didn't understand what the heck they were reading. And some of them couldn't *doven* either! Great numbers of them! I wouldn't even say that they were literate. No. No. A great number of Jewish *tates* and mothers and *zaides* and *bubbes* didn't even know how to write in Yiddish. Don't believe the story. Quite a number of them—not all of them, but I would say the majority—were illiterate.

However, I would say that the overwhelming majority were politically more conscious and politically to the Left because they came out of revolutionary backgrounds; because the October Revolution carried with it a lot of promises for the Jewish people. But, unfortunately, not all of them have materialized.

I think the values that we taught our children when we came to this country have left such a strong impact that it is coming back now at the present time in the second generation and it will be stronger in the third generation. That's why the children now do not accept what their parents give them. Look at hundreds, if not thousands of boys—particularly, men—that do not want to go in with their father in their businesses. They could have it very easy. Yeah. Their fathers came with a great sense of justice and they left it behind because of their change in social conditions. And that's why the children don't like them! That's why the children are against them!

Take a man like that poet, Cohen, Leonard Cohen. You know he comes from one of the richest families in Montreal? His father and others were founders of very important Jewish organizations. In the clothing industry they played the most important role in Montreal. And here they give birth to such a man like Leonard Cohen! He has developed in a different direction, but he is a revolutionary in his way. He's a rebel. He is against the Establishment. He is against the whole way of life. The faulty values that his parents and his grandparents tried to give him. He just said: To heck with you! I don't want it!

The process that Canada is going through at the present time—even amongst people who are leaning towards the Establishment, or want to be like the Joneses—the process is not the same as it was years ago. It is more than a different form. It is a different thing.

Jennie Zelda Litvak

Jennie Zelda Litvak was born in Warsaw on 5 August 1910. She came to Montreal in 1925.

In 1974, I interviewed Jennie in her small backyard, with the breeze rustling through the many trees, trying desperately to hear her stories and praying the tape recorder was doing a better job than my ears! The movie Blazing Saddles will always remind me of Jennie, because she took me out to see it after our interview ended.

Jennie Livak died on 27 August 2003. She was ninety-three years old.

MY NAME IS JENNIE LITVAK—by second marriage. My maiden name was Switzman. Actually, my first name is Zelda. It's an English name. By coming to this country, a lady decided that it should be Jennie because she wanted to give me a ring—a golden ring. My father was a boarder there in that house and in those days, fifty years ago, this lady, her name was Mrs. Barzer, kept a boarding house so she could educate her sons—she had four sons. And each one was a professional. Not only did she keep boarders in those days, to keep a Jewish boarder was also hard. But she kept a negro man—a dark fellow. I remember it like today. So her sons today are professionals: one is a druggist, one is a famous Dr. Barzer in Montreal, the other two are engineers—four of them.

Oh, I remember everything. When I was a kid I seemed to have noticed, to have observed things. I was born in Warsaw, Poland. I'm named after my paternal grandmother. My father was an only son. He had two sisters. At that time Poland belonged to Russia—so, when they had to serve in the army, they served in the Russian army. My mother had a son whom she lost after he was one year old, and I came only five years after their marriage, I was the special thing! So my grandfather cherished me very much. I carried his wife's name. I was the little special thing, although circumstances at home were quite hard.

In those days people were poor, just like today, although my father had a dream. My grandfather had a *droshke,* he had a coach with a horse, and he had a number. In those days they were forced to have a passport and a photograph, and I think it was the first time in his life that he took a photograph. He was what you call a progressive religious man in Warsaw. And I have a photograph for that number on his hat with the peak.

My father always had a dream. He used to always tell me about his dream, that he wanted to be a doctor. And he used to sing very beautifully. So, at six years old, they brought him to a school and they put him into a choir, but it only lasted till he was nine years old. When he was nine years old, they gave him to be an apprentice in a home in leather goods in Warsaw. Now, not only did he have to ... he actually wasn't learning anything ... he was like ... he rocked the cradle; he used to go for all the messages for the lady of the house. They probably only had one room and this is how his education stopped at that time. But he was a self-educated man and, since his dream wasn't fulfilled, he always had a dream for his children. When he married, he was already an efficient and also a very creative person in leather goods; because, to him, to handle a piece of leather was like somebody handles a beautiful piece of brocade or a diamond.

I remember my brother Harry, who is next in line, although my mother lost the first one. I do remember when my sister Pauline was born—she was four years younger than I—we lived in Warsaw in the Jewish district[41] and I was a little girl. It was 1914. So when she was born, I remember my mother just fell into bed, nobody was home, just my mother and I, and I was a tiny little one. My mother sent me upstairs to call the neighbour, to come down to call the midwife. Then my father came home, he was out for the evening, doing business.

But things were not very good, and my father was working in the house when I was a year older, let's say I was four, because I remember distinctly the table where he was working and there were two beds and a sink and ... well, this was the whole business!

As time was passing, the Germans occupied Poland. And my father had a diary, only from one year, 1908 to 1909. I have it. It's in Jewish. It has to be typed. Nobody has ever done it. My father is dead six years, seven years now. Well, at the time, things were very bad, during the 1914–18 war. There really was no food. So my father had an offer—he met a man—he had an offer to come to a place called Yablonka Yeganova. It's a half-hour drive by train from Warsaw, where he was promised a job to be a bookkeeper. This man had a place where he received coal and wood. He was a supplier and receiver and distributor of coal and wood, and my father worked there. We moved out to this area. At least he had the security of a job there, and we were given a little house, and by then we were four children. There was myself, there was Harry, there was Pauline, and there was Sarah that was born already. And this was a place where the trains were right nearby, and across the track were the barracks, the soldiers' barracks. During that time, 1916–17, there were a lot of interned soldiers in this area. There were all kinds of interns because it belonged to Germany—not German interns—other nationalities, and probably Polish interns too; and let's say it was five minutes walk from our house.

I was a little girl, so what my father did then, was he used to go to the neighbouring countrysides—outlying areas—and bring black breads and beautiful cheeses and eggs, and my mother cooked hard-boiled eggs. We used to go with my aunt to the barracks—my father's sister who perished in the Warsaw Ghetto. We used to put this stuff, the food, in the apron: a quarter of bread or a piece of bread, a piece of cheese and something else, and hard-boiled eggs, and we used to get money from the soldiers across the barbed wire. We used to get the money and give them the stuff. Well, it happened on several occasions that my aunt, who was an older person, she was fooled: they took the stuff from her and they wouldn't give her the money so my mother was very, very furious about that, you know. They thought my aunt was not capable, that I was an example—like I did better than her!

And this is where we went to school—in that area, Yablonka Yeganova. We used to spend beautiful summers there. Winters were cold, but children don't feel the cold or poverty as much. Now I remember during that year, between 1917 and 1918, there was very little to eat. We had already moved to another place. We actually lived in three homes in that area until 1925–27. In 1917 there was very little food, and every Jewish family—rather than Polish—was favoured by the Germans! In that war, the Jewish people were the friends of the Germans. The Germans were very happy to come into Jewish homes. They didn't trust the *Polaks*. They were happy to come into the Jewish homes and be welcomed as part of the family. So every family had friends among the soldiers, and the Germans would bring us a sack of sugar, a sack of peas—split peas that we had to pick. I remember sitting with the family picking—there were a lot of wormy beans. They used to grab this away from the Polish peasants, you see, and give it to the Jewish families. And there was a time when we had no milk. My mother would give us tea with saccharin. I remember complaining to her that she begrudged me another cup of tea. I wanted another cup because it was very sweet, but she didn't want to give me tea because saccharin was dangerous for children. So I remember that incident.

However, in 1918 the Germans supposedly had lost the war and they were leaving, and the trains were leaving through our area into Germany, going west. So at the time, the *Polaks* took over again, although it was their liberation from the Russians and the Germans, if you read your history. The Polish people came to our house and actually made us move out from this house we lived in. So we got another house through somebody but they really took away a lot of stuff—they came with guns, you see. The Poles for sure never forgot. They never forgot that the Jewish people were friends with the German people and German officers in the First World War. But it didn't last very long.

So we found another home and by then it was the last house. My brother John was born, and then there was Rose, the last one: we are six living. Two children my mother lost—the eldest and the one in between my brother Harry and Pauline.

At the time, my mother had a nephew in New York who had been writing to her, and he told her he wanted to bring my father over and he sent affidavits—or visas, at that time—that we should come to the United States. But my father refused. He really didn't want to leave Poland. He was a Jewish patriot, what they called it then, and he struggled.

Now at that time, after the 1918 war, my father established himself in the house with machinery that he needed. He used to make the tops for shoes, what you call? … they were tops for shoes, leather tops … well, they're called in Jewish *kamashen-makher*—*kamashen* means the top part of the shoe. After the top part is made, you give it to an expert shoemaker, who would do the bottom part. It was all hand work, you see. So he was really an expert on a piece of leather and on the top part of the shoes. He would take a measurement and make designs, colours, beautiful. Yes, he was really an expert designer in this.

By 1920, things were still restless. My father, in fact, was a very progressive man, you know, in his day and age. The Polish neighbours called him communist. So we had to be very careful, you know. Although he was not a left-winger, he was a progressive man. He was not religious, but he was not a left-winger. In fact, in Canada he was busy in the Labour Zionist movement because it was labour, that's why. And he was very devoted to Jewish cultural institutions in Montreal as much as—maybe I'm jumping over too far?—but sort of to give a thought that he had certain … that he had certain ideas about culture and education. That was his life, and he was well-read, and in his 1908–9 diary he begins with a poem by Heinrich Heine on peace—in Jewish, translated into Jewish [Yiddish]. My father worked at home and the children at home used to help him out in different ways by doing little things that we found interesting; or a punishment was that if you didn't do your homework well you had to sit while he was working. You did some of the poetry by heart, and things like that.

Besides having a nephew in New York, my mother also had a sister in Montreal—Mrs. Opolsky, and her husband. They were here before, and their three sons came into the millinery trade in Montreal. They were very well known in the Montreal millinery trade. Now one of the Opolskys, the eldest, went to New York to work in the millinery trade as a blocker. My father didn't want to go to the United States, to this nephew of my mother's who was my mother's age—they grew up together in the house. He decided he wanted to come to Montreal, and when my aunt sent an affidavit from Montreal for my father, I remember that the decision was made: he is going to sell all the machinery and everything and he is going to go to Canada!

My father came to Canada in January 1924, and in his diary of three years he describes the hardships then. It's in Jewish, and I wish it was in English. It was meant to be translated afterwards to incorporate it into the book that I would like to write—starting in three or four years, if I live. But my sister started to type it and she gave it up. She's the one who knows the Jewish language very well—she's the Jewish typist.

My father came in January and he went to work in leather goods, of course. And he was supposed to earn four dollars a week, but somehow the boss thought that he didn't do a good job and gave him the little pieces that he cut of the leather and told him that that was his pay. And he had no money to live on, and my uncle was not a very nice person. He was a miser and he wasn't even nice to his own children. So naturally, my auntie, being a weaker person, used to give in to my uncle. And my father had a very miserable time.

I, being of the age of thirteen, was very unhappy at home in Europe and wanted to come to my father. I preferred to be with him. So my father decided that he is going to bring me over. In those days there was the Holstein Company—the travel agency which is still in existence. They would make out all the affidavits and all the papers and everything, and you could pay them back a dollar a week. And they were very good because there were so many immigrants—and the company really did favours. I met these people because I used to go down with the payments.

Where I came from wasn't what you would call a village. It was a train and soldier area. It was a very busy little area with schools and other places. Sure, as a matter of fact, there was a time, if you read the history of the Jews in English, you can find there were pogroms there. There were pogroms there too in Yablonka, because there were a lot of Jewish soldiers and families who used to come from Warsaw to bring food and things for the soldiers. My mother had an open house for these soldiers too. I remember that there were pogroms in Yablonka—it isn't a pleasant history for the Jews of that area. It's a very famous place. I revisited it, you know, in 1964.

So when it came to leave this area, you had to go to Warsaw. My mother brought me to Warsaw, to the Canadian consulate, and there she met the family by the name of Yakobovitch—the lady was travelling with six children to Montreal as well. So I sort of became part of this family too for the trip. I left home—mother took me there. I travelled with this family to Danzig—that's where you took the boat.

[At this point we gave in to the rustling outdoors and went into Jennie's den.]

The trip was an overnight train to Danzig on the Baltic coast, and there we stayed a day in what must have been barracks. A very funny incident happened, too. One of the kids in this family, the Yakabovitch family, his name was Koona—so the mother was calling: Koona! Koona! So people thought that they were calling for the Cunard Line, so those who were there for that boat got up and started to run to the boat! These are some of the things that we remember too.

When we went on the boat, I was very sick and they took care of me. I was lying most of the time in bed and remember they gave me candies with lemon. I arrived in Montreal. It took a week. No. We first stopped in Liverpool for a day. We were in a hotel, where I lost a precious umbrella that my father had asked my mother to buy for someone here—for me to bring. And in all the almost fifty years, I'm still broken-hearted because those people gave my father the money so that my mother should buy this umbrella, and I lost it. So many things you live with. We stayed there a day in Liverpool. I remember going on this double-decker bus that is so famous for London, England, and then we went on the boat and we were coming to Canada!

Now we come to Halifax—the trip took eight days. We came to Halifax and we also stayed there in barracks overnight. Those days, from Halifax to Montreal took twenty-four hours by train. It was too early to come to

Quebec City, because the St. Lawrence was still frozen. At the time I didn't understand it, but I learned later on why we came to Halifax instead of Quebec. This was early April and there was still snow in Montreal when we arrived, like a late winter. (We had a very big snowstorm on April 11 this year, 1974, a huge storm in Montreal. So that probably happened then too.) However, I arrived in Montreal at the Windsor Station. My father was there with a cousin of my mother's, also with the name of Opolsky—a brother-in-law to my aunt. And they took me to their house. We travelled by car to Papineau. In those days, Papineau was an outlying district, very far out in north end. And I stayed there for three weeks. I went to school with the children there. I was grown up already but ... I was very much impressed with that home because they had a piano for the only girl! There were three boys and one girl, and they had a piano. They learned to play "*Hatikvah,*" the Zionist anthem [*and which became the Israeli anthem in 1948*]—it shows you the potentialities in a person, you know.

I was thirteen or fourteen at the time. I had finished grade six in Poland you see—I was well advanced in schoolwork, according to the curriculum over here. I was much advanced even for today. So I went to school and, by July, my father had decided that I had to go to work because he didn't have the means ... like my father was making four dollars a week, eight dollars a week ... that's all. It was horrible. I remember that. And so I had to go out to work. Then we took a room on Henry Julian with a family. There was no bath in the house. Oh, he was probably paying ten dollars a month, according to the wages.

When I started to learn the trade, I got acquainted with two girls—one of them is the one that you [*referring to me*] met on Pratt Avenue. She was nineteen at the time, a few years older than I. And she was an operator in the millinery trade. My father's ship brother (what they call a person who was with him on the boat) brought me up to that factory to learn the trade. His name was Handler and I knew how to sew, because they teach you in Polish schools how to do fancy work, sewing, embroidery, that sort of thing; and my mother used to teach me too. So, at this place they teach you how to put a lining in a hat. In those days you wore hats with lining inside. And I was very good at that and the name of the place was Monarch Hat Company. It was a Jewish outfit, the boss's name was Max Solin. So there was Max and Jack. Jack was in charge of the people and Max was the one who was doing the cutting. So Max was the quieter person and Jack was the very aggressive one who would try to get the most out of the youngsters. Now the forelady at the table was a girl who was two or three years older than I. Her name was

Lucy Goffman, and she was very nice to me. She taught me different tricks to begin with. I took very fast to the work, so that when we had to work on a Saturday morning, which meant coming in from eight to one, she would choose me because I was very fast.

In those days we worked forty-eight hours a week. For the first two weeks they didn't want to pay me anything, but this Mr. Handler (and of course I cried, I was miserable) … so this Mr. Handler spoke to the boss and thought that I should get four dollars for the two weeks. Then he paid me four dollars a week after the first two weeks. I worked up to eight dollars. I remained there for two years. I used to take to work a lunch, which consisted of bread and butter and five cents, That is all we could afford. Sometimes I had a piece of Kraft cheese.

At the time I was getting eight dollars. The forelady was getting married and she went on vacation. So I guess I must have been so capable that the boss made me in charge of the few girls on the table—and I was only getting eight dollars. So I wanted a raise of three dollars to give me eleven dollars, which would mean an awful lot of money for me at that time.

He didn't want to give it to me, so I left. And he was furious. I left and I went into work at that time to New York Hats, which was controlled by the Leopold family. The Leopold family had a hat factory, The Canadian Hat, and this was called The New York Hat. I didn't only get eleven dollars, I got thirteen. Had I asked for more, I would have got more. That's how good I was! I was very advanced. I had terrific speed and was very qualified. At this time I was seventeen years old. It had taken three years, you know, to get up to thirteen dollars. The foreman changed places and went to work at another place and he took me with him. I got seventeen dollars right away. Seventeen dollars by then—I'm talking—another year had passed. I worked there for about a year and couldn't produce a quality hat to sell. That was a place where they made very cheap hats.

Now those days there was no union. We were not organized at all. My eldest cousin was getting married in New York. Time was passing on and I was already nineteen and I decided—and my father agreed—to go to New York. By then I was still not using any makeup because, well, in those days the father was the boss and I was not allowed to use any makeup. So I used to use a little bit of powder.

When I went to New York I started to use lipstick. I preferred lipstick to powder. Anyway, I was supposed to stay there for a few weeks and come back home. Through my cousin I came into a place called Alfreda. The name of the factory was Alfreda where there were girls that worked "week work" and girls that worked piecework. Now I worked piecework and my cousin took me up to Alfreda and I remained there. That was the beginning of the Depression years. That was 1930.

I was able to work there in New York because in those days one could stay six months without anything like papers; you just passed through from Canada to the United States without a problem. But you had to come home after six months. So that's the way it was. I went back to New York, though. I worked in this place and the owner was a lady who had no children and she was very fond of me. I was making at the time fifty-five dollars a week. I even have my book from those days. Honestly! I could even show it to you; but it's in the basement packed in a trunk.

I was making fifty-five dollars a week doing piecework. What they did was they gave the hats that took much longer to work on, to the girls who worked at the week-work table. They used to take me—I was so fast and good— that if they had extra work, like the hats that took longer, they would put me on the week-work table and pay me one dollar an hour. In those days I could stay doing this sometimes for two weeks straight and make fifty to sixty dollars a week. We would work overtime and get paid more. There was enough for our meals and everything. And it was just beautiful. I lived with a family who were friends and relatives from Europe yet. So they were very good days. I used to send money home.

I lived with those girls—the mother lived in Philadelphia because the father had a butcher shop there. So we lived in Brooklyn Borough Park and we shared expenses. No rent—the mother paid the rent—but we shared expenses for the telephone, the electric, the gas bills, the food. And I used to send home one hundred dollars every month to help the family here in Montreal. By this time my whole family was here. We brought them over in 1928 and we paid out a dollar, two dollars a week for their travel tickets. All this is written down in my father's diary, which he stopped writing in when the family came over because things began pressing and demanding for him, you know.

There was a Peretz School at the time, and so my father immediately enrolled the children into the school, although he couldn't afford to pay. But, he said, Someday he would pay it back—and he did. He brought children into the school and he paid for them too. These were the beginning years.

I came back to Montreal. I worked for a while here as a forelady in a place—I was very young, about twenty, and I was a forelady. I was then offered here twenty-two dollars a week but I went back to New York. I made a fortune and I helped my father here in the Depression yet. Then the Depression really came. The Crash really came. And I came home. At times I also worked in New York. Three times I went back and forth to make money. I came here because one of my sisters who had remained in Poland with two aunties (they perished in the Warsaw Ghetto)—she was arriving here—and the year must have been 1932. She was sixteen years old when the family left, so she was going on twenty-one years at the time.

Times were very bad, but I managed to bring back enough money from New York. Then I was invited to a wedding in Montreal, a friend of mine also in the millinery trade, and I remained here after that because I met my future husband—my first husband, named Rashcovsky. I worked here in those days as a plain worker, a draper, and was getting fifteen dollars a week. And I was making sixty dollars in New York, and that's a fact. Can you believe the difference? And then there was the Crash. Finally, when we did get married, I went to work and my husband went to work.

I met my husband at the wedding of my friend. He was a furrier and he was very busy—but still he made a date with me. His mother ... was very dominating and she was the boss in the house. She couldn't understand how he met a girl at this wedding and right away made a date with her! Then when she heard that I came from Poland, she really didn't want me. She was from the Ukraine. They were very narrow-minded people—very, very narrow-minded, reactionary people. She didn't want a Polish girl because they didn't like the Polish Jews. And, also, she had heard that I came from a working family, a working-class family. So did they! But they had a store, a little stationery store, so they thought they were rich, you see. She knew that I was not going to bring any dowry. So then she certainly didn't want me. But he cared very much and I was spiteful. I figured since she doesn't want me, then she will have me. But I suffered for that. I paid the price. [*Jennie chuckles.*] I did. This is what happened then.

I got married in 1932 and it was a very hard time. My father didn't even have enough money for the wedding. I had a beautiful lady make my wedding gown and other things. I held on to the marriage with three children for twenty-two years because I wanted them to grow up with a family, you know. I thought, maybe he'll change ... I could go on and on, but ...

At the time when I got married in 1932, we had boarders. My mother had a widow, Miriam Goldwasser, with a little boy named Herschel. This woman was also working in the needle trades. My mother actually brought up this little boy. Later on, this Miriam married a Mr. Shatsky. (She died of cancer later.)

You will meet Mr. Shatsky tomorrow; you will be walking around and you will probably be introduced to him. He has his own home, a car, and he has already married a fourth wife who also died, but of a heart attack. Poor man, he had a very hard life. You'll hear from Shatsky that Miriam Goldwasser was a Shatsky. In fact, this white vase is from her. She gave it to me. She said, I want you to have it. She was part of the family after all.

My mother also had a girl, another boarder, and all these people—my parents and family, the boarders. I was married and lived with her also. We all lived in one house. The rent was all of thirty-five dollars a month. Yet altogether we couldn't afford to pay that rent and my mother used to cook for these people as well as do other jobs. It was one house. We were six children, plus two parents, my husband—that's nine. Mrs. Goldwasser and her son, that's eleven; and the other girl, that's twelve people. And we all managed. My parents never had their own home. People lived in rented houses with boarders and they lived on the east side.

My mother cooked for everyone and lived to a ripe old age of eighty-three. She would have lived longer but she died as a result of an accident. My father worked all of his life. He was secretary of the leather-goods union in Montreal—and that's quite a piece of history there.

I had friends in the millinery trade and there was a girl named Dora Lazar who came from Lithuania. The Jewish people from Lithuania were very cultured, educated people. I got involved with her, and through her I met many teachers who were teaching in the *Folkshule*, the Jewish Peoples' School, then on St. Urbain Street in the east end. You see, they were very much Zionist-minded, these people from Lithuania. They belonged to organizations and so through her I came into the Labour/Poale Zionists, they called themselves. And I was there for a while. I met many people through the years. I was a member of the Zionist organization through my father, just to honour him when he formed the Pinsky branch of the Zionist organization—but I was never active in the movement. I was active in the left-wing movement, and I was in the Communist Party after the war, the Second World War.

Let me talk a little about the question of classes. It didn't matter if you were a Jew or not—even today. It still stands that a Jew, or even a brother against a brother ... if one is rich and one is poor—there is that difference. This is my opinion and it seems to be proven in society that money influences many people and their character—it proves their character.

When the Jews came here, they felt that the only way they can make money is by exploiting the people. Now I remember being very miserable and crying every single day of work because, first of all, I was very lonely. I was new here. I was very sensitive. I wanted an education. I couldn't go to school formally, only at night. We were very poor. At night I used to go out and buy bread from the day before—which I don't mind eating, even now. But those days, if you bought some rolls you paid a penny a roll, and you bought a herring. It was very cheap, you know. I used to go to bed hungry many, many times. I used to buy bananas. Our meals consisted of things like that: bananas and Kraft cheese, and bread and rolls from the day before, which you got for next to nothing. Those days bread was five cents, so you got bread from the day before for two cents, three cents, you see. These were horrible times. I still remember we used to go to bed hungry. Even my brother Harry, who came here alone, after me (because my father couldn't possibly bring over a family of five people all at once, so my brother Harry came next), even he recalls going out to pick up some food for the next day late at night.

For breakfast we had coffee and bread and butter, probably a black bread. For lunch a banana, bread and butter with cheese. When I was making four dollars a week, I used to get a nickel every day. I would buy a couple of biscuits, or even you could buy a bag of french fries for five cents those days. That made up part of the meal, because I brought the sandwich from home and so the chips helped. We used to go into my friend's sister's home. They had a little store on Notre Dame Street, where they served food and things— so we had the privilege of getting a drink. We would go upstairs to their small kitchen and finish our meal. Those were good days!

At night for our supper we sometimes had—I learned how to cook on the weekends—a soup with a piece of meat in it, or sometimes had a stew. Sometimes we would just eat herring, tomato, an egg, and things like that. We would have a decent meal when we went visiting my mother's cousins, the Opolskys on Papineau. Also we used to visit the Goldenbergs once a week on the weekend and there we (my father and I) would get nice food.

The Goldenbergs had a wholesale grocery, so there was no problem having a nice meal or a nice sardine, and something like that. Not only that, I used to bring my ironing there once a week; take a good hot bath in their home. So I was privileged. The mother, Mrs. Goldenberg, who died of cancer at forty-seven, used to sew; and the first dresses she sewed was for me. She would pick out for twenty-five cents a piece of material and sew up some clothes for me. I was still going to school at that time.

It was very tough, very tough times. My father was a very strict person. I remember at the age of seventeen, I wanted to have a date with someone and he didn't allow me to go with this person because he worked for a butcher. This boy used to come to collect at the place where we lived. In those days, no one paid cash. My mother never was able to buy groceries for cash. She used to buy and mark everything down and at the end of the week, when my father got his pay and I brought home the few dollars, then we figured out how much we can pay this week. You see? And many times my mother needed an extra dollar for, let's say, for us to buy something or something extra that she wanted—she would add on a dollar to the whole figure so that my father wouldn't even know. Well, she had to do it, to get an extra dollar. And the man in the grocery co-operated. It was the corner grocery. She needed that. And that went on for quite a few years!

Hyman Leibovitch

Hyman Leibovitch was born in 1896. He came to Montreal with his young sister in 1914, a few months after the First World War had begun. Hyman was a fine cabinetmaker from the Old Country; however, he serendipitously found himself in the building trade, where he flourished.

I met him in the summer of 1974 at the Young Men's Hebrew Association in Montreal, where he kindly gave up an afternoon of card playing to talk to me.

I COME FROM ROMANIA. When Romania started to fight Bulgaria and Hungary, I was only eighteen years old and they took me to the army for three months for training. This was in 1914. So I made the three months in the army and I left because they gave me my privilege to go home. Instead of going home, I went to find work to the Romanian border and I passed to Chernovitz and when I came to Chernovitz[42] I have nothing left—no papers, no passport, nothing; only my uniform from the army. That's all I had. I didn't have a penny in my pocket.

I came over to Chernovitz and there was a man standing there with a little horse and a wagon. And I was talking to him in Jewish because I didn't know whether he speaks Romanian or not. I was speaking to him Jewish and I told him, Please, I want you should take me to Jewish people, I should be able to stay and have at least a cup of water, because I have no money to buy anything. Anyway he said, All right, I know a person who lives not far from here who has a farm, no children, and I'll take you there. He took me there, I come, a man comes out; I would say, he is only about four feet—not tall, not fat. So the man said to the other fellow, he was speaking like an Austrian, he was a Jewish man. I said, *Far vos?* Why don't you speak Jewish? He said, I'll talk in Jewish. He asked, where I had come from? I told him I had come from Romania, I had passed the army, and I don't want to go in the army further because I don't want to go in the war. In Romania the Jewish people have no opportunity to do anything, to go anywhere—the same like in Russia.

So they took me in and I was sitting outside in the balcony and I was waiting there, and a lady who comes out—I would say about three feet higher than he is—a lady, a fat woman comes out. She says to me, You would like to have something? I was waiting, maybe she was gonna ask me because I want to ask her to give me at least a glass of water. Because they don't have like we have around here, a tap and go take some water. No, there is a well, you have to draw with a pail a bit of water. She went there, I said, I don't want nothing, I just want a glass of water if it's possible. She said, I'm going to go to the well and I'm going to get a pail of water and you are going to have water. Believe me, if I didn't drink four cups of water, not one!

I was hungry like a dog. Then she asked me, Are you hungry? I said yes. I was very, very hungry and she said to me, we'll wait for supper. Until supper, I thought I'm going to burst, because I was hungry. I asked the lady to give to me to eat, something, a husk, anything, I'm hungry. I'm waiting for the moment when she called me in for supper. There was potatoes and what else there was didn't matter—I was the happiest person—I filled my stomach.

While we are eating the meal she asked me from where I'm coming. I told her I'm coming from a small little city near the Russian border—Stephanitz. She asked me, Was your father born in the same city? I said, No, my father had been born near the Austrian–Hungarian border. He comes from Bordejen. When she heard that my father had been born in Bordejen, she said, I am a Bordejena myself! What is the name of your father? I said, My father is Benjamin. She said I'm coming from the same place, yeah! Yeah! Your father had any relatives around there? I said, He hasn't got any relatives. He has a sister and he has a brother. The brother is a shoemaker and he is in the States (Canada, New York, is the same, it's combined—it's called America) and I managed the name of the brother. I didn't manage the name of the sister because I didn't know the name of her. She asked me, How long your father stays in Stephanitz? I said, We are already six children. He is married a long time ago. She said, Well, manage me another couple names. I said what kind of names I could manage? I know he comes from Bordejen and he has a sister and their father had a home and they sold it and they didn't even let him know.

She jumps up and she falls down from the chair. I thought she had started to faint. So I went—I was a young boy and I was strong. I could pick up three women like that. I was a very husky boy. And I picked her up from the floor and I said, Madam, what is wrong with you? I want ... I feel like I want to cry, the way she talks. She told me, I want you should call your father here, right away. I said, Why? She said, Your father is my brother. I said, You want I should call my father? But I haven't got money. I haven't got nothing. She starts crying. She said, Come with me.

We went to the post office. There are no telephones around in the house. We went to the post office and we sent a telegram to Stephanitz and my father came the second day with one of my sisters. And they come there and she grabbed my father—and there was a lot of field, a lot of bush, and they went away and they was talking for hours and hours and hours. They wanted me to remain there as her child. She will give everything over in my name that I should remain her child. When my father came and told me the same story, that he wants me to remain there and everything belongs to me because she didn't have no children, I said to my father, Look, Pa, I am a man who is a mechanic with golden hands. I would never be lost in Romania and I would never be lost somewhere else and I intend on going to America.

Anyway, they kept me up for a week's time. They tried to talk me into it and I said no. My mind is made ... I didn't have any money. She said to me, I will give you some money. You go to America, and I want you to come back. She give me money to go to Germany. I went to Germany and took my sister with me. We rented an apartment with two rooms—she was living in one room and I was living in the other. I couldn't live with my sister in one room! And I was working for one of the bosses. I started to work for him. I was a cabinetmaker, a good cabinetmaker, because I used to work piecework. I told him in the beginning, I said, If you want I shall work for you as a pieceworker. I'll try and get me a boy for helping and the rest, just give what you want and tell me what you want, give me the measurements and that's it.

He started to give me some cabinets to make. I said, give me the material, that's all I want from you. I want a boy, a young fellow to work with me. I started to work and I worked over two, three days. The man doesn't see any material coming out like to show some work that I had done. He comes over to me in the nighttime when I finished my job, he tells me, Look now you worked three days, I don't see no work.

[*Hyman asked me, Are you rolling cigarettes? Since when? For years, I told him. I used to do that many years ago, he said.*]

Anyway, I said, Look, my work is mostly done; then what you think about it? Because you're never used to that kind of work. He was a good cabinetmaker. Everybody works in a different way. And I was working in a different way. I had got a good cabinetmaker to teach me, and there was a German fellow working then when he teached me the trade in Romania. I said, Look, my work is going to be done in a couple days and I am making all the framings and everything completely and then I start to put it together. I put them together. He saw it was growing. Everything was getting ready. He never thought it would go so fast once I start to put them together. And I used to polish by hand and scraping by hand. Not like today, a machine with spraying and different altogether. There everything was by hand. Anyway, I was working there and I made a nice dollar bill in Germany.

He had a girl there, the boss man, he had a nice girl, a young girl. And I was a stranger in the country. The girl comes over and says, Look, you're a stranger in the country, how about going out to a show? I said, I don't mind. What I could lose? And she was a very young girl, a very nice girl, an educated girl, and I went with her to a show. I remember like today. I went into a show, she started playing around with me, and I figured what could I lose? I intend to go away anyways. So, one time, second time, we went to a different show every night and my sister was waiting for me. I used to go, but I told her [the girl], If I go, I cannot leave my sister. I got to take her once in a while. I cannot leave her in the apartment. She hasn't got nobody to take her out.

At once, comes the boss to me, and says, Look, I want you should get engaged to my daughter and all the shop what I have around here, I give it to you, over to your name. I want you to get married to her. I said, I'm only a stranger around here and I cannot give you that kind of answer. I can't give you no answer for that. I'll have to think it over, think about it before I'm going to make that move.

That was in 1914. The war was not yet (I came to Montreal only six months after the war broke out). So anyway, I said to him, I will give you an answer. I'll have to think it over first before I give you any answer. So, I come the second day I want to try to finish up my work, because my mind was already to move out from there. In the same time, he owed me a lot of money. So I come over to him and I said, Look, I have to pay the rent to the hotel for me and for my sister, and I need money. He said, Yes, I'll give you some money. He give me some money and I figured he still owed me still more yet. Well, I'm not finished with the work. I'll try to finish up the rest of the stuff and try to get my money out and then disappear. At the same time, the girl tells me the second night she wants to take me out. I said, I don't feel like to go out as my sister is not feeling so good and I told her a story. I didn't want to go out. Anyways, they make me to go out with her. The father and the mother. I should eat supper by them and, if I wanted, I could stay even in their own home instead of in the hotel. I said, I can't do that. My sister is still there in the hotel and I can't do that. So I finished up my work and I said I need some money again. And he gave me another little bit and left some owing so not to give me the whole thing. So I figured like that, I said to my sister (her name is Arke), I say, Arke, you start packing up tonight everything because from Germany to France goes a train, right through from Germany, right through to France. You'll pack up everything, your stuff, my stuff, in the valises. We'll have to go away to France tonight. I didn't tell her nothing about the other business.

In the morning I was suppose to come to work. He is waiting and it's eight, it's nine; because seven o'clock in the mornings we used to start the work and it's eight, it's nine and I'm not there. He knows where I am living. He calls up to the hotel. He calls up to the hotel to go and see what is wrong with the man—maybe I'm sick, maybe I'm in the bed. The hotel didn't know when I went out. They thought maybe I moved out. I didn't tell them where I am going. And I took the train and I went to Paris with my sister.

I came to Paris, couldn't talk no French. It was very hard to get Jewish people to talk to them, or to talk to Romanians. I went in from one store to the other till I got one person to talk to in Jewish. And I remember the name of the firm was Le Bouha. So I figured, it's a French name—I could try. So I tried and I went in. The boss was alone, like he's a manager and a boss himself. I talk to him that I want to try to get a job around here because I just come from Germany and I intend to go away to Canada—they call it Kanarda, not Canada. Anyway, he said, I'll try to locate you to a job. I have a customer of mine—he's a good cabinetmaker.

I went down there and I was working there about four months, and then I made my mind I had enough money and I went to change my money into gold—the twenty francs into gold. My sister was seventeen at the time. She was a young girl, skinny. She was not working. I made up my mind that I had to start going away. I changed my money into gold at the bank. I didn't deposit my money in the bank. I used to keep it in the valise. So I made up my mind that I have to go away from here. I took the train and went over to Antwerp in Belgium and there I find another job. So between the boys who are working there, they was talking that there's a Canadian passenger boat what goes to Canada in five days. So I left the job and went over there to the boat and I bought the tickets—and in five days it was a pleasure for me to go. And I said to the boss, I'm going away to Canada. I want to get paid for my work. He said, You'll have to finish the whole thing. You left me in the middle of the road! I said, I cannot finish it because I bought tickets. I show him the tickets (for me and my sister) and I have to go away. Anyways, little by little I talked him in, and he gave me a few dollars in Belgian money.

And then I came to Quebec. My ticket was to take the train and go right to Montreal because I bought the tickets to Montreal. So the tickets was good enough for the train too. And they asked me for money coming into Canada immigration. I took out a bunch in gold and said, Is this enough? So they pat me on the back and said okay. So I passed through in Quebec. They didn't do no examination, nothing at all.

I come into Montreal and I find a man from the Old Country who used to live on the third door in Romania next to us. And I was the happiest person that I meet somebody at least to know, somebody to talk to. So I was talking to him and I said—his name was Mascarinin—and I said, Look, Mascarinin, I'm looking for a job. I have a few dollars only because I had to show thirty dollars for me and for her thirty dollars. I tell him, It's no use for me, I'm coming from Europe, different dressing. I didn't have no clothing. I only had the uniform from the Romanian army. I want to change my suit.

I went in to buy something, so I said, How much is the gold worth? I took out twenty francs, what I thought I'm paying up with one gold—twenty francs. He said it's not enough. So I went to the Bank of Montreal, this bank was on the corner of Pine Avenue and St. Lawrence, to change my gold. I gave him the gold. I count so much gold, and they give me a few dollars and no other money. I look over and said to her, I give you so much gold and I've got only a couple paper bills. Anyway, she said that if you don't want it, don't take it.

So I went back to the same guy, the same Mascarinin and I told him, I have so much gold and they give me in the bank nothing at all for it. I should at least buy a suit but I'm left with nothing; especially the girl. I've got to put on her a dress. I am coming in here, it is the cold weather. I need a coat and she needs a coat. And I couldn't buy nothing. Anyways, he said, We'll wait. Don't spend your money now. I'll lend you a couple dollars. I'll lend you fifty dollars and you'll give me the gold and when you'll have your money back, when you'll have your fifty dollars, you'll give me back and I'll give you back the gold. So it was an idea.

He called up to a guy in the trade and he said, I need a good carpenter, a good carpenter. And they start to build a store in a building on St. Catherine West. And what happens? We start to work but a couple of weeks and nobody got paid. And he failed. He failed and when they closed up my tools and everything, they said, can't touch nothing and he got no money either!

Bankrupt. Because everything that is in there is responsible for the rent. So I went over to the … I couldn't talk in fact, no English. I talk a couple words there … so I told him that it's my tools, I have to make a living. I cannot leave my tools. I have no money. Anyways, then I wait a week, two, three, then I took my tools out. Well I couldn't get no money from the guy. So I figure I will see what I can do again.

I went to look for a job, and I look for a job: a month, two months, four months. I couldn't get no job. You know how boys are! So I went to a show— in St. Catherines? St. Lawrence? The Midway, I think they are calling it. It used to cost fifteen cents to go to see a show and I went in there and I meet some boys—and we made a friendship. And one boy, he said, I'm looking for a job. He's looking for a job. And I am also looking for a job. If we could find some jobs. Where could we find some jobs? They are looking for young boys to carry advertisements around to the houses. I said, I'll go down. We could lose nothing.

We went down there and we took the jobs and we didn't ask no price and they didn't tell us what they gonna pay. We were working out two weeks carrying around the advertisements—steps up, steps down—and I don't have no coat, no jacket, just a uniform jacket, and there it was cold, wintertime, freezing. I had a big handkerchief, a red handkerchief, and I cover my mouth, my face. The hat I pull down. I have nothing else. I just had a hat. So I'll just pull it down over my ears and we went down to carry the advertisements and we finished two weeks. I'm waiting for the two weeks to finish already so we should get some money out. I come to the end of the two weeks. They give me $1.30. I look them over and I said, What is that? Charity? I worked two weeks! That's the price. You like it, keep it. If not, go. I take the $1.30 and I throw them right back in the face. I was not scared. I go away from there and I say to the boys, What are we going to do? We were working two weeks and we cannot, he does not want to give us no more than $1.30 a person for two weeks. I said, I'm not going to collect. I'm going to knock his teeth out. I'm going back and I don't give a damn what is going to be!

The other boys were like Canadians already, a long time ago. So they said, Don't start it, you could get arrested. And who is going to take you out? You going to be in trouble. So I went back to him and I said. Look—and I give a hammer with the hand on the desk—and I said, Are you going to pay me or not, once and for all? He saw me, I was mad. He went and he took two dollars and throw me in the face. So I took the two dollars and went away. I come home. I nearly cried. I have to keep up my sister and myself and I was living in uptown with a poor family—the name was Mrs. Breitman—and

this woman said to me, Don't worry. You're a young man. My son is working. He's a presser. He makes a living for us. We'll give you to eat. We'll give
you a room. We'll keep your sister and don't worry about it. I said, Look, I
cannot let you should keep me up when I haven't got the money to pay.

So what I used to do? I used to get up in the morning, six o'clock in the
morning, and go looking around for a job. I see I can't get no job. So I find
a job in St. Dominique and corner of St. Clair—a piano factory. I come in
there, in the piano factory, and I ask for a job. I couldn't speak no English.
So they had a foreman, an Italian foremen, and the Italian foreman was
working in Romania, in Bucharest, and he was speaking Romanian. So they
called down the foreman that he should talk to me. He asked me what I am,
what kind of work I could do. I said I'm a cabinetmaker, I could do any kind
of work. I'm a responsible man and I want work. He said, Here in Canada
there is only one thing. You do one kind of work. We'll give you a job to
make only the doors for the pianos. I said I could do the whole thing. I can't
work on only one piece. I'll get sick and tired of it. He said, Well that's the
law around here. That's what everybody works on, one piece: one makes
drawers, one makes the top, one makes something else, one glues them
together. Everybody does his own work—special. Anyways, I said, I'll take
it. Better than nothing. Better than walking around in the streets. I took the
job and I was working a week, so the second week the foreman told me,
You're not getting paid. One week is going to always stay. I said all right. I
was working up two weeks. The second week he brings me in an envelope,
the pay. I open the envelope. I see five dollars. I start to scratch my head. I
said to myself, What the hell is going around in here? They told me in Canada
that you sew me up a button and you make five dollars! I'm a cabinetmaker
with golden hands. I can't make no living around here. What am I doing
around here? I think I'm going to try to get out from Montreal and go over
to the United States.

It was so strict. You couldn't pass to go on to the United States. You
couldn't pass for no money in the world. I was trying every way to get out
of Montreal and couldn't get out. So here is the job, I don't want to work for
five dollars.

I was working there from seven in the morning to six. So I figured myself,
I'm not going to work here for five dollars. I'll starve for hunger and I'm
not going to work for nothing. Because I was gold in Europe. I make a golden
living there. What I need to come to Canada and work for nothing? To give
away my strength for nothing. And have to keep my sister, a woman. You
know a woman needs clothing. A man can put on any pair of pants or suit.

Anything at all would be good. But not for a girl. I was worrying about her more than my own father. Anyways, I left the job and was going around over a year and a half I couldn't get no job altogether. A year and a half! That woman Mrs. Breitman kept me up. I'll try to see what I can do again.

I never knocked in a nail in my life since I was in the trade. We used to work only in dowels. No nails—dowels. Drilling the holes and making passing dowels. Not nails. Comes a man from Prince Arthur Avenue, name of Yankele Swartz. He said, You're a carpenter? I said, Yeah. I have a job for you, he says. You have a job for me? I'm happy. What kind of job do you have for me? You come with me.

At the time this man had a car and he was a rich man. A rich man! He took me down to Prince Arthur and he had houses there and he wants to make a store from the basement. He wants to make a store. So you have to break down the wall, preparing for a window, a big glass window, and an exit door for going in the store. I never done this in my life. I didn't even know where to start.

So he said, Well, can you do that job? I said, I'll look over the job. (I figure I cannot stand with my back holding up the building!) I'll see what I can do.

He said, How much do you think it will have to cost me for that job to be done? I said, The glass, I'm not going to put it on for you because I don't know about glass. The job I'll do up to the glass. So he asked me, How much you want? I said, I want six hundred dollars. I didn't know how much to charge. One hundred dollars or charge a thousand. Still, I took the job. I didn't have no contract with him. I figured like this: I'll go over to any lumber yard and find out if I can get somebody who knows the trade because I didn't know what kind of trade. I've never done that kind of a job. So there was a man, name of Shlucker in St. Lawrence, and I went over there and said, I want to talk to the boss. So they sent me in to another office and said to Mr. Shlucker, There's a man who wants to talk to you. He saw me I was a greenhorn and I was talking to him in Jewish. I said, Look, I am living in Montreal. I am a cabinetmaker. I never did this kind of work in my life. I don't even know how to start it. It is for a man name of Mr. Swartz. He wants me I should make him a window from a basement with a door and entrance and I don't know where to start it. So he asked me, Did you give him a price? I said, I told him six hundred dollars. I haven't got no contract with him. And I told him that my mind said six hundred dollars, but maybe it's worth more and maybe it's worth less. I don't know. So he asked me for my name and I told him my name was Mr. Leibovitch. So he said, Look, I am going to go over with you to see the job.

I bring him right there to the spot, You're sure you told him six hundred dollars? I said, Yeah and then he agreed with me that I should do the job for him. Okay, he said, don't worry about it, you have a good price. That's what he told me. I said to him, No glass—he wants a glass door. No glass, nothing at all. I told him that all he has to supply is the door and the material for the building and making the framing and that's all what it is. He said, You have a very good price. I'll give you a labourer and I'll supply you with the materials, and I'll come and show you how to do and don't worry about it.

I see he sends me a truck with posts and wood and bolts and kinds of stuff I've never seen in my life—and never done that kind of work in my life! He said, You put a plank on here, you'll drill a hole up there, and you'll push through the one post this way and a post the other way. He told me the whole story the way I should do it. And I was young and I took it into my head. And now, he said, I'm going to be running. You going to work and you do what I am telling you. You jack up the building with the posts on both sides.

I done what he told me. It took me three days. We made the job. The whole thing, the framing and everything. I spent on material, with the labour—it cost me two hundred, nearly three hundred dollars. And when I finished the job, I made three hundred dollars profit!

Well, when I see three hundred dollars profit, I said that this is for me a good thing. I think so. I am going to start in the building trade. I have somebody to show me what to do. It passes about two or three days. He calls me to the lumberyard, the same Shlucker. He says there's a Chinese man down near St. Catherine, he wants to fix up some double windows. At that time it used to be with a sash cord to pull up the windows. And all these sash cords were broken by him. I had never done that job either. I never knew which way to pull on these sash cords. I could take off the moldings and take out the window, but when you take out the window, you must put in the wheels because through the wheels is the sash cord and there's a weight inside. How do you take out the weight? I don't know which way.

Mr. Shlucker come and showed me what to do and what not to do. So in the beginning I didn't take it too serious. So I said, All right, show me how to take out the weight so I'll know what to do. I'm no dummy. So I went and I put in a big sash cord. I tried to put the window in. The window doesn't move because the sash cord is too long. I start to cut off two inches, three inches, five inches, six inches until I come to a size. Then I figured it out that I have to go up as far as the wheel, leave only about six inches, lower the cord, then you make a knot, and then you put it on to the window. And this is how he trained me and this is the way I made a living. And I have made good money setting in the windows; and since then I started in the building trade.

And I say, thank God for that. I could thank Him a thousand times. The man, Shlucker, is dead a long time now. I would say that he is dead about forty-five years already. All the time I remind myself of that: that the man pulled me up in a way that I made a living.

Later on I see that I'm all right and in good condition. I was already twenty-six years old. This was 1922. I have to build a home for myself. I found a nice girl and I got married. But she was from Galicia and I was Romanian, and we were living in happiness. I had six children with her and I was the happiest man. We lived together for forty-two years and we had the happiest life.

It happened, unfortunately, that she got arthritis of the feet and the circulation of the blood was bad—it couldn't pass through. They took her to an operation. I had to bring doctors from the States. It cost me over ten thousand. At the time there was no medicare, of course—so I had to pay always cash. I paid a doctor in the US for transportation, the plane back and forth, five hundred dollars, Victoria Hospital over two thousand dollars. The doctors had to take out both feet, have to make an operation and take the chances. They took a chance and made the operation and overnight the thing got black, and the second day she was dead.

This was for over, say, about four or five years ago. I did not want to go to my children. My children were okay. They had a good living, and I figured I will try to build another home. I got married again. The second wife, she never had any children. She comes from New York. She married in Toronto with another man. Her man got killed by a car. What happened was, I went to Toronto for Rosh Hashanah and Yom Kippur and I met her there. And in eleven days I got married. I didn't even think about it because I figured, Look, my wife, my woman, how long you make a living for her? You give her everything ... now be satisfied. So I married and I said to her, Look, can you travel, because I give up my trade now. I don't want to spend the rest of my life to make a living. The only thing is, if you could travel, we get married. You can't travel, forget about it.

She said, I'm a good traveller! My honeymoon I went away for six months. I went away in October and came back 15 April. I was for five months in Miami. I saw from the beginning it was no good: life between me and her. Her name is Victoria. I was about seventy years old and she was fifty-nine. She was much younger than I am. I got married in eleven days. I didn't think around because I figured, Why should she not be happy with me? So we went away to Miami.

The first day, the second day—a new life. Then I went away for about a month because in that hotel, I said, I couldn't sleep. So then I went away for nearly a month, nearer to the ocean side and I went down to the ocean every night. And I was standing at the beach all night. I couldn't fall asleep—not in the daytime and not in the nighttime. But in three weeks, nearly four weeks, I went and got some pills—you know, some sleeping pills. I took one night four pills. And she got up from her bed and she saw the pills on the counter, she started jumping, Where do you get them pills? I said, A month's time I am not sleeping. What kind of wife you are? Are you married to me for love or for money?

She said, Well I was living with my husband for so many years and don't need no more of this living together. I said, It's no life for me. I figured maybe she still has in her mind her first husband. I figure I'll try. I went away and I bought her a golden watch. But the man wants two hundred dollars there. A beautiful watch, in gold. And I bought her the watch to make her happy, for a present. Here's a nice present. I tried different ways and then she accepted. When I came back from Montreal, I went to Toronto with her. She had a friend who was a goldsmith. He used to make diamond rings. I went and made her a diamond ring there and I order a diamond ring for her and he charged me reasonable, about seven hundred dollars. It was a beautiful diamond ring with a large diamond in the centre. I figured I would try something different, try a different way altogether. I bought her golden earrings. I said if you make holes in your ears, I'll buy you diamond earrings. She was like a young child—she has to have it. She used to wear always earrings with clips. One of her friends said she would try her earrings in my wife's ears and pushed the earring into the hole—saying it still must be good—and so in a year she had diamond earrings.

After all of that I find out she has a friend, a Christian boy, a married man and that man ... how did I find out? I got a heart attack on account of her! Six years already. When I used to drive the car she used to make me nervous all the time. There's a cat! There's a dog! There's a man! There's a ... I said, Look, you cannot sit in the back. I don't want to get nervous. I don't want to get killed like your husband. You cannot drive with me in a car. I am driving already so many years, since 1926. You cannot drive with me or I'll sell the car and if not, I'll throw you out from the car. One or the other.

Well, she said, that's the way I am and I can't help it. I am very nervous. I said, You're nervous? Go back to Toronto. So the married boyfriend's wife had a mother in Montreal. And he came in Montreal to see the mother. And he come to see her, my wife, he come into my house and I was laying in the bed. He come in and says hello. And he was standing by the door of my bedroom, he was inside. And I feel like to go to the washroom, you'll excuse me. I went to go to the washroom and I see she fall on top of him, with the hand, and start kissing back and forth. I didn't make any fuss and I went into my bathroom. When he went out, she took him right downstairs with the elevator, because I am living on the seventh floor. She took him right down to the car and she pulled him out from the car—I was going out on my balcony—and she kissed him ... she didn't let him go. I see something wrong goes on. Maybe she lives with him? This was the only way to believe it. And since then I make my mind like that [*uses some Yiddish expressions*] ... she's only working for me. I give her so much a week and I live in the apartment and that's all what it is and that's all I want. I don't want to fight. I say, You don't feel like to stay here in Montreal, you want to go back to Toronto, the door is open. Anytime when you feel like it, you could get out. I am not keeping you. You're not under the Russians. I'll keep my doors locked. You could get out anytime you wish. And that's the end.

And since then she doesn't want to go home. When I told her to get out of the house, I don't want to see you anymore, you're not my wife. I want a wife and I'll get a wife. I don't need you anymore. What I bought you, all the gold and everything, I leave it to you and that's all. I am living with her eight years and I never touched that woman yet and I'll never touch her.

She doesn't go anymore to see this other fellow because his wife sent her a letter to Montreal. My wife didn't close the letter and I read it. She intends to leave him—the wife intends to leave him. And that is the reason she never goes back. I told her, Your friend, she is getting so sick (this is another friend). Why don't you go to Toronto? She said, Well, I don't feel like to go. You see, that's the only thing. She feels that if she'll come there to Toronto, there will be trouble, something will happen there and that's the reason she doesn't want to go.

I give her so much a week and that's all. No more. She cannot get a penny out of me. And I would be the happiest man if she would leave me.

Ena Ship

Ena Ship was born in 1911 in the Ukraine and came to Canada in 1928. I interviewed Ena in Montreal in the summer of 1974 as we sat enjoying the sunshine in her backyard.

Ena and her husband, Dave Ship, whose story follows later in the volume, were long-time supporters of Jewish progressive organizations in Montreal.

I COME FROM A SMALL TOWN in the Ukraine, the Soviet Ukraine. We were not exactly working class because there was not much of an industry, but there were some people, shoemakers, and all kinds of tradesmen. I went to a Soviet school and was very much involved with activities around the school. After I finished school I joined an adult drama group and had a more progressive upbringing than some people coming from a background like that—like not a really working-class background.

The idea to come here was because my oldest sister and brother had left the Soviet Union during the civil war and went through Romania to the United States. Part of the family was there and when the United States was closed for immigration,[43] they brought our older brother to Canada. The family, the whole family, was supposed to emigrate to Canada, but my father took sick and so my younger sister and I came here. This was in 1928.

Like all other people, if you know somebody, they take you in. You have no idea what you're going to do here in a new country. So people take you in and try to find you work. They try to fool the boss that you know something when you don't know anything! The first job I had was just pulling threads out of the pants and it paid a high salary, like three dollars for the first week. You see, they used to baste the pants, the seams of the pants, and after they stitched them, we pulled out the threads.

It was really a very dinky sweatshop where we worked—on Main Street, downtown—just a little tiny two-by-two place. In fact, one of the girls who had taken me there (she's still in this trade and never married), when we recall sometimes the way we worked at that Mr. Stein's place ... well, it was a wooden table, and the girls that used to pull the basting out, we worked from 8 a.m. to 6 p.m., and lots of times we had to work overtime. And if he wanted us to come in on Sunday, we had to do so or else we would lose our jobs. Later on, when I was working in other places, there was no question of coming in on Sunday. But then we had no choice.

I was staying with my younger sister and my brother. We all stayed in one room. Things were not like they are now. They had, sometimes, more than three people living in one room. Or you'd be living in a room and the lady of the house used to serve us meals for so much per week. In this house there was just the three of us newcomers. But when we moved to another place, it really was like a boarding house. She liked us because she had no children of her own and she had sort of adopted us. But she had other roomers—Ukrainians—some were the real fascists who had connections with the fascist movements all over the world.

When a new immigrant would come, a friend, or somebody who was staying where you were staying, would know somebody who works in the trade, and so that is how you found a job. You had no choice of what you wanted to do. You just had to go to work. First of all, we didn't have the language. You can't learn anything if you have no profession or skill, if you don't know the language. It takes at least two years till you get up enough courage to speak, even if you understand what someone is saying. And then, also, we found that the progressive movement and Jewish culture in the Soviet Union and everywhere else that was blooming was here too. We came with our traditions, you know, like cultural values and things like that. And we pursued it here and so we could get along. If it was for the work, we could get along in Yiddish only—because the choir sang in Yiddish, the dramatic groups were in Yiddish—so it slowed us down to learn to read and speak in English. You had to go to school to be able to converse in English so it wasn't much of a choice. Some of us had to do it.

I was seventeen years old at the time I arrived and my sister was younger. But she went to work too. There was no question of going to school because nobody will be able to keep you up. So we went to night school. We did our best. We got acquainted with the progressive movement. We used to come to the cultural centre. We started to sing in the choir and got involved in dramatics. It happened that Mrs. Massey's sister worked in a factory, and she took me up and helped me get my first job. After this first job, somebody took me up to work on ties—we made them by hand then—and of course I still didn't know how to do anything. But after a while I acquired the knowledge of how to do things, and by the time I finished working on the ties I got married and I had to stay home. I was going to have my first baby.

At the time I was really playing one boss against the other. I was so experienced that if he didn't give me a raise, I would go somewhere else. They wanted to teach other girls. So I left and got a better job. I used to get twelve dollars working on ties. It was piecework, so it would work out to twelve dollars or fifteen dollars a week, which was all right then. We would manage between the two of us to save up a couple of dollars.

I met David, my husband, in one of the clubs. It was a [Communist] Party club in which we met, a political party, before he went into the army. He was training here in Canada. By the time he had to go overseas, our daughter was born. She was five and a half months old when he left. At that time there was no fuss made about your politics, not in the air force. There were a lot of our progressive boys who volunteered. And then there was, at that time, the idea that we were helping the Soviet Union because they were fighting the same battle against the Germans. There were Russian aid committees and things like that here. So there was no discrimination in that way.[44]

When I got married we divided our big capital! Then my sister got married and then the Hungry Thirties came. Two of us were working. The men couldn't get any jobs! My sister and I, the married women, we had to go to work because a man couldn't get any jobs at all. They hired women because it was cheaper, and in the tie industry there was no union at all. But being in it, I used to always talk to the girls wherever I worked. In fact I missed out on learning French because the French girls, who was also cheap labour, wanted to learn English and so I tried to correct their English as much as I could. So I lost out on learning French.

We got together with some other shops and formed a local. We asked the Amalgamated—since ties is mens' articles: bow ties and handmade ties were our specialty. And then there were some machine-made ties. And there were pressers and cleaners and workers like that. We had a local in the Amalgamated Union and then the war came [World War II] and the men were mobilized or they joined up themselves.

During the Hungry Thirties there were soup kitchens. People who were unemployed could line up in soup kitchens to get a bit of soup and a piece of bread. There was nothing. I worked in a children's camp in those years.

It was a workers' camp. It cost $2.50 a week for the child and, if you didn't have the money, the organization paid for them. It was an international camp. We had at one time as many as ten nationalities in that camp. We used to go to the farmers and ask for food, and if they gave us bacon, we used to tell the mothers, who would come visit on Sundays, that it was good chicken—because we couldn't tell them we were feeding their kids bacon! Some kids used to gain something like ten pounds in the three weeks because they were so hungry at home.

In the children's camp I worked for quite a few years. I worked as a financial secretary in the city and as a counsellor, as the mother of the camp. And it was really wonderful. The whole week everything was fine—ten nationalities, eight nationalities—the children got along beautifully. On Sunday, when the parents came out—it was a little different already! Everyone had their little prejudices … but it was worthwhile. In fact, none of us got paid at all for doing the work. Later on, we used to get a dollar a week allowance. The cook didn't get paid and the manager of the camp did get paid. We used to call her "Mother." She is still around.

I got out of the trade. In fact they wanted me to do the work, and so my last boss used to bring me the work while I was in the house in bed. Never mind the house! I had to stay in bed for a couple of months because the child was late in the game and I was afraid to lose it. So I worked because from what my husband was getting in the services we would send some to his old father, and part of it to me, which was not enough to send parcels overseas all the time. So I still worked at home.

We used to help out when there were strikes in other trades. We would go and picket and sometimes get arrested. There was once a strike in the dress industry, in a building right next to us on St. Catherine Street, and we were asked to come and help. So they used to send the girls because the police would not do the things to girls that they would do to the men. And they were bringing in scabs. It was in a building where there was the elevators on a higher landing, with a couple of steps down in the front. There was a big foyer where they had a little restaurant there, and the police were watching the girls, the scabs, go in and we wouldn't let them go into the elevator. Then a fight started. The police—we were so many—they wanted to get rid of some of us. So they pulled us to the door and threw us out. Pulled us to the door! Pushed us out! The two that were left inside was my sister and another girl, and they were arrested.

Imagine, in those days, to ask for twenty-five-hundred dollars bail! Where would anybody have twenty-five-hundred dollars bail money? Some of the sympathizers would sort of sign off their property to take the two girls out. You see, there was no such thing as keeping them separate in the jail because they were strikers or political prisoners. They kept them with the prostitutes and drunks and everybody else. The food that they got there … when they came out their faces were all pimply. They were there for over a week.

I was arrested too, but I was never in jail. Do you know Misha Cohen from Toronto? He just left for the Soviet Union. He is leading the group. So, it was a demonstration for the unemployed and we were to protect the speaker [*Ena laughs*] and I was yelling on top of my voice, saying, Leave alone my brother! And I hung on to Misha. So every time he comes now to Montreal, he says, Hi, sister!

So I was arrested and a priest came up—it was in the paper, you know—and a priest came up and spoke to my boss and he spoke to the foreman, and he said that there is no reason why they should keep me at the shop, a troublemaker like me, and showed them that I was not even in the trade! So what business did I have to poke my nose and do things like that? But the boss didn't fire me. And when the trial came up, the lawyer told me, You keep quiet. I didn't know that much English, so he says, You keep quiet. I am going to say that you're only sixteen years. Well, the judge gave me a good talking to. He said, You came to Canada, you want to be a Canadian, you should be a good Canadian and not get involved. A kid like you should not get involved in things like that against Canada and against the government. And they dismissed the case because I was a youngster supposedly. I must have been twenty-two then!

My sister was a dressmaker—and this happened also in connection with this strike. One of the men went with two girls to the homes of scabs to speak to them that they shouldn't go to work because it was to their benefit too that they should have a union. And my sister was stabbed with scissors in the back by one of the scabs. They had to burn it out so she shouldn't get any infection!

Things like that happened. Police were always there, breaking up the strikes, breaking up demonstrations. Even when we went to choir practice, plainclothes policemen would stand and watch, they would stand downstairs and watch who is going in and they would sit in at rehearsals. Can you imagine how we felt to have the Red Squad sit at rehearsals and watch us?

You know that up until then I was the manager of the *Vochenblatt* and *Outlook* and a lot of people changed their names. First of all, the Red Squad used to come to homes and make a mess of things and take away books and take away belongings. And people couldn't get into the United States. So people used to change their names. They were known as So-and-so in the movement. Up until now, I still have people that have their old names in my little book with the names of the readers. We had built a beautiful centre in Montreal, a cultural centre. A lot of people donated money, big sums of money, and this centre was padlocked!

There was discrimination against the Jewish girls because they knew too much and they wanted better conditions. So the French Canadians who came from farms or from big families that they had, they couldn't go to school, so they went out to work. You can say they didn't discriminate against Jewish girls—whoever wanted to work, they could work. But if they have somebody cheaper, they tell the Jewish girl to go! Some bosses would not take Jewish girls at all.

We had a progressive man who was giving donations to the *Vochenblatt* (his second wife still gives a donation of one thousand dollars every year) and he had a box factory. I was like a friend of the family. They had no children and when I had nothing to do, no job, he took me up to his place and there I was the only Jewish girl because his staff was all French Canadian. They didn't know from nothing. They didn't know from unions. And this is a progressive man that came here in 1905. He ran away from Russia and he worked up—now it's a very big business. He retired and gave over the business to his nephew, and his wife I suppose will have a salary for life.

Now on the question of exploitation—they didn't discriminate. The bosses exploited everybody! They didn't come as bosses but, because they didn't have the background of being workers at home in the Old Country, each one tried to better himself: to get out of the shop and become a boss for himself, even if it was only with two people, three people. Then by exploiting the workers, they got bigger and bigger.

There were non-union shops until before the Second World War, but they were not like the shops now. Some shops today are air-conditioned! Then the shops were in old buildings.

After the children were born I did not go back into the trade at all. When the children were small, my husband was asked to give up his job and to go to work for the *Vochenblatt* magazine for a year. And I have now been working for the magazine for nineteen years and have not gone back into the trade.

Masha Goldkind

I met Masha Goldkind in Toronto in 1974 at the home of Lil and Albert Abramowitz. (Their stories appear earlier in the volume.) She was reluctant to speak to me; she felt there was nothing important in her life to relate. However, she kindly sat down and talked to me.

Masha, who was sometimes called Mashinka, meaning the youngest (which she was in her family), was born on 15 May 1907. She left Vilna, which was in Poland at the time, in 1924. She was fifteen when she tried emigrating for the first time. During her lifetime she married and survived three husbands. Her son, Bernie Zuker, a long-time dear friend of my own family, is sorely missed. Masha died on 22 August 2001, at the age of eighty-four.

I CAME HERE TO CANADA because I had my sister here, who was also in the same tailoring trade. And I had my brother too. I didn't know them, as I was little when they left. They all left. They wanted to get away from home. It took me a long time to get here. I went through the war, the First World War. I left the Old Country in 1924 from Vilna—it was in Poland at that time. I was left an orphan. There was another brother and he went to the States and he came here later on. And I came here to brothers and sisters and their families. When I came, I was a very young girl. I was only seventeen years old. I couldn't even go to school because I had to go out and make a living. But I went to night school because I had the ambition to learn.

My father was a tailor and my mother used to help him out because she had quite a few children—nine children. I remember—I remember so much! My mother had bought a big fish, must have been about twenty-five pounds It was a hake—you know what a hake is? Like a pike. It was so huge that it made me a little bit afraid! I remember that.

I started working here in Toronto—my brother took me into a place where he worked. I lived with my brother, upstairs in an attic—I don't know if you have it in Vancouver—where the ceiling is bent. Well, that was not important. Now I say it wasn't important, but when I first came, I had a hard time. I didn't look like a tailoress, and I was returned back to Poland. They told me I didn't look like a tailoress.

I got sick on the way back. I had typhus and was in the hospital in Poland for months. I didn't have where to stay. Then my brothers and sister here made out new papers for me and I returned again to Canada after one year. It took me two or three weeks to travel. I remember the boat. And I had experiences there on the boat. I wasn't a bad-looking girl and the doctor started up that I should stay with him. I had a translator at that time, I couldn't even speak—he spoke English ... and this and that—I shouldn't say anything! Well, I was a young girl here and until I struggled through, it was hard and it took me a very long time.

Then I landed in a shop. I was very, very unhappy to be in a shop and I couldn't tolerate that. I didn't have a very good education and it hurt me. I was very hurt by it. I was very unhappy. I was in men's clothes in a factory. I didn't know anything. We worked nine, ten hours. I learned a lot of things in the trade, to work by hand, by machine. I was okay—I was capable of doing it. I struggled through with it, without happiness. I went to night school as much as I could.

I met Karl and I got married. He was in the jewellery business at the time and he was making seventeen dollars a week. Then I was pregnant and I had my son, Bernie, and we were living in two rooms.

I was working and getting paid about ten dollars or twelve dollars—that's what they paid for us as finishers—and then I worked myself up to $22.50. That was big money. I didn't work for a few years because I had my son. And then I separated from my husband, which wasn't a pleasant thing for me. It was a hard time getting along without money but I had my family here: sisters, nieces, brothers. Sometimes I lived with a sister or with a brother. I had a very good sister-in-law. I would come into the house and she had a cake—she was a good baker. When I went to work I knew there was somebody to look after my son. And that's how it went.

I looked around for a job. The boss I worked for was very good to me—he treated me very nicely, he looked out for me. I used to take the same bus from the house to work and back again. Most of the time I had Jewish bosses. I can't remember having any other. Sometimes there was no work. You worked two hours, three hours. There wasn't such a thing as steady work. You worked a few hours, sewed this and this garment, and went back home.

That was the life: without any interest or any progress—what shall I say—of anything that pleased me. I hated it—the profession. I was very unhappy about it. I used to read and people were nice to me. And I struggled.

In the Old Country, when I was a young girl, I couldn't understand it at all—the question of politics. But I had a brother who was involved. I remember there was a big, big strike. He used to make the tops from shoes and it was some kind of a demonstration, and they were running after him—I think it was a May Day demonstration or something; and he was hiding. It was in Lithuania at the time—after the war [World War I] it was belonging to Poland. I remember him running away to somewhere where they used to have fights, boxing fights. I was a young girl then, I always remembered that happening.

We had a big strike here in Toronto—the Shiffer & Hillman strike. I lost my job at that time. People wanted a better living and better conditions and the union were not united and there were different opinions. I can't remember how many weeks—it was a long time ago.

If I had the choice I would have gone into another trade. But that was not possible at the time.

Mary Kevalko

✤

Mary Kevalko was in a seniors' home in Montreal when I talked to her. She was born in the Ukraine in 1899, and came to Canada as a young girl of thirteen. She didn't have much of a childhood, as she helped her mother run a grocery shop and tried to learn at night school. As with so many other Jewish immigrants, Mary ended up working in the needle trades.

I'M FROM THE UKRAINE—my name is Ukrainian: Kevalko. We came in 1912 right before the First World War—because in 1914 already the war started, and I don't know anything about it. What I know is from the papers. I was interested to know everything—but we came before the war and the revolution which was in 1917–18. When we came here to Montreal in 1912, I was thirteen years old. Where we lived, in the Old Country, I was very happy there. It was full of flowers and trees. It wasn't a big city—not on a farm but a small city. And because I wasn't so old I didn't suffer so much. But in 1911, my father died. I had brothers here, who went away four or five years before; and they wanted my mother and me, and my younger brother, to come here to Montreal.

I came first. Montreal at that time—it was a very small, a very funny city: no sidewalks, no electricity. In 1912 there was no electricity! We had gas lamps: little lamps with gas—don't know how to call it. But it didn't take very long, about a year or two, when they made sidewalks and we got electricity too. And while I was young, my mother came. We didn't know what to do. She brought a little money. No matter how much you brought you know it was half here. My brother said the best thing is to make a grocery [shop], make some business, because we had a business at home, in the Old Country.

When we came from the Ukraine we took a house, me and my mother and my younger brother, and I had an older sister from me, not married yet, and we stayed together. We took a grocery shop—we were helping. My sister was working. Then she got married. And after she got married, at that time, you know, young married women didn't work—no matter whether it was good or not—but they didn't work. It would have been much better, but they didn't work

So we made a grocery and my mother was green, a newcomer. She didn't know the language and I was too young. I helped her as much as I can. You come from Europe, you are thirteen years old, you are not a baby no more. Thirteen years is a big girl. So I helped her for a few years and then she got sick. It wasn't for her that kind of business. We had bigger business at home. She got sick and she couldn't do it any more and we gave it up.

I tried to do something, to work, you see. I helped her and at night I went to night school to take up a little English. So that means that I didn't have much education to work in an office or places like that. So I tried to go to a factory. My relatives' friends took me up. So I got four dollars a week. Four dollars a week at that time! None of our relatives or friends were tailors. They didn't know anything about that. But here you come to America— you call it Canada—you can do whatever you want to make a living.

And so I was a button sewer. You'll be surprised. Lots of people work in it. You have to know how to do it. It's not just you sew a button on. You have to know how ... well, in the summertime you work on big coats, winter coats. In the summer you work on the winter goods to prepare for winter. And in winter you work on the summer clothes. So I became a button sewer and I worked a few years. I work myself up. And before I came here, there were all kinds of people working here, at that time, in 1912.

People were working very long hours before I started to work. The men came even before the women, and even the women worked more than fifty hours a week. I mean, they were doing this kind of work, tailor work, and they weren't tailors. There were lots of people came from college and so on—they were looking for work. It wasn't so good. So they went to whatever they got. Some went to the CPR [Canadian Pacific Railway] or the CNR [Canadian National Railway] to look for work until they got the language. And then some of them went back to college. And they learned. But they had to eat. They didn't come rich. Very few people came rich from Russia.

So then I worked myself up and made twelve dollars, fifteen dollars. But there were lots of times when there was no work. You didn't get paid when you didn't work—slack, they called it. Slack! When I came I was working forty-nine hours a week—that was six days a week.

Then all of a sudden a strike came out. And people were striking for weeks and weeks and weeks. And we had a big manufacturer here in Montreal, Weinberger was the name. The building is still here. But the strike was so long that they broke Weinberger's business.

The workers went on strike because they wanted more money and less hours. So it took an awful lot of weeks, maybe sixteen weeks. Sixteen weeks was the strike and we took off one hour! I didn't work that time, just I am telling you what happened. I worked later. But they took off one hour! That means forty-eight hours. One year we didn't strike even a week and they took off four hours, you see. Times change. Times change. Oh, people were struggling terrible in the slack time of the business.

Then they were organized. People got organized. It was a different thing entirely. Now they work—I don't know how much they work now—forty hours in the tailors? In the rest of the industry I think they work less.

Anyways, the unions are very strong today and people that worked a long time—they are different people entirely. Now they have doctors there in the factories and they have insurance and when they work a certain time, they stop. They get pension. We have people here that get pension from the union. That doesn't mean that they get the whole cheque from the government when they get pension from the union. It is different.

Now the tailors are not what they used to be. Now they live very nice. They got for vacation, paid vacation, and you look at a tailor today—they aren't even tailors! They're not a *custom* tailor. A custom tailor makes a suit altogether. But in a factory you don't have to be a tailor—you learn only to make one thing. One is an operator, one is a cutter, one is a designer—naturally, you have to have a designer! But cutters and pressers, and ironers—you know, the ironing? This is not for custom tailoring. And everybody does something else—like me—I was working the buttons. You need buttons. But years ago you had to do it with your hand. Even now there are some things that you have to do with your hands. But now they have lots of machines that sew buttons; and before you put it on it falls off! I just helped an old man—two buttons I sewed on his clothes. And there are finishers, they finish here, they finish there. I was never a finisher. I know only one thing: button sewing. And I was a very fast button sewer. I was respected. I didn't suffer in the factory.

There was supposed to be a foreman in the factory, or the boss. There were lots of people who were not satisfied. The foreman used to say, Work harder!

Go quicker! But I was all right because, first of all, I was a very quick worker. Even now whatever I do—I'm working here, you know, an hour, an hour and a half, for therapy—but whatever I do I do it quick.

So sure, there were lots of trouble in the factories. There was a time before they were organized, before the unions got so strong and rich too— one for the mens' and one for the ladies' dresses, etc.—I worked in a union shop. I belonged. I paid my dues but I didn't work long enough because I took sick—my heart is not very strong—so I didn't work long.

Before the union was so strong, when you went down on strike, the boss didn't want to take you back, you know, and it was terrible. Like the French-Canadian people; it was very hard on them. They didn't want to strike. It's all right, they said. But the Jewish people were all the leaders, they were the union leaders and organizers and everything. It was so much trouble with the French people. Now there's very little Jewish people in the factories you know. The second generation, the third generation, they are all professionals, all college students. I don't say it is so good. There are plenty of college students who have nothing to do, but they are all educated. The father could have been a real tailor or shoemaker but he didn't want his son should be a shoemaker or a carpenter. Everybody send their children and grandchildren to school. And it's a different world now. In everything now most of the people are French and Italian in the Jewish tailors' places.

Maybe you know the German people came first—not what I saw but what I read—and I suppose you read maybe even more than me—the German people came rich here and more educated. In Germany they had good education. They did everything—they built the Shaar Hashomayim Shul— that was a German *shul* [*Gate of Heaven Synagogue, built in 1846*] and they made it beautiful and they helped a lot to build many things. In the States they built railways! You know that? The Jewish people built railways. But here in Montreal were mostly the Russian people. Russian people came, not very rich; they were poor. No matter how poor the first thing they made then was a synagogue and also here was a *folkshule*, a Peretz Shule —you know what I'm saying? Yeah? And all kinds of organizations. And no matter, with a few cents, a few dollars, they started that. They were poor immigrants, and believe me, if you know Montreal, and you see it today, you go, Hah! It's very nice.

The people that come now, they are different, they come rich, they don't call them greenhorns because they know so many languages. They were all over, what you call them?—refugees, refugees.[45] You don't call them immigrants. They suffered maybe more than we suffered but they also have money, they came with money. And even now some of them get money from Germany. I don't blame them. They saw so much sorrow and other things. They travel. Every month they go to Israel, they go to Italy, they go here and there. But for people years ago the biggest enjoyment was to go up the mountains; and every cent went for organizing another synagogue, another *shul*, you know. I think that was very nice of them.

I quit making buttons when I was in the hospital. I had worked in buttons for years, worked in mens' clothing. It was very bad times then. Came a certain time, it was very slack, you know, so I got a job at a shop—Laytons' Clothes, I think—also sewing buttons … after all, I had learned to do that. And I worked on this for seven years.

That's what I remember now. There are some who remember much more.

Max Povitz

I spoke to Max Povitz in 1974, in Montreal, when he was seventy-seven years old. He was born in a shtetl *called Dwinske, in Latvia, in 1897.*

Max has repeatedly said how bad things were in the Old Country when he lived there from 1897 to 1925.

I REMEMBER A LOT of things. When I was nine years old, my father gave me away for to be a tailor. It was a military tailor in the Old Country and this was in Latvia. At that time my father was not so rich. I had three brothers and one sister. They worked in a match factory. My father was a tailor. In winter he was a tailor and in summer he was a peddler. He bought chickens and sometimes apples, and this and that in the market, and this he would peddle. He made a poor living. My mother helped him a little bit but she passed away when I was very young. She was about fifty or fifty-one years old.

I was very young, just a schoolboy at the time, and I had to help my father. My brothers were working in the factory and so they decided I should be a worker, I should be a tailor. It was a big thing in the Old Country. So I was given for a tailor for three years. I worked for three years for forty rubles. It was a small factory, about four people, not like factories in America. In the Old Country we didn't have factories like that. I am now seventy-seven years old. I'm not a youngster. I am now retired seven years, but I want to say, so they decided to give me away for a tailor. So I had a very, very hard living, you know.

They give me away for a tailor to learn the trade. It was that time very bad. I helped my father a little bit—whatever I could help him—he was a tailor—in the winter—and if he maybe made a dollar a week, then it was a good week. It was very good.

So what could I do? I work in the shop and the boss—it was very bad at that time, very bad. The boss I work for didn't even give me a piece of bread.

They didn't want to. But they give me an old pair of shoes. I haven't got good shoes—with torn shoes I went to work.

Until I was ten, eleven, twelve, thirteen years I am working there, and I learned to make a pair of pants. A pair of pants to learn, it took three years. The boss didn't want I should learn at that time. The times was very bad. The boss's wife hollered at me as if I am a maid in that home. She had four children, four small girls. I have to look after them. I went with them in the park, and I had to do this and that. And they scream at me what I should do to learn. That was my life. And for forty rubles that they give me for three years. You see, the boss himself was a poor man. He was Jewish. He was in the army. It was a poor life.

Anyway, I was ten or eleven when my mother passed away. My two brothers went away to America, to New York. One brother, the older one, was still in the Old Country, and also my sister. So I am left with my father, my brother, and my sister. My brothers decided when they come to America they will be better off. But they were poor at that time, in 1906. Maybe they make a few dollars more. And they send home five dollars, ten dollars. So father was better off. We paid, at the time, a ruble a month for rent.

Can you imagine what kind of life there it was at that time? I remember just like now! I work for the three years and I don't think he give me all the forty rubles even. I went away from that boss and I went to another because I wanted to learn the trade and how to make a pair of pants. I was thirteen or fourteen years old. My father went and found another woman. He took another woman and she was at the time about nineteen or twenty years old. She didn't like that we only had two rooms and six people: a kitchen and a room, that's all we had. She didn't like it. What can we do when we live like that? We had a poor life there.

When I was young I was here and there; not just a sleeping boy. I was always happy. What did I do? I learned a little more at another tailor, a little more of the trade, and I start to make a few dollars more. When I was fourteen, fifteen, sixteen years old, I was helping my father a little. He was a very, very honest man, very honest. *Frum*—you know what this means? He was religious. When he went to the market, before he bought anything, he would ask the farmer or the woman: how much it cost you? And he would always say, I give you so much—maybe it is a half a ruble—and he would give it away—the whole thing sometimes, so the other one should make a living too. Such an honest person.

But what I want to say is that I lived like that. I was fourteen or fifteen at the time. I would make maybe four dollars a week. Four dollars a week!

I learned to make a vest. When I was seventeen years old I learned how to make a suit, a whole suit. All of a sudden, it's coming (I'm seventy-seven years old now), and I remember it's 1914 and it's coming over, the war, the First World War. And the Jews, we must have been forty miles from the war, from the Front. All the Jews in our *shtetl* from Dvinske, in Latvia, were sent out. The Germans had bombed Nikoleiyev where the Jews were staying. The Germans didn't kill us. They put us on empty trains and said to go where you want to. So they sent us away to Siberia, to Yekaterinburg. I was about seventeen or eighteen years and I remember it was Yom Kippur. I had left already. I was without my family. All of a sudden I saw my father and my brother and my sister and brother-in-law—everybody, you see, was on the trains— and I see them in the middle of nowhere! So I go with them to Siberia.

I was in Siberia for seven years. I was married there and I was a tailor. I know how to work there as there were no tailors in Siberia, no Jewish tailors altogether. And I had a job.

My wife, she had a father here in Montreal, and they sent us the papers and visas to come here. It was 1925 when we come here. I had a child. We had eight children, but six died and I had only two left, just two boys. It was very, very cold there in Yekaterinburg.

So I came to Montreal and my life here was very good. We lived with my wife's parents. My father-in-law was a shoemaker. He didn't make much. He didn't make much. He made five dollars a week. It was enough for him. In the Old Country a shoemaker make a little store and he make a living. He worked at Clarks. He made their shoes. It was a second cousin of his and for years and years he work for five dollars a week. When I came over and I said to him, *Shver*, what are you doing? You work for five dollars a week? He was a poor man with a long, white beard; a religious fellow and he went to synagogue. Friday twelve o'clock and Saturday and Sunday the store is closed and that's what it is in the old days. He went to synagogue in the afternoons, and that is the life. Go make a living!

I was a good tailor here and I went right to the union and the union give me a job. When I came in 1925 they gave me five dollars a week. I was screaming, I want to go back home! So my family said stay. Stay. Maybe you know the Smollas family?—they are grocers—they talk to me and tell me to stay here. I found another factory in ladies clothing and they give me seventeen dollars. I was the head operator. Myself, I am a tailor, but I know the operating business too, so I made a few dollars. I also worked for S. Ruben.

Then was born to me another child. I start to make a little more money working with S. Ruben and then I am getting thirty dollars a week. That time there was a strike again. We were striking because there was two unions: the Canadian Union and the Amalgamated Clothing Union, a US labour union. And they took us up on strike, 105 people, and we all lost our jobs. One side wanted the Amalgamated and the others wanted the Canadian to take over the union. It was fights in the street. I don't think that you remember that! It was fighting on St. Lawrence. There were fights every day. Oh, it was fights, plain fights, with sticks, knives ... you see they wanted to take over the union, the Canadian union. It was Hart, Morris Hart—he was the manager and he wanted the Canadian Clothing Union to take over the Amalgamated which was American. It was a good thing but the Amalgamated had thousands of people and they were millionaires. They were not poor. They could take over. It would have been better to have a Canadian union, but they had no money to hold on to. It was not a union just in Toronto or in Hamilton. It was for all over Canada. It was hard to have to make a union. So they took over, the Amalgamated got back. We lost the jobs of 105 people. They fired everybody. I had two boys at that time. You know if there's a strike, somebody takes over your job. They are scabs sure. But what can you do? You fight and they take your jobs away. I had a few dollars. I eat them up.

It was ... it was in 1929, 1930, during the Depression. It was very, very hard. With two children what should I do? So I took ... I got a press machine in my home—I live on the east side where I have lived for twenty-five years— so I bought a press machine and I try to make custom work. Not in a factory but at home. I am a tailor myself, so I make a little living. Meantime, it was very hard to make a living. I had the children, they were small but they couldn't go to higher schools. They finished high school but they couldn't go to college because I had no money to send them at that time. And, *danke Gott* the boys are okay. My wife didn't work. My wife was pregnant, and then there was this and that—and the children passing away ...

Anyway, by the Second World War I had this job, a good job as head operator at Shiffer & Hillman, and that is the best job in the factory. I made a little money at that time. I bought a house in Park Extension in 1951. I had a brother-in-law, a carpenter—he built me the house. It was very cheap at the time. It cost sixteen thousand dollars, it's a duplex, and I rented the upstairs. I was so happy. I work at night, trying to pay the mortgage, but I didn't pay it off. We had a garden in the back, a little garden with a pond, and this and that. The children were growing: eighteen, nineteen, twenty years old.

When I first came over I worked nine hours a day, not more. Later we worked eight hours. At that time, I want to say, there was no unemployment insurance. They don't give unemployment insurance, they give relief. You know how much they give? For a family, five dollars a week. That's what you call welfare. It was no money to pay—to pay the taxes, the water taxes (you have to pay twelve to fourteen dollars for the year) and I have no twelve dollars to pay. No money for coal. Coal was twelve dollars a ton. Rent was very hard. We live very humble until the Second World War. After the war it was for the workers a little better. Not much, but a little better in the shop.

I am a union man and I am involved in the union. I get one hundred dollars a month now from the union. I was not an officer in the union. I don't know how to write in English. I had no chance to learn. I was nine years old when I have to go to work. That, by me, is the worst thing in the world! If I would know how to write, I would be rich. I would be in Poland. I would be a boss because I know the trade 100 percent. I know how to make the best garment in the world, the best custom work. I'm a tailor, the best tailor, but if I would know how to get on with customers—to write and read—that is the main thing. But I was nine years old when my father gave me away for a tailor—they gave me away for three years like a slave.

I was never involved with the Communist Party or with politics. I don't like them. I was in Siberia and there I didn't like that. I worked for them. I worked in good faith. I didn't go into the army because I was a tailor. I worked for the army there. I made the coats and the uniforms.

That was my luck at that time, you know. That was my luck! But *danke Gott,* I was a little smarter than my father-in-law and I tried to make a living, to make a few dollars and pay off my house. All of a sudden my wife passed away! She was sixty-seven years old when she passed away. Very bad for me. And what shall I do with my two boys? *Danke Gott* I am making a nice living. And when my wife passed away the children told me, Pa, come to us and sell the house right away. (If I wouldn't sell it, I would be better!) So I came to them and it was no good. It was very good, very good—but I am alone. What should I do all alone? So what I do? I married again. I find a woman and I married again and she's not so good for me. I was six years married with her but it was not so good. Not so good. No. No. No.

I spent a few dollars and I came back to my sons. They like me. They hug me—like a daughter, like a father. They don't know what to do with me. Now I go every year to Florida for six months and this I am doing for six, seven years.

And that is my life.

Art Browner

Art Browner was born in a little town not far from Lodz, Poland. By the end of the nineteenth century, Lodz was the leading centre in Poland for the production of cotton textiles as well as wool, silk, jute, hemp, leather goods, and the manufacturing of clothing and other materials.

Art immigrated to Canada in 1923 and spent his life working as a pocketmaker in the needle trades. I interviewed Art Browner in Toronto in the summer of 1974.

I WAS BORN IN POLAND in 1900 ... I'll be seventy-four in a few days, on 10 July! I left the Old Country and came here because I had relatives here. I was already working in the Old Country. I started to work when I was eleven years old. I came from a little town where I learned the trade, the tailoring trade.

I was born in a little town but worked in Lodz, and soon the war started, the First World War, and I went back to the little town because they expected that the war would be worse in the big city. But in the little town I couldn't find anything interesting. So I went back and worked in Lodz for a while.

In Lodz everybody was interested in politics. So naturally I was also. In the beginning I was a Poale Zionist. Then I became a Left Poale Zionist, because they were more progressive. I think it was in 1922 or 1923 that I went out on a May Day demonstration. On a May Day demonstration different parties went out on demonstration, and I was with the Left Poale Zionists. The police concentrated on the Jews, and they organized, I would say, a pogrom.

When we went to the demonstration, they cut off a whole group of about six hundred people—even the communists went through. I mean it was something! That's why I am telling you this. And they hit us and they came out from all the houses, the people, Gentiles, with sticks and bars and everything, and they hit us. I was nearly killed by a policeman. He gave me a knock on my head with the other side of the gun. I couldn't move my hands. If it was not for another policeman, a mounted policeman, who came over to tell him to stop, maybe he would have killed me. So this one saved me. Then they took us to a place where they washed us—we were bleeding.

I was overnight in the police jail and then my father took me out. When I came home I was two weeks in bed because I was beaten up black from the bars they hit on my head. I had about eight bumps. I took out the bumps, I had them removed, when I came here to Canada—here was one, and a few more here. This is what happened there in Lodz.

Somehow my uncle found out over here in Canada—it was written, this demonstration, in the Jewish paper—so he tried to bring me over. My uncle was living here in Toronto and he brought me over. I was a tailor then. This was in 1923. As a Left Poale Zionist I went over to one of their meetings after I came over here. I didn't like them! They looked to me like any other Zionist organization. So I left them after a few meetings. I got connected to the real left-wing movement and then I had to find work. So I started. I was in men's clothing and I lived with my uncle at the time.

Before I left Poland I had a girlfriend, you know. We got married about a few months, about six months I think, before I left and I came here by myself. I liked my wife, and like every young person I wanted to bring her over. I had in mind to save enough money to do this. I looked to get a job. I was acquainted with a couple of people here and so I got a job. I went to work in a shop for twelve dollars a week. It was already a good beginning and I worked myself up. I got another job—this was as an operator of a machine. And then I got a job working by hand, finishing cloaks, and was making nineteen dollars. That was a good wage but I didn't like working by hand. I like the machine because I knew that a machine operator was better than a hand operator. I tried to look for another job and I got one in a cleaning and pressing store. I did both things: cleaning and pressing. But it so happened that the shop closed up. I went to the union. They put me on a list. I remained without a job. Then the union called me up and I got a job making twenty-two dollars the first week. This was a steady job. I worked myself up to thirty-two dollars a week. At that time it was still time work. You got paid for how long you worked. It was not piecework, where you get paid for how many pieces you finish.

Then it was that I joined the union and found out what was going on. There was already fighting between the left-wingers and right-wingers and I naturally leaned to the left. We started to work together to organize ourselves. We organized ourselves for better working conditions, you see—and not just for the sake of left-wingers.

In the meantime I saved up money and I went to an agency. They gave me a ticket for to bring over my wife—there was already a baby—and in eleven months she was here, my wife and baby!

I was living with my uncle. He gave me a big room, like this maybe [*he waves his arm around*]. We lived there in one room. The kitchen and the bedroom was in the same room—everything was in one big room, and the baby was there also. We lived there for a while, and after we saved up something we moved into a rented flat with two rooms only.

Back to the trade union. We organized for better conditions and also to change the system from time work to piecework. We, the left-wingers, were against this because we knew that the piecework people will lose: they have to work harder to make more—like a speed-up system. So we were fighting and it was a big fight in the union. People lost their jobs. I was expelled from the shop and lost my job. It took a while but they start to oppress or suppress the left-wingers. It was a bitter fight and they decided to expel, to throw people out of jobs, and I was one of the first to be expelled from the shop and I lost the job with the union. I lost the job there! This was 1930. Then came the Depression time, and you couldn't get a job without the union. You couldn't get a job because there was no trade, there were no open shops. The union was organized. So for a few years it was very much suffering.

You want to know what is an open shop? An open shop doesn't belong to the union. The union doesn't control it. Sometimes there are small open shops, but in a union market and during the Depression you couldn't get any jobs. I managed to get some time. But for a few years I couldn't get anything. So my wife had to go to work.

She used to work by shirts at home in the Old Country, so she went and got a job in a shirt shop. She worked a few years there. This was in the 1930s. I was expelled from the union because I tried to distribute a newspaper, *Der Kampf* [The Struggle] in a shop. They knew that I'm a left-winger. I tried and I did sell a paper in the shop. The union executive told me that if I want back the job I should sign a paper. We used to call that a Yellow Dog Agreement. It was called that because it meant you sell out yourself. If I sign the paper then they will give me back the job. So I told them that this was out of the question. I have nothing to sign. I still believe in it. I didn't sign.

At the same time the union went to my wife and they told her that I am not a man interested in his family because, they said, one would think that I would sign a little signature and then get back my job and she would be all right.

My wife was pregnant with our younger kid. She went to the hospital to have the baby and I didn't have a job. We didn't have anything to live on. I used to go to beg for something from the Jewish Federation to give me some relief. I used to get something. It's not important about how I got it. I got some relief but not enough, naturally.

So my wife told them when they came to her, that she leaves it to me, that if I think it's not good to sign this paper then it is good for her too. This was that!

A few years later, around 1933–34, I got a job in a small shop, a non-union shop. Then there was a movement in the union to organize all the small shops. This was 1935. In my shop we talked it over and all the people in the shop agreed with me to go to the union. So the union organized us and I was still not a member of the union yet. But when we called a shop meeting to elect a shop chairman, I was elected. The union office objected to this and said I can't be chairman. They had nothing against me but that I'm suspended, so I haven't got a right to be a shop chairman. The union insisted and they appointed a shop chairman. Appointed! An old man, a plain—not a left-winger—old man. He didn't want to accept it, so they were forced to take me in as the shop chairman. Then, as the shop chairman, I had a right to go to the executive meetings of that local, Local 211 of the Amalgamated Clothing Union. Naturally I did everything to find out what is going on in the rest of the movement.

We became organized, we were a big group in the union, and for a time we elected a left-wing executive in that local.

Where I was working was a Jewish shop. The boss always liked better to get in Gentiles. He took in Jewish workers because they were … well, he couldn't get anybody else sometimes to do the work!

It happened so in a shop where I was working—I don't know how or the reason—but they took in a woman; she was a fascist. So the workers told me about this, as I was the shop chairman there. I went over to the boss and I told him that this woman is a fascist and that he should not keep her in the shop. He knew me and my political stand, but he liked my work and we became friendly—the boss and the shop chairman! You should know, I didn't get my job because of that!

Anyway, to get back to the woman. The boss said, I need a person to make buttonholes by hand. (Today this is made by machine but then we made them all by hand. It was a good line of work. The boss got paid good money for it, for the suits and for the garments.) So he said to me, Find me anybody else and I'll send her away. I said to him, You phone the union and ask them. But they didn't have anybody. Anyway, I spoke to the boss' wife, telling her what sort of woman this was, what she did when the war was on, how she was always happy when she heard that the Nazis are gaining and when it happened the other way around, she got upset. But the boss said, Can't help it. Got to live with it.

Now it so happened that this woman was brought in by a Jewish person who was in love with her and he wanted her to work there. He was the foreman. One morning he called to me in the restaurant where I was having my breakfast on Yonge Street. He knew that I go there in the morning. So I come in. He said, Browner, what have you got against this woman? She is a fine woman. I know her for a long time. So I told him, Mr. Cohen—that was his name—to you, maybe she is a fine woman. If you would know what we went through, that I lost all my family—my father, my sisters, and my brothers, and all the families killed by the Nazis—and when you know who she is, that she is happy at the time when this happened, then you can't blame me. He said, But she is this and this and this.

Anyhow, I didn't agree with him. He even called in the manager of the union. The foreman worked with the union offices hand in hand. I decided that I'm going to take a big gamble. I went over to the boss and told him, Mr. Keylis (he died, he's dead already, and the other guy, the foreman, is also dead), I told him, Mr. Keylis, I can't help it. I tell you that this woman makes me nervous when she is in the shop because you know what I lost. I told him the whole story about my family. If you think you've got to have her then I'm sorry, I have to leave the job. That's what I told him. Aw, you wouldn't do it, he said. I'm telling you what I think, I said.

So he was forced to send her on. And the other guy, the foreman, was so mad that he nearly killed himself! This was during the Second World War. For the First World War I wasn't here. I came in 1923.

It was at this time, during the war, when we stopped making civilian work. Everybody—all the places—went over to uniforms shops and military work. So a lot of things happened. It happened that everybody came in, from the cloakmakers and others, and came into the trades of the mens' clothing to make uniforms. Military work. You see, things like this happen when you work piecework. You make more. You get more. You get paid for how much work you are doing. I was so experienced and I was working in a place where there were different kinds of people. The foreman was a Jewish fellow and he liked to drink. He had a lot of people around him that he used to like to drink with—in the shop, outside, anywhere. So they were all good friends.

But I made my job in a certain way and that took me faster. I knew a few tricks—like I didn't change the foot on the machine by doing certain this and that. Others had to change, and my work came out straight. The workers complained to the foreman because they couldn't make as much as I did, and the foreman came over and said, Browner, why can't you do like everybody else? Why do you make an exception? The other worker was also a pocketmaker, so I told the foreman, Take this or any coat, is it straight or not? He said yes. So what's the difference what I do? I can make it under the table even! I still give you the job. He could do nothing.

During the war we also made summer suits for the soldiers. So we changed from civilian clothing work to uniforms. These suits had patches on them and, since I was experienced in men's clothing, I could work on these patches fast. I got paid better than the others as I worked faster and it was piecework. But it was the same thing. People kept complaining how I stitch the patch. I start here, go all around and finish. That's all. Others had to stop and straighten it out and spend more time. They even complained to the foreman—the brother of that other guy who was friendly with that woman. I told the foreman to look at it. The government examines everything, you know. They examine every stitch. Did you get anything back? I ask. No? So why are you bothering me? The others are killing me, Mr. Cohen.

Finally they saw that I was making notes for one of the union leaders so they decided to get together to rearrange the prices. Instead of staying at the same price, they cut my wage down. I used to get about ten or eleven cents for a patch, so they cut it down to six or seven cents on account of the other people. This happened, and this was initiated by the union, and there was nothing I could do, naturally. The people around, they were glad. Sure. The union is always ready to cut prices—I mean the boss complains that it costs him too much. They didn't call it cutting price. They called it rearranging the cost and straightening out the cost of everything. And so that is how they managed. They always did this.

I had this also in another shop. It was called British Brands. They are still there on Spadina Avenue. I was working there and the same thing happened. I worked by myself. I didn't care what the others did because there will always be people—I wouldn't say crooks—but they were less than honest. They would always sell out to the boss. They always worked with the foreman or the boss, and got favours. But I didn't do this kind of things. So they gave me some material to make up coat pockets and it was a different kind of material. And they tried to divide it equally but they did not divide it right. So they gave me to make the coat pockets. It was a different kind of cloth, soft, and it was hard to do it. So, I said, I didn't want to make it. And I didn't make it. They went over to the boss (I knew him from years before he worked here), and they told him the story that I don't want to make it, and it's a rush coat, and this, and this. So the boss comes over to me and says, Browner, you're making always trouble. Yeah, I says, what kind of trouble? It's a rush coat, he says, and you don't want to make it. So I told him, You think I make trouble when I told you that I made a coat like this before and they just put it off against me? You think I …? He said, You know what I am going to do? I'm going to phone the union and tell them that they should change you and put you in another shop!

So I stood up and said, Listen, you don't have to change. I'm not changing—a horse changes! I can go out right now without changing. And I stood up and I was ready to go. So he says, No, no, no. Don't go. Sit. Sit here. He didn't want me to leave because he was short of people.

The workers were exploited by the bosses. The bosses do this because they are bosses. A boss is a boss, like they say. It doesn't matter if he is Jewish or not. His interests are more important to him than all the Jews all around. He doesn't care about this. Never. And this I got experience a lot of times. You see, they are not interested in the workers. They are interested to make money, sure, and always. That shop where I was shop chairman? It was maybe 75-percent non-Jewish people, because they couldn't get other people at the time as it was right after the war. It was prosperity. They had to take in anybody.

I was out on strikes. Not big strikes at the time. Just small ones. My shop was out. Sometimes individual shops went out; or if the unions are organized for one reason or the other, they called out strikes. We got some strike pay from the union. I don't know if you know about it but there was in New York a few weeks ago a strike, a general strike, and this was the first one in fifty-three years. They didn't call a strike. Nobody believed that Amalgated Clothing will pull a strike! But it happened. There was no strike here—just some small shops but they were nothing.

Many of the Jews went into the needle trades because they found Jewish people there, to communicate with each other. Yes, this was one of the main reasons I think. Also at that time, some of the shops were closed on Shabbes and open on Sundays. And some workers—religious people—liked that at the time, but later on—the people didn't care about working on Shabbes.

These are the little things that happened to me as a worker in the trades. I can tell you dozens, but they are not such important things really.

Bertha Dolgoy Guberman

❦

Bertha Dolgoy Guberman was a staunch union worker, a feminist before her time, a fighter for human rights, a wife, mother, and a member of a large family. She was born in 1908 in Dagda, a shtetl in Russia, emigrated to Winnipeg in 1922, where she received a short education, and then went out to work.

Some years later, Bertha moved to Toronto, where I had the pleasure of interviewing her at her apartment over afternoon tea. Later, she settled in Edmonton, where her daughter and family lived. She died there in 2004, at the age of ninety-six.

Bertha is the sister of Nina Dolgoy Ullman and Max Dolgoy, whose stories appear in this volume.

MY MOTHER MADE ME a new winter coat and before I left my *shtetl*, my village, in Russia to come here, my mother said to me, Leave your coat for your cousin here. You are going to "America"—ho! The sky is the limit! So I left my coat behind. I arrived in Winnipeg in August 1922. The whole winter I went in a little spring coat that was a hand-me-down because we couldn't afford to buy a coat for me.

I can remember when the First World War started—that was in 1914— and you know when you live in a small town the Jewish children didn't have any education; they didn't take in Jewish children in the public schools. We had to have private tuition. You live in a village here and you are cut off from the rest of the world and you don't know anybody in the immediate vicinity. But when the war broke out and you started to listen: cities here, cities there … and to me it was … I couldn't visualize this because this little *shtetl* was my world!

As far as education was concerned, my mother used to sit nights and pluck feathers—you know, for the teacher, for cushions—so that she should give me private lessons; that I should be able at least to write an address, because my father, my two brothers, and my sister were in Canada and we three were left at home. We had to go to the pharmacist so that he should address an envelope for us to send to Canada. And the main dream was that the children should at least be able to read and write—well in Jewish too. It had to be all private tuition. They only took in 4 percent of Jewish children in high school and you had to prepare them for high school by private education.

So the few, the rich people in the town—there was always poor and rich—so they had the learning already. They would go to the gymnasium in another city and they were exceptionally good—the ones they did take into high school had to be top notch—and top notch financially and bright. They would come back to the town and be the private teachers for the other children.

The population in our town was predominantly Jewish, but they took in the children from the countryside into the elementary school. I lived in Dagda. It's in Latvia. Until I came to Canada my education was practically nil, but the desire was so strong that when we came to Canada in [August] 1922, I started school in September in Winnipeg, in King Edward School, I was fourteen. In one year I made six grades, not even knowing the language! My teacher used to be amazed. I would sit over the dictionary and try to be able to figure things out, and when she would ask for a definition of a word for the Canadian-born, they wouldn't know and I was too shy to pick up my hand. If they don't know, so my answer must be wrong! But finally, when I did pick up my hand, and I remember one word stuck into me, and she said, What is "din"? You know, when you are reading a poem: the din of the city? And she said, what does din mean? And I said, Noise. She couldn't get over it: that I knew and the other children didn't know.

You see, because the desire for education in Europe, particularly amongst the Jewish people who were discriminated against and oppressed, was so strong that the main thing was to get an education, to be able to read and write.

Economically, we were down and out because my father was here in Canada and my mother had to raise us and provide for us. My sister Nina (the one in Vancouver) started to work when she was nine years old, and she worked for ten rubles the whole year to learn how to be a dressmaker. And my brother Max started in a place where you make—I don't know how you call it in English—the tops of shoes, when he was ten years old. And my other brother who was with us in Europe, he started to work in a bakery, working nights when he was ten years old. We always used to tell this joke about him. He was kneading the dough when he was asleep and whenever he felt a lump he threw it on the floor. So in the morning they found all the raisins on the floor! So they discharged him on account of it. Can you imagine? He was ten years old! Because he didn't know that there were raisins in the dough.

So under such circumstances my generation, who came to Canada, feel that it's a sacrilege, and cannot understand it, when you hear now about people dropping out of schools. We were dying to go to school and we couldn't and here you have all the possibilities and you don't want to go to school.

Now you can understand why when I came here I was dying to go to school. Education was very important to me. I passed from Grade 6 to 7 with first-class honours, but when I started Grade 7 in September I had to quit and look for work.

When I came to a cloak shop and I was asked how old I was, I said eighteen. You don't even look sixteen, I was told. Can you sew? Are you experienced? That word, "experienced," didn't ring a bell with me. They said, We only need experienced help. I said, oh, I can sew (because I used to help my mother sew on the hand-machine since I was eight years old). So they took me on and I started to work in that cloak shop for eight dollars a week, and that was considered a terrific wage at that time because I know when my husband started work in Montreal, he was getting only three dollars a week.

The first day I started I had to work overtime. Now my mother didn't even know that I had started working. So I begged the foreman to let me go home. He said okay. Today you are forgiven. And what kind of work did I have to do that first day? I was sitting with a big stick turning over belts—heavy belts from Ulster coats (nobody wears them today)—and my shoulders were aching from sitting and doing that work. You have a belt, it is sewn along the seam, you leave a little space open at one end, and you push the stick in from the other end and pull it out, and the seam remains inside.

I immediately registered for night school, paid in my two dollars, and I was supposed to go Mondays and Thursdays. So it happened Mondays and Thursdays I had to work overtime. And the foreman said, Either it's your job or your school. Do what you want. I don't have to tell you that it was the job not the school. I cried my eyes out. I lay at night and I'd ... you know the desire was so great and whatever I've learned I've learned it through the hard way, as they say, through the university of hard knocks. I read a lot and went to every available lecture that was possible and then, since 1928, I was active in the union, helping to organize, and for a short time I was helping in the office of the union.

I didn't stay long making belts because I did know how to sew and I was quickly promoted from one section to another. I worked in that shop—I started in September and December was slack, and I didn't know there was such a thing. So I was out of work until the beginning of February. There was no work! And there was no unemployment insurance.

When I started work again I went to another shop. I asked for a raise and they wouldn't give it to me. So I went to another shop and they gave me nine dollars a week and I was by then a fully qualified finisher. People who were working there for years got more than I did, but being a teenager they wouldn't give me a raise. I worked in that shop for a year.

A girlfriend of mine, who lives in Montreal now, told me about T. Eaton's—who had a cloak shop at the time, and children's wear also—so we went to Eaton's to apply. She was tall and more stately, and I looked puny. The manager says, This girl I'm going to take but (to me he says), her I don't want to. So my friend says, If you don't take her, you can't have me. Either we go together or we don't go at all. He looked at us. He thought we were nuts. Then he says to me, If I would take you and I wouldn't take her, what would you say? So I said, I would say the same thing. We are together. So he employed both of us and we got twelve dollars a week, and I worked at Eaton's for three and a half years. I was raised already to fourteen dollars and at that time it was a fabulous wage.

But I was fired just like that! We had a strike and I didn't take notice of the precautions. I went around collecting money for the strike and they spotted me. That's all they needed at Eaton's. At the time I worked on special machines and, after I left, they had to employ three people to replace me on account of that.

And then it was tough. It was tough going from one shop to another and then it came into the Depression years already, which was very tough, you know, as far as work is concerned.

You want to know about a typical working day? A typical working day started at eight o'clock and finished at 5:30. You want to know what we had for breakfast? We couldn't afford oranges, I can assure you. I used to have a cup of tea and a slice of toast; and for lunch we took along sandwiches. And you come home you had a supper of whatever mother prepared. It isn't like nowadays, as soon as you are old enough you move out to your own apartment. I lived with my parents and my brother. My brother was already married. So we lived. We kept on moving from one place to another. Living conditions were very hard: wherever you moved there were bugs and cockroaches, or what have you. And no bath. Once a week I used to go with my mother to a steam bath—every Thursday—you know, to the *svitz.* Then my brother moved into a house with a bath so I used to go and bathe there. But, as far as sanitary conditions is concerned, it was everywhere then in Winnipeg, the same conditions in the old houses: no bathing facilities, just a washroom, a toilet. We have three rooms and we were four people.

In 1932 I went to the Soviet Union to learn about trade union work and my parents moved into one room because they couldn't afford anything else. When Nina, my sister, came to Winnipeg with her husband and girls, we had a cottage with four rooms and so they stayed with us for a year until they moved out on their own. Nina's daughters were born in the Old Country and they spoke a beautiful Russian. Now they don't remember a word of it.

A day at work was "speed up," but not as bad as it is now. Now it's piecework, and one chases the other (the pieces you are working on are fed into the machine without a break). At that time it was time work, but you had to produce. You couldn't talk to your fellow workers who are sitting right beside you. If the foreman would spot you talking you would hear a real tongue-lashing for it: You are here to work not to talk! And there were no coffee breaks. You worked from eight to twelve, then you would have an hour for lunch, and most of the people brought their lunch and you sat there with the dust and dirt and everything—you know, like here is the work table, you push away the things into a corner and you sit and eat there. Then we would work from one o'clock to 5:30. And on Saturdays we worked till one o'clock. It was a forty-eight-hour week at that time. And then gradually, gradually, it was reduced, but not peacefully. It was reduced through struggle. Nothing came easy.

I got involved in union work through my brother, who belonged to progressive organizations. My brother Max and his wife belonged already and also my older brother who is now in Winnipeg—they all wanted that I should *oisgreene,* become—how would you say it in English?—become Canadianized. So they took me all over. I joined youth clubs, and then we had the International Ladies Garment Workers Union, which was a dead duck at the time because they had a general strike in 1923 and the strike was lost and the union went *kaput.* My brother was secretary of that local. After the strike everything broke down, and the head office didn't bother, and we didn't pay them.

So we started in 1928 to build the Industrial Union of Needle Trades Workers and that was mostly under progressive leadership—Communist leadership, if I may say so. So we built. J.B. Salzberg was appointed the national organizer and he went to Montreal to start the office there, and he came to Winnipeg to help us start. And we started. We took in not only cloakmakers but all the needle trades workers: garment workers who worked on overalls (Winnipeg had no tailoring shops), and furriers. These were all separate locals but one union. And J.B. stayed for quite a few months in Winnipeg—he lived with my brother—and helped us organize.

The union dues at the time was ten cents a week and the people did not have the ten cents a week to pay for it. And there wasn't such a thing as a check-off system that you have now, where the employer takes off the dues before you see your paycheque. At that time, you had to go with the list and stand near the shop and whoever felt like giving you the ten cents, it was given. You had shop stewards. It was all underhand because if the boss discovered we were organizing a union in the shop and if somebody undertook to be active, their jobs were in jeopardy. It had to be done quietly. So until we had some strikes, the conditions didn't change. (The furriers had strikes in 1926, a general strike where Joe Gershman[46] and others, anybody who was active, was discriminated against at the time and he had to leave the city because they were blacklisted.) It took years. We went on and we built quite a union. And then we had a strike in 1934 from the cloakmakers. And the strike was lost due to lack of finances because there was no strike benefit and how long can people carry on? And the employers knew that. They knew that once they would starve us out, then we would go back to work.

The result was that at the end of 1935—and this was after the CIO-AFL [Congress of Industrial Organizations and the American Federation of Labour] was organized—the CIO and the ILGWU [International Ladies Garment Workers Union] sent in a business agent to Winnipeg to organize the trade but only the cloak trade. So a fellow by the name of Sam Herbst came, a real ignoramus, you know: no reading, no writing—did you ever hear of him? [*I knew of him because I had worked in the head office of Sweet 16, a clothing factory in Vancouver in the mid-1950s.*] And then it was a question … we could have chased him out of town, we could have! … but it was a question of organizing and they, the AFL-CIO, had the funds to do it. So we had a united front. Herbst had nobody. The employers had a lesson with the strike and they knew that with the ILGWU they could manoeuvre better than with a communist-led union. So the first thing Herbst did was to go to all the employers and he sold them a bill of goods that he will deal with them—no strikes, no whatever—so long as they sign an agreement. We got organized and we won minor benefits—they had to give some increases, you know—and so we worked together.

My husband was from the Industrial Union and he came to Winnipeg from Montreal in 1933 and took over the leadership of the Industrial Union. The fellow holding that job before him was starving because all the organizers of the Industrial Union workers didn't get paid. When I left the shop, I was getting fourteen dollars a week; and a year working in the union office, on an average, I got $4.20 a week, because the union had no money. It was voluntary work! Sacrificing work! So I know when my husband became the organizer of the United Garment Workers Union and he started to get twenty-five dollars a week, we thought it was a fortune. And that was in 1938, 1939, 1940, the years that we were crawling out of the Depression.

I met my husband—Louis Guberman was his name—in 1926, when he was in Winnipeg working for a season. And when he came in 1933, we started going out together. In 1934 we got married. I had already gone to the Soviet Union. At that time it was a very hard year. It was one of the worst years economically. That was the time I met Sarah and Sidney Sarkin in Moscow. [*Sidney's story appears earlier in this volume.*] The purpose was that I should go and get a trade union education there. I was there for four and a half months, and I saw that they had no time to devote. I mean I got some education, but it wasn't really what I expected. Conditions were so bad—I didn't leave on account of the bad conditions—but I felt that it was not serving the purpose for which I went there. We were supposed to learn about practical trade union work and we did not because their system is entirely different than ours. So I went in May and came back at the end of September.

Conditions as far as female workers in the shops? Well, the wages were very much lower than what the men got. Men were underpaid but the women were paid still less. Like, for instance, you take a day of work: each operator had two helpers. He was the qualified person, but it didn't take long that you, the helper, acquired the experience and you would do the work. But you wouldn't get paid for it. Like, for instance, in 1937 I got after the foreman, I said, I am working with the boss's nephew and he sits around and talks, smokes, and I'm doing all the work. I'm opening the bundles and doing it and I'm not getting paid. So I insisted that they should promote me as an operator, which they did. So as a helper I had sixteen dollars a week. As an operator I got the magnificent sum of twenty dollars a week, you see. And I had the responsibility of producing. Then they gave me two helpers and I had to teach them from scratch, because usually they came in as inexperienced girls and you had to teach them how to make a straight seam, how to make a loop, how to do some of the things.

In a big shop, like where I worked, there were some thirty to forty machines at the time, so there would be a good fifteen operators, then helpers. There was a whole section of finishers and pressers and cutters. Cutters were the aristocracy of the trade. It still is. It still holds true and the cutters are getting the best. Of course, now they have all the modern equipment, automation with cutting machine, and what have you. But in those days, they didn't have them. And now it's all piecework. The only section that is not in piecework is the cutters.

But right now, as far as the union is concerned, unfortunately, there is the trade union bureaucracy—you know that there is no democracy in the local—but otherwise the unions are strong. They had their strike here in Montreal—the tailors—for three weeks and they won terrific conditions. It was the first strike in a long time. Even as far as pensions is concerned. I get twenty-five dollars a month from my local in Winnipeg and they get one hundred dollars a month now! The ILGWU started making pensions when I was at their convention in Atlantic City in 1937. This was at the time of the civil war in Spain. It was the most progressive convention in the history of the ILGWU. It was at the height of the CIO campaign. John Lewis and the Spanish ambassador, and many others, addressed the Convention. You know what conventions are like: big circuses!

So the pensions started in 1937. They accumulated a lot of money in the treasury for pensions and they can now pay out more. The pension in the fur trade in Winnipeg started in later, after I went back to work and after raising a family in 1950. So we started a pension in 1959, and we had to pay ten years to accumulate a fund. So we haven't got enough money to pay more.

When you came from Europe, in the towns we lived—not only in my town, any other town—there was no industry. So what did you have in order to make a living? You had hand craftsmen, like shoemakers, carpenters, tailors. And what do you do when you come to the US or Canada at middle age, like my father who was a peddler? He used to go around in the Old Country, in the town, amongst the farmers, and sell them needles and thread and bring back hides from calves, as well as fresh mushrooms which we used to, as children, sit and string them together, you know, to dry them out. And he used to eke out a living from it. So when he came to Canada, what could he do? He became a peddler here. What did he peddle? He peddled with vegetables.

So when these people come from Europe, they go into the next industry that they can possibly do. These people were tailors from the Old Country, and they went in there. Very few people went into heavy industry. You will find some that went into the railroads. They couldn't go into heavy industry because, first of all, they were not physically strong enough that they would be employed. Now, take when the Ukrainians came to Canada—in Winnipeg there is a noted railway centre—they either went into farming or they went to the railroads. Now, if a puny little Jew would come to the railways to ask for a job, they wouldn't employ him. He wasn't strong enough to do physical labour. So he would go into a needle trade shop or he would go open a little store if he had the means, a corner shopkeeper; or maybe he'd be a capmaker or a shoemaker, something of the sort. That is why most of them went to the needle trades.

In Manitoba they had some farming settlements, like Edenbridge, where the Jews struggled as farmers. And there were Baron de Hirsch colonies. But they didn't survive. The Edenbridge settlement lasted the longest.[47] When my sister, who is in Los Angeles, got married, she lived in Edenbridge. The conditions were very harsh. Excellent histories have been written; unfortunately, they have not been translated into English.

There was a time when a tailor had a growing son or daughter and he would do everything possible for the employer to take the children in to learn the trade. Even in my time there were people in the shops who came in as small boys and girls and stayed on because their parents won the favour of the employer to take in and teach the child. You don't find young people in the needle trades now; not the Canadian-born. And this is not only Jewish, but generally so. You go into a needle trade shop and you think it is a senior citizens group! And it hasn't changed. Mind you, the wages right now are comparably good, but the young people will not go into the trade for some unknown reason.

At that time, other ethnic groups found other professions: they became carpenters, they became bricklayers, miners. In mining in the West you'll find Poles, Ukrainians. But the needle trades was a too light industry to which they did not adapt themselves. You'll find a six-footer sitting at a machine? You'll find Jewish people who went to the railroads who were well built and strong. There were a number of them but not as many as you would expect.

As far as sanitary conditions in the needle trades were concerned, they were bad. I don't know. I have been in one shop here in Montreal where they make dresses today and the sanitary conditions here leave a lot to be desired! But the conditions at the time when I first started were awful. You'd find only one toilet for men and women in any of the shops. The shops were mostly located in dilapidated buildings, which were firetraps. In one shop where I worked on the fourth floor, the toilet was on the third—so it served two floors of shops, where there was a cloak shop on top and then there was a cap shop—and when you came to the toilet, you had to bring your own toilet paper and soap. I always had a container of soap and a towel. I would say that, on an average, some thirty to forty people would use the one toilet. And if you went to the bathroom there was no time for stalling, you know. In my last job, the employer would stand and watch to see how long you go to the washroom. And he'd ask, Did you smoke in there? Well, most of the people when we had a coffee break, everyone would run (but by the time of my last job there were two separate toilets and washbasins). So everyone would run at coffee break, then lunch hour, and in emergencies you went during working hours—but only if it's an emergency because you would be stopped!

For instance, if a woman went into the washroom and if it took her longer to do her duties … the employer went by once and he saw that the lights were on, so he closed the lights on [a woman] and she got scared and she fainted. They had to call the ambulance. I mean this is a true story. It impressed everybody in the shop and they were up in arms. He never did it again. He never dared to close the lights even when he saw the lights on.

As far as stories are concerned, the girls I worked with—you see, some of them didn't know the language and would stick to each other. We were not only workmates but we were chums out of the shop. After work we would go out for supper and take in a movie. Or if a girl happened to have got married, we'd all chip in and make a shower or take her out. The atmosphere was much friendlier than the present. You felt a kinship to each other, which I think is lacking now. If somebody missed a day's work, you'd right away phone up and find out what happened? Why didn't she come in? Or go and visit. But now I doubt if this happens.

You want stories? Listen, there are so many comical stories, I really don't know where to start. We used to have picnics. One we had was in 1929—my brother has a picture of it—and there were hundreds of people because people had no money for entertainment as you do now, and so you had to congregate in groups to entertain each other. As youngsters we used to go out toboganing or tramping. Tobboganing cost money, so it was mostly tramping in the snow. Or we'd gather in a house and we'd sing and drink tea, and eat potatoes and herring, and we'd have a gala time. Nowadays, if a teenager hasn't got ten dollars in his pocket he wouldn't think of going out of an evening. In the summer we'd go to the parks in groups and we enjoyed ourselves.

The times when we were on strike—the CLDL [Canadian Labour Defence League]—they defended strikers when they were arrested. The police on the picket line were in full force, sticking with the employers—same thing as right now. In 1934, when we had a general strike in Winnipeg, the public was with us, and we had headquarters in an old church—the company, the Workers' Relief Organization, bought it but they gave us the church, and they would go to shopkeepers, poor shopkeepers, who would give us potatoes or whatever they could spare. And we had meals prepared for the strikers.

We had to be on the picket line at six o'clock. They would come and bring the coffee and breakfast and then again at lunch. We had a conference organized of citizens (at that time we had the Independent Labour Party—like the New Democratic Party now). Some of them helped and food used to come in from the farmers from the countryside and the meals were quite adequate. As far as money was concerned, we had conferences from societies—the Jews are over-organized!—and all the societies would send in a little bit of money. So we'd give a family three dollars for immediate necessities because there was no money at all. Those who could afford it, did without it. Our main problem was the question of finances—to keep the strikes up. But the response from the population was very good. Of course, I'm not talking about the rich or the employers. They, of course, stuck together. But, particularly in the north end of Winnipeg, we got very good support in every strike. Because they felt we needed halls for meetings, we'd get them free. A lot of strikers went scabbing: either they were forced, or they were bought out by the employer who promised them pie in the sky.

The question of Jewish bosses and Jewish workers! I'll give you an example. A girlfriend of mine died on account of the strike. She was Freda Coodin. We were on the picket line and the boss was Jewish and the workers were Jewish. This was during the furriers' strike. And the scabs that they had, they provoked the police. Now Freda, she was such a gentle girl that she wouldn't touch a fly. So one office worker from the boss said that she attacked him and the police arrested her. She had a trial and she was a year in jail. And in jail she contracted TB and she came out and she died. On her tombstone it was written that she was a victim of the strike. So, do you know A.A. Hertog? They broke the tombstone because it said that she was a victim of the Hertog Strike. Atrocities like this. So we had victims. The strikers were arrested left and right. Freda Coodin actually was a bystander—she had come to support the picket line for the furriers' strike.

To understand how Jewish bosses exploited Jewish workers, you have to bear in mind that there is a class distinction amongst the Jewish people—and as a matter of fact, the Jewish manufacturers are better exploiters than the Gentiles that we had and it was harder to deal with them, the Jewish, than with the Gentile employers. In the garment trade there were a few Gentile employers, but the majority of them were Jewish because they themselves came up from the ranks of the workers and they knew the tricks of the game. It's the easiest thing. A miner could never dream of becoming a mine owner. Or a railway worker can never dream of becoming a railway magnate. But a needle trades worker? Their psychology was not of a worker at that time. It was a psychology that *some day I'll get out and become an employer myself*—which is what a lot of them did.

What do you need? You buy a machine and you have a corner in your basement and you start working. And you enslave yourself day and night, and when you have a little cash you rent a dump someplace, and you open a shop. So the Jewish employers in the needle trades, most of them came up from the ranks and they worked themselves up, and they know how to exploit.

You see, some of them are mechanics, like those from my generation and older, they were mechanics and they knew the trade. But their grandsons are the worst to work for because they don't know, their knowledge of the trade is not the same as their father's or grandfather's. So the old man died who was a good mechanic, his son learned a few tricks of the game, but his grandson they make him a manager of production!—that's because he went to university and he only took up space and is as dumb as you make him! So he, this manager of production, gives you something to do that would take an hour and he'd say, Will you be finished in five minutes? Now his grandfather wouldn't say that because he knew it would take an hour. And something that took five minutes, he'd say, I'll be back in an hour! You see what I mean?

As far as the class distinction between the Jewish workers and the Jewish manufacturers, was worse than in other trades. There was no respect. They didn't value a worker. The grandfather valued more the good help because he knew he needed it but the grandchildren, well … it wasn't a question of religion, because most of the Jews that came were religious and they probably went to the same synagogue in which the employers would go only on high holidays [*essentially three or four days of the year*]. Even in the synagogues there was a class distinction. As well, there were very few places where you didn't work on Saturdays. You were forced to work on Saturdays. The employers knew that if you had to make a living you had to work on Saturdays, and those who did not—well, in my time, I didn't come across those that didn't work on Saturdays.

When I came to Canada, all the cloak trade and the fur trade were predominantly Jewish manufacturers. They started the trade. It wasn't in English hands before. The trade was initially just a few people and they started it. For instance, in the garment trade there was a demand from the farm population for work shirts and overalls, particularly Monarch Overalls. Monarch was a Jewish manufacturer. J.L. Morton was gradually taken over by Jewish employers. If they weren't originally owned by Jews, they were bought out. Now Western Garments, I think, is still in Gentile hands, but it's very small. The other thing is that the children of Gentile employers didn't come in to take it over.

The shop I worked in twenty years ago, there were 110 people. When I quit there were twenty-two. With automation, where it used to take a good worker three to four hours to stretch and block the fur, with staples it took half an hour. To tape a fur coat, to tape a mink coat, would take three to four hours by a fast worker. Now they have sticky tape and you just hold down the roller and you go to the seam and it's on. (Of course, they wouldn't put this tape on a good fur, as it would rot the fur.) The shop where I started used to have six to eight girls who would sit and just tape, and when I left, there were only two and those two didn't have enough work during the day to do just taping. The better garments they tape by machine.

I started to work in 1924 until 1972, with a twelve-year break from 1938 to 1950 when I was a homemaker and raised my family. When my little girl died I went back to work in 1950. My other daughter, whom you saw, she was twelve years old when I went back to work because I wanted to give her an education and you needed two pay envelopes to make a living even then. Now you need more than two.

My husband too was in the needle trades. He struggled all those years. He was arrested in 1940 when the Communist Party was illegal. And when he came out, he went back to work in the fur trade at twenty-eight dollars a week, and with a sick child it was, it was a struggle. When I see now the way the dollar is just flying … I was just saying to my daughter that her father used to walk to work—and he was flat-footed—in order to save the nickel that he could buy her an ice cream. So my son-in-law says, No wonder she has an inferiority complex! You shouldn't have told her her father was sacrificing for her. I said, We did not consider it a sacrifice. We considered it a necessity.

This is how we had to guard our pennies, and even with this inflation today, which is sky-high, still the dollar is easier than when there wasn't inflation because the wages are better now and people have learned to live differently. People don't save. People used to save for a rainy day. Why not save for a bright day?

Max Yellen

Max Yellen was born in 1899 in Russia, and came to Montreal before the First World War. He was thirteen years old, straight out of a yeshiva, a Hebrew school.

Max spent his formative years involved in the start of the unionization of the garment industry. While others his age were getting a formal education, he was getting an education of a different sort. He subsequently spent his life in the needle trades.

I interviewed Max in Montreal in 1974, when he was eighty-five.

I ARRIVED HERE IN MONTREAL in 1912 from Russia—at that time it was Russia—before the First World War, and I was thirteen years old then. I got to be an orphan: no father, no mother at that time, and I was raised by my grandfather and grandmother. They died off, and so a cousin of mine took me over to Canada.

I came here from the yeshiva—they call it at that time, Hebrew school— and at that time the only jobs for the immigrants was the tailoring trade. Nothing else. Either you became a peddler—I was too young for this—or you went into tailoring. I came into such a place at the age of thirteen and I was working there a month, I think, without anything, without pay. At the end of the month, I got $2.50 to three dollars a week ... something like that. And there was no union shop at that time. It was starting to form, the United Garment Workers' Union. So we were, some of us, starting to form. And there were right and left [*politically*] too at that time.

A strike broke out in Montreal. We were working at that time, if I'm not mistaken, fifty-two to fifty-three hours a week. The majority of the shops from the tailoring manufacturers then was in Jewish hands, with the exception of a few Gentiles. So our week consisted of from 7 a.m. to 6 p.m. each day except Saturdays, when it was closed. Saturday we worked after Shabbes (the Sabbath) at night. That was in the winter. In the summer, Shabbes did not finish till 9 p.m. But in the winter days we had to go back to work after the Sabbath and I think we worked two and half to three hours, and on Sunday half a day. That was the way at that time.

So, naturally, that was the time when the strike broke out. We had a strike, I think, in 1913 for nine weeks. Majority of these people were elderly people. That's the way we were working for three, four, seven dollars. Ten dollars was the highest pay at that time.

At the time I was living with my cousin in a house. You would like to know how many lived in that house? [*Max breaks out laughing.*] That's a good question and I'd like to tell you. I think we were: the cousin of mine who was single (his wife was in the Old Country), his two brothers, and me, and the family itself was a couple [*whose house they all lived in*] with three children. Nine of us. The house consisted of two bedrooms and a kitchen and a living room. All of us stayed there. The rent at the time, I think, was ten dollars a month for the house. I paid two dollars a week and that included food.

I stayed in the needle trades practically all of my life. At the very beginning, I was working there as an operator until 1929. There were big factories at that time, and I am not talking about contractors—those were others who contracted work out to people in their homes—I am talking about factories. The big shops consisted of one hundred and fifty to three hundred people. Oh yes!

I wasn't in the contracting at all. I stayed in this place until 1916. Then I got into the International Garment Workers, in the cloakmakers' trade, and I was working in raincoats at that time. That was a big industry here in Montreal, which it is still at the present. And it was better pay at that time. I used to make about thirty-eight dollars a week, which was a very big pay until the end of 1917—until the war ended in 1918. During the war it was prosperity, you know. Every war it is prosperity. I used to make around fifty, sixty, seventy dollars a week, which was very, very good in the years 1922, 1923, 1924. Then starts the Depression years. At that time, the clothing industry was the first industry to feel the Depression.

I met my wife in 1917, and in 1918 we were married. The Jewish community in Montreal then was just like a ghetto. The community started from the waterfront on up until about Sherbrooke, from the west to the east as far as St. Denis. There was nothing else about. My wife was in ladies' garments. I met her there, in the garment industry. She wasn't working with me. But, as I say, it was a Jewish community, and we all met each other and got acquainted. I was not living with my cousin anymore because, as soon as I was making seven, eight dollars a week, then I moved out. I got another room.

The moment I got married I moved out again. I got a place—it was twelve dollars a month, and I furnished it and we brought up a kid down there. We had three kids altogether, but we lost a son in the Second World War.

Not all the shops I worked in were Jewish; some were not. I worked for Canadian Rubber Co. Not a Jewish boss. But most of the years I was working in Yiddisher factories. The needle trades was the only industry at that time in which you could go. Take, for instance, in the time of the Depression, at that time the season used to consist of six or seven weeks. Eight weeks was all finished up. So we used to try and get some other jobs, which I did. I used to work at the CPR, the railway—it was hard labour and we got twenty-five cents an hour.

Now, I remember we had a strike at one time. We were working fifty-two to fifty-four hours a week and the strike was for fifty hours. Most people stayed out. We had meetings, it was in the Coronation Hall on St. Lawrence. They were very well attended, as far as I am concerned. There were wonderful speakers. We also had a meeting, which they called at Prince Arthur Hall, and we made a collection, I think, of one hundred seventy-five to two hundred dollars. That was very good at the time. Many people did not have any cash and they took off their rings and gave. The strike lasted for nine weeks. That was a long strike, and we were fortunate that it was not in the winter months. After nine weeks, the strike was settled.

There were no political parties. We were just trying to form the unions. Everybody was a socialist at that time, although most of the people didn't know what socialism is. They were mostly from *shtetls*, small towns, and didn't know very much. They only know that they have to make a living, so that was the best way. Anybody approached you in a socialist way, you took it.

I remember at the time the manufacturers were trying to break the strikers. They brought in people from Toronto which they didn't know—Toronto had already formed a union by then. As a matter of fact, the people they brought in to break the strike were union people. Oh yes! And they placed them in the finest hotels here in Montreal. And the next day they are supposed to come to work, but instead of coming to work they came to the meeting at Coronation Hall! We had a good laugh at that. I like to remember that incident. It is worth mentioning.

There was such a thing as dictatorship when we worked then: if you don't do it the way *I* do it, then out you go. So, in the time of the Depression, naturally the first one to suffer is the union man. And at that time, the manager and the foreman was working hand in hand with the boss.

I was for many years in this trade. They gave me a lot of respect. But the rest of the people, they really did suffer. In order to get a job—there always had to be a payoff somewhere else.

I have a son of mine who is a commercial artist and a daughter who is married. Not one of them went into the needle trades.

Dave Ship

Dave Ship was born in 1915 in the White Russian Republic, not far from Minsk, during the First World War. He lived through pogroms, the Russian Revolution, and received his basic education in a White Russian school. Dave Ship arrived in Montreal in the middle of June 1930. He spent most of his life in the garment industry except for the four years he served in the Royal Canadian Air Force during the Second World War. He was still working in the trade when I interviewed him in Montreal in the summer of 1974.

Dave Ship is married to Ena Ship, whose story appears earlier in the volume.

I WAS FIFTEEN YEARS OLD when I came to Canada from Russia—the White Russian Republic, not far from the capital city of Minsk. Life in my early years was very interesting. The times were of great importance to Russia because those were the formative years of the new republic. I was born actually during the First World War, and then followed the revolution. There were counter-revolutionary attempts; there were White Guards and pogroms by various bandit groups. They tried to take advantage of the weakness of the Communist government [*the Soviet Union*], and they robbed and pillaged the population. In the small *shtetl*, the town where I lived, there went through a pogrom where eighteen or nineteen people were actually murdered. That was about 1919 or so. I remember it very distinctly. I was carried on my father's shoulders to run away, you know. It is vividly imprinted in my memory. I will never forget that occasion.

Then there were periods of stabilization of the government: setting up schools, opening avenues of education to most of the people who wanted to take advantage of it. My parents did take advantage of it by sending me and my brothers to school and I actually finished there seven grades. This was a Russian school, a White Russian school, and I had every opportunity to pursue my education and continue it further to university level. I am sure I would have done that had I remained in the country. But my parents (and I was the youngest in the family) decided to come to Canada.

My mother was the oldest in her family and she had to be a mother to her younger brothers, who eventually immigrated to the United States and established themselves there, and became quite well-to-do. They were in the dress-manufacturing business and they regarded my mother as their mother, not as a sister. My uncles wanted to bring the family over to the States, but immigration was closed by that time and so they brought us over to Canada. My mother did say to them in letters that her youngest son (that was me) would have a good opportunity to go to university in America. They replied that there are plenty of universities in Canada!

My mother's brothers were here to meet us. They established a home for us and then they went back to New York and continued to live there. However, life did not turn out to be exactly so. We came in 1930, in the middle of June. That was during the Depression period and those were hard years, naturally, for most of the people here, especially the immigrants. It wasn't that difficult for us since we had support and assistance from my mother's brothers who were sending us money. I went to school for four years. I went through high school and during the summer months I used to work as a delivery boy in a grocery store. My older brothers went to work in dress factories as cutters.

As it so happened, during that period, there was a good deal of discrimination against immigrants and Jewish immigrants. It was difficult to get into the professions and not so much in the professions but just to get a job in other industries. About the only place you could get a job was in the needle trades. So, naturally, through some recommendations of acquaintances, most of the youngsters ended up in the needle trades.

I started out when I finished school, beginning at the end of 1934. I went to work in 1935 as an apprentice cutter in the coat and suit industry. A friend of my brother's got me into the cutting room. It wasn't difficult. They needed somebody, so they took me in as an apprentice. I was not too slow in learning and I picked up the means and the knowledge of how to work the machinery and I suppose I qualified in the industry.

In the trade there was no prescribed period for apprenticeship like you find in electrical or plumbing, where you need so many years until you get your journeyman qualifications and a certificate of craftsmanship. In the needle trades you were dependent on your personal ability—how quickly you learned and how well you advanced. Then either it was recognized by the bosses that you are qualified and you asked for an increase or, if you didn't get it, you went to another shop. There were so many shops then in the needle trades industry; many small shops, that you could move from shop to shop. If you proved your ability and delivered the goods, you got paid well.

At the shop where I worked for a time, there were about three cutters. Then I moved to a smaller shop where I was the only cutter and was able to fulfill all their needs: I cut up all the cloth they required for manufacturing.

I worked for three years as a cutter and I was making something like seven or eight dollars a week at the start, and then I progressed rapidly and I was making much more by the time I left the trade in 1940 to join the war. My salary was close to forty or forty-five dollars a week.

I was never involved in strikes. It so happened that a shop I worked for was not organized [*not unionized*] and I helped by going down to the union and telling them that I would be interested in having the shop organized. We succeeded in organizing the shop without too much trouble. You see, it was a small shop and when most of the people signed up and the union representative came to talk to the boss and the boss saw that the workers were with the union, he couldn't afford to object. That was shortly before I left for the war.

You have to understand that at that time there began the rise of fascism on a large scale and the threat to peace. It occupied the minds of most young people who were taking an interest in the world around them. I was very much impressed with the role of the progressive section of the Jewish community, and this is how I sort of drifted, moved ever more closely, to the progressive left-wing section here.

Shortly after the war broke out, I volunteered into the service, into the Canadian air force. However, because of my eyesight—I had to wear glasses—I was not accepted to the air crew, so I worked as a mechanic in the ground crew. I attended classes for eighteen weeks and then further periods of time to learn the principles of aerodynamics and hydraulics to be able to service the airplanes. I was already married when I joined up and I left my wife, Ena, with her sister, who was also married. About two months before I left to go overseas we found a small flat, a three-room flat, for thirteen dollars a month. Ena was getting a serviceman's-wife allowance; she rented out one room and so was able to manage.

I spent something like two years here in Canada training, but the remaining two years of the war I spent overseas: first to England and the invasion of Normandy, then the campaign of western Europe, right through Germany, until the war ended and we met up with the Russians in the centre, about forty miles east of Hanover.

I was away in the war for four years and I came back in January 1946. Shortly after there were elections, and I was elected to the executive board of my local of the International Ladies Garment Workers Union [ILGWU]. It was a credit union and various crafts belonged to different locals. I was in the Cutters' Local No. 19. I was also elected to the joint committee [*made up of union and manufacturing representatives*], where I served for two years. I had many hassles there in the union with the official leadership, including a Bernard Shane, who was the Canadian vice-president and representative of the national executive. I became known as a communist, and when the next elections came around, they organized a vicious campaign against me: that I was a communist, a traitor to the working class here, to the people of Canada; a traitor to everything that is good for the country! And they spread such rumors against me that I was not elected again. I did receive one-third of the total vote, though, and the nearest opponent was elected by not too many more votes.

I continued being a candidate in subsequent elections with the same, more or less, procedures, and later on in 1948, when the State of Israel was established, that became a factor too in the Jewish community: they tried to scare away the members from voting by saying we were not only traitors to Canada but also to Israel. So using this sort of manoeuvre, which was actually foreign and damaging to the best interests of the union, they kept away the progressives from being or serving on the executive boards and the joint boards.

As a result, progressives ended up fighting on two fronts: the union and the bosses. Matters that needed to be brought to the attention of the union, to the executive board, so that the union can take up the struggle with the boss in order to correct the violation, or to stop them ... well, what happened was that the union business agents were not happy to fight with the boss. The leaders were not militant at all. Let's say, for instance, they give out contractors' work at cheaper rates, or scale was not paid, full scale as specified in the contract was not paid, the union leaders and the organizers (business agents, is what they called them) were not going to search out these violations and start a fight unless they were compelled to do so, unless it was brought to their attention in open meeting and pushed. They were more or less glad to formally go slow, to formally carry on negotiations with the bosses for a contract. And they prided themselves on the fact that there were no strikes in the industry!

And for umpteen years, you know, they had no strikes in the industry and they brought about improvements peacefully through negotiations, etc., etc., which meant that they compromised a great deal and an awful lot as well. As a result, conditions in the industry deteriorated as compared to conditions in other industries, whereas during the heyday of militancy in the union, in our industry, in New York and in Canada, they were amongst the highest paid. After a number of years of such policy by the union leaders, the position of members in the ILGWU sank to something like the seventeenth level in the rank of wages. It also resulted in the fact that no new bright young people would enter the industry, especially in the cutting trade—which required skill, ingenuity, and intelligence, to a certain extent—only immigrant people would come in. And now it is very difficult to have qualified people in abundance. We don't have enough. Very rarely will local-born young people come into the industry and as a result, the industry suffers a serious shortage of highly qualified people.

I am still in the industry here in Montreal. The majority of people are women, and they are immigrants, yes. We had at one time a substantial percentage of French Canadians. Now the French Canadians do not make up the majority either. There are French Canadians, Italians, Greeks, and very few Jewish people in the industry. We have quite a number coming now who are West Indians, and from Trinidad, from Tobago, from Jamaica, and even we had several hundred people come in from Haiti. They came to Quebec and settled in Montreal because they speak a sort of variation of French, which they call Creole, and it's easier for them to communicate. And they are here—not so much in the cloak and suit industry—but they are in dresses and sportswear, where they also manufacture, of course, ladies' suits and coats. And, naturally, manufacturers pay them the lowest wages permissible.

Recently there was a reporter, I think her name was Sheila Nupalus, and I would say that she did a very accurate and truthful report. As she says, it is not a general picture of the working person in the industry, but she did try to bring out the fact that many immigrant workers are taken advantage of and they are exploited particularly the new, the immature, those who are not in the union, not fully skilled, etc. They are the ones who are exploited. In that sense she was absolutely correct.

Even though people today are getting $1.85 an hour, conditions today are far better than thirty years ago. Thirty years ago there were no minimum scales, you see. Now the provincial government here and in Ontario and elsewhere, have minimum-wage scales. Don't forget, thirty, forty years ago, when people came, immigrants came from Europe and were first thrown into the industry, they were getting three dollars a week—a week!—for forty-eight hours. Now figure it out and you will see that they were getting exploited much more then than now. And sometimes they weren't even getting paid at all. They were told they were learning a job.

So I would say people now, in this generation, immigrants who come, those that enter the trade generally, are better off than the immigrants of thirty, forty years ago. Because the immigrants then, the militant immigrants, together with the militant section of the workers, fought to organize the unions for the very process of fighting for unions! And when unions were organized, they fought: they fought for pensions and for the reduction of working hours, and much more.

The people who are coming in now certainly enjoy the fruits of the struggles of the previous generation. There is no doubt about that. And this is what we call the process of civilizations!

Ben Abrams

Ben Abrams's father came to the United States in 1906 as a tinsmith. At some point the family moved to Canada, where his father and brothers carried on working in tin. Ben, however, worked in the needle trades for about six years, left, and then returned to it in 1949, at which time he opened his own shop.

The interview with Ben took place in 1974 in the dining room of a cultural organization where pots and pans and plates were being banged and stacked. This noise was further exacerbated by the shouting and shushing of volunteer workers. Someone kept saying that she had the money!

I WENT INTO THE NEEDLE TRADES around 1928 as a pleater working for other people. It was not a union shop. There were about twelve employees: pleaters, button makers. My job was calling on the trade—the dress trade and cloak trade.

About 1928, I started working for eight dollars a week, as a delivery boy. Then I progressed to pattern making and about 1930, I was making approximately eighteen dollars a week.

Patternmaking was designing the pleats that they used on dresses at that time. I didn't open my own shop until way after. In between, I got out of the trade. I left the needle trade about 1935. I went back into it in 1949, when I had my own shop, and I went into manufacturing children's wear. We had approximately 120 people working for us—50 percent of them were Jewish and 50 percent were from all religions. It was not a union shop at that time until 1949, when, without our knowledge, they had been organized and, without even coming to us to ask for demands, they just walked out on strike.

We came in one morning and they were picketing the place. Then the union organizers contacted us and we had a meeting with them. The demands that they made were no greater than what they were getting at the time. So, consequently, we signed a union contract and they all went back to work after being out about three weeks. And they found, at least our employees found, that they were making less money under the union than they were making prior to joining the union. Unbeknown to us, a movement began amongst the employees after several months and they all decided to withdraw from the union, which they did. And we continued in business after that for about—well I did—for about two years without it being a union shop.

In those days, it was go to work, and work, and go home. That was it. We worked a normal day. We worked till five o'clock. Until, it must have been about 1930, when flared skirts came into style—and they were making them by the thousands. And for about one year, we worked about fifteen hours a day steadily for an entire season, on flared skirts. I'll never forget that. Some days we worked right up to midnight from eight o'clock in the morning because of the volume. It was no union shop that I worked for, but we got well paid. I worked for Jewish bosses and most of the employees were Jewish.

Strike? No, I never did go out on strike. And the shop where I worked they never tried … the union never even tried to organize the pleating industry and we were never approached to organize. From the time I got in to the time I left, we were never organized. Although the garment industry was being organized, we were a separate entity from the garment industry itself.

My father came from Russia, originally to the United States. He was a tinsmith and the stories he tells me—he worked for two and three dollars a week—and that was pretty good. He came over, I believe, about 1906.

My grandfather, my father, and the entire family were all tinsmiths back in Russia. They had their own shop there. Consequently, when my Dad came here, well, he worked for a while and then opened up his own shop. His upbringing was tin: tinsmithing and that's what he did. They manufactured in those days: baby baths, washtubs, boilers, ash sifters—which are unheard of today. They are all antiques today.

There was, in my day, at that time, everything was quiet. Strikes were almost unheard of then. The needle trades was getting organized and being organized on a peaceful basis.

Approaching the Depression years—and of course during the Depression—jobs were hard to get. Salaries were very low in those days.

I met my wife in a bowling alley. She went after me until she caught me! My wife was a sales girl in a store, I believe, for some time and then we decided to get married. She never worked. For many years she didn't work. She just became a housewife.

I got out of the needle trades and went into the dairy business, and for several years I made a fair living. It was a fair living for those days.

Abraham Taylor

❧

Abraham Taylor was born in 1886 in Kishenev, Bessarabia. The pogroms of 1902 forced Abraham's brother to emigrate to Canada and Abraham came to Montreal in 1904, accompanying his brother's family. I interviewed him in Montreal in 1974, when he was eighty-eight.

IT'S NOT OF MUCH INTEREST to say how I was born in a poor family. I was handicapped. I was short-sighted from birth. You couldn't fit me with any glasses. The first glasses I got was over here when I was eighteen or nineteen years old. And they didn't give me 100-percent sight, but they helped. When I was in school, I couldn't see what the teacher marked on the board.

I was born in Kishenev, Bessarabia, in 1886. Why I left the Old Country is a good question. If you are at least familiar, in 1902 there's a pogrom where they killed the Jews. Then there was a wave—I don't know what you call it—a rush, to move as many Jews out as possible and take them to Canada or the United States. Why we picked Canada, I don't know. An older brother of mine, he came here in 1903. He didn't make a living. He was struggling. His family was not here. They were back in the *shtetl*: his wife and three children. After being a year here he and some *landsleit*, Jewish people living here from our village, advised him to bring the family over. He had no money for the tickets, so they decided I should come with the family. It was on the weight of me being a young fellow that I'll come, I'll work, and help pay off for the papers and tickets. You see, my brother didn't have any money to *buy* tickets.

This was in 1904. I came to Montreal and I brought his wife and three children here. You know this money for the tickets?[48] Not only the passage was involved, they also paid from port to port. They took us from the house, they paid for smuggling through the border, they give us an envelope with money, they come to us: you must go to Germany, from Germany to

Antwerp, and from there to Liverpool. We all had envelopes with money. Luckily someone had made a mistake, and at some station they gave me change. So I had enough money to come here.

I come here. My father in the Old Country was in barrel-making, and did a bit of this and that and, like my father, I was also in the field of barrel-making. You know what that is? Coopers. There used to be barrels, everything was in barrels, and they used to be made of wood. I come from a place where the main industry was wine, and of course my brother, my father, my brother-in-law were barrel-makers. In English they call them coopers. At the time I came, my brother had some job here and I wanted to work with him, so we will be a little together for each other and fix old barrels.

My brother took me along with him to work. They gave me a job too, but he had no tools. I had no tools. Somebody loaned us some. Most of the people had tools—different kinds of tools—but we had none. So we waited. The foreman wanted us to come back on Monday with tools. My pay consisted of $1.25 a day, six days. I decided that I'm not going to buy tools. I didn't like the work—it was dirty work—as barrels are always. I think I got up at five in the morning to catch the first street car. We lived on a little street south of Pine Avenue, small little blind street. The trees on the street were just shedding blossoms, cherry blossoms. The streetcar didn't come to our street and we had to walk a little ways in order to catch the first street-car. I had to be there at seven in the morning in order to start the work. This was way out, and I would have to go to the end of the line. I didn't like it.

I had a sister who was married. Her husband was a tailor and she was a dressmaker. They were both successful. He conducted men's work and she conducted ladies'. I used to watch. I was interested. When he cut the cloth with the cutters—something rang a little bit inside of my head and I wanted to be a cutter.

I had to start to work. I had to pay up for my tickets. Same *landsleit,* same people, they find me a job to learn cutting. But I had to work three months for nothing! It was in a factory in a clothing store. The boss had a clothing store but he made his own clothes. Instead of buying from factories, he had a table at the back of the store. He used to buy cloth, cut it, and send it out to be made. For example, he would send the vests to a vestmaker, pants to a pants maker and in this way he saved the profit in manufacturing. He knew as much about cutting as I knew about diamonds! He was supposed to learn me about cutting. So I worked three months without pay. I had to go and ask permission from the ticket agents that I could work for three months without paying.

You see, the ticket agents who gave us the tickets to come here—we had to pay them back. So I needed their permission that I can work for three months without paying them anything. They gave me the permission and I worked there without paying. Then I started to get three dollars a week. I needed a few cents for to save to send my family. So there were some people here from the same country with family there, so we used to send the money through them. The second three months I got three dollars. Then another three months and I got four dollars. The last three months of that year I got five dollars. And this was in 1905. When I reached the end of the five dollars he wouldn't give me anymore—he looks already for another man.

So I start to look for another job and I found one. There was a firm called the Munshaw Waterproof—I don't remember the name—they used to make raincoats. The factory was on Papin, between Ontario and St. Catherine—there's a building there. I got a job there. I learned a little bit how to use scissors And I started there again for five dollars a week. To make the story short, he was my teacher and I picked up the trade fast enough and kept on and got a raise, a dollar a week; and when I reached thirteen dollars a week, I was the head cutter. There was ten or twelve cutters working there and I was the head. The cutter who was the head left for a better job, and I took his place.

I got married in 1908. I got married and they gave me two-dollar raise. I was the highest-paid man in the cutting room and I stayed fifteen years in that place. When I left I was the head designer/cutter, and got sixty-five dollars a week. And in those days, in 1920, sixty-five dollars was a big, big wage!

This was a time when the unions were being organized, to become unions. They had a strike here and there and they never won a strike. I remember one strike—this was in raincoats season—and we belonged to the International Ladies Garment Workers Union. We didn't make any cause, any trouble, and we were on the job and they didn't take us out on strike but we paid 25 percent from our wages for how many weeks, I don't remember, but for a long time we pay 25 percent [*in order to help the strikers*]. I myself was never involved in any strike. I was a union man.

We started making different ladies' coats. It wasn't a raincoat, it wasn't a cloak, it was an in-between raincoat.[49] It had rubberized material and I think they would bring this material from England or the States.

The needle trades was never good. It was bad! The work for ladies' garments was more in demand for the simple reason that their season was very short. If you could work for ten weeks or six months, it was a big season. So the wages for ladies' garments was almost double than the men's clothing. Men's clothing was more stabilized. Women didn't get double wages—they had stinking jobs! What I mean is that the wages that the ladies' garment workers settled for were double that of what the men settled for. The men's clothing operator—if he made thirty dollars a week, it was a lot of money. A ladies' operator in those days was making fifty to sixty dollars a week and some even more.

When we joined the cutters' union and the International Ladies' Garment Workers Union, I was secretary at the time. In 1917, I went to a convention in Philadelphia to represent the cutter's union as a delegate.

My wife comes from the same town as myself. I met her through *landsleit*, coming together here and there. She had no relatives here. She had nobody. So we used to get together in big groups, have a gathering like on a Sunday, have a little bottle of beer—in those days you could buy for ninety cents a lot of beer! So everybody chipped in ten cents.

My wife was a finisher before we got married. After we got married, she didn't work. Those days, of course, it wasn't the style for women to work.

Simon Harris

I had the pleasure of meeting Simon Harris and his wife, Zelda, at a dinner party given by a cousin of mine in the summer of 1974. I was in Montreal then, conducting my interviews. Simon is not an immigrant. He was born in Canada, but his parents came from the Old Country.

I interviewed Simon Harris in Montreal at his place of business, Dominion Clothing. He was about fifty-nine years old at the time.

I LEFT SCHOOL and I went into the woollen business. This was in 1932 and this gave me a background on cloth. I never intended ending up in the clothing business except that my father at that time—it was during the Depression—was not successful; having gone bankrupt, he went in with my uncle—went to work for my uncle, which is more accurate—and had to close up his business. My only brother was with him in that business.

Some three months later, my uncle asked my brother to come in with him. I at that time was working in the woollen business, which is cloth being sold by the yard and learning about cloth. I had no intention of going into the clothing business. I had no intention of going into *that* clothing business because my father and my brother were there. About a year or so later, my uncle approached me to come in. I didn't want to tell him why I wouldn't go in, but I just said that I hadn't made my plans for the future and that I was still staying in the woollen business. Then I guess, possibly as Jewish people do, I don't know, but he worked on my mother and my father and gradually I agreed.

We were extremely close with his sons—he was a religious man who used to come into *shul* every Saturday, and used to come up to the house for tea every Saturday afternoon. So there was a lot said possibly every Saturday afternoon when I was never there for tea! And I would get these bits of pressure talks. I lasted another year without doing anything. Then my uncle's wife started on my mother, and they were pretty close. I guess it swayed me or I guess I didn't have at that time very much else to foresee, so I conceded one time and went with them. I gave up my other job.

As soon as I came in with them, they decided it was a good time to move because moving a plant was a very, very difficult thing, and he had some young blood there so I guess my uncle didn't want to wait, and they moved to St. Catherine Street after he had been on St. Paul Street for some thirty years.

This was 1935, when I got into the clothing business. At that time it was quite common for anybody who was starting in the business to go out travelling, if you cared to travel. I was very young at that time, almost the youngest one among those who were travelling, and it was glamorous—I thought it was—for the first year. But that glamour wore off. It isn't surprising that I got to like it because I do like people. I also went to Ontario. I liked the people there and I liked the country.

I ran into a bit of difficulty there after a while because I had red hair and they didn't believe, in Ontario at that time, that there were red-headed Jews! I would get many derogatory remarks about Jews and I would tell them immediately that I was Jewish. I mean, I tried to clear it up because I didn't want to hear their remarks. But I did like the people in Ontario and that remained on until after I took over the business. And even to this day I still travel for two weeks in the spring and two weeks in the fall. As a matter of fact, just before you came in, I got a long-distance call from a person I used to sell to in Ontario, and although he could have asked for anybody, he asked for me. And so there was a certain climate arranged between ourselves, and I like that type of people.

At that time, I must say, and before I got married, I travelled twice a year and I would say it was then eight to ten weeks, which meant a total of twenty weeks. I cut it down to about six weeks—but if you talk to my wife, those six weeks always sounded like twelve—and I'm sure it did to her. Those six weeks were not six weeks continuous—I always came home on the weekend. I always left on the Monday morning. I was always home Thursday evening. That I considered a week. And that went on.

We stayed on St. Catherine Street from 1935. In 1953, my aunt died and my uncle wanted to sell the business. We had shares in it and I was in this business with my cousin ... wait ... it is all coming back. There was my father, my brother, my cousin, myself, and my uncle's brother-in-law! My uncle wanted to sell it five ways. So we immediately bought out my uncle's brother-in-law—who I am quite sure was happy to get out of our family! [*Much laughter.*] As long as his brother-in-law was there, he had a tie-in. So we bought it that way. Later on my father passed away, and my brother and I bought his share. So that left three in the business.

During all this time, I have to say that I ran the business because I ran it ever since I got into it. In 1969 or 1970, I decided I wasn't going to go on this way. The usual story, you see that you are doing everything. You've carried them long enough. Period. So we separated without any problem whatsoever. I think everyone felt this way. I assured them both that they could and would have a position here. My cousin was not young and stayed with me some two or three years until she got married—it was her first time getting married—so she was very happy to get out. My brother, unfortunately, when we split up, was already sick and had a stroke before we actually separated, and he has not been back in the business since. From that time I have been running the business myself. [*I ask, And having fun?*] Having fun, yes. Up until now, up until the last few years, when labour has become such a problem; it really hasn't been fun anymore. But I enjoy it.

From the stories I heard, apparently when my uncle came to Canada, he peddled eyeglasses. According to the story, he bought them at the fifteen-cent store—Woolworths—that they were magnifying glasses and he went out from place to place in the country. How he actually got into the clothing business, I don't know. But it was a family affair because all his brothers, with the exception of one who became a dentist, got into the clothing business. And, actually, they all started from one or two firms, which they had started together, and couldn't stand each other, and after three or four months the business broke down! But what caused them to go into this whole business, I don't know.

It could be the one thing that I think started everybody in this whole business. It was a type of business that you could go and buy cloth from a jobber and pay them in sixty or ninety days, or give them a note. The uncles were contractors and they would make up the garment for you. There was very little money involved. I heard stories from the time when they started, that they used crates in which the cloth had come in for counters, and didn't have a phone for maybe a year or so afterwards. And it was a business at that time that you could get into with extremely little capital, and is maybe one of the reasons why they chose to go into it. But all of my uncle's brothers, with the exception of the one who became a dentist, went into it.

[*I ask him when Dominion Clothing actually came into being.*] In 1903. That is seventy-one years in the same family.

My father, on the other hand, came from Austria. He landed in a place called Boystown, New Brunswick. I hope it's New Brunswick and not Nova Scotia! But it doesn't exist today. He opened up a small store there. He often told the story that the door was never locked, and he'd go for a haircut or he'd go to the bank, and nobody was worried. It was one of those small places. It was not a grocery store. It was a clothing store but I would say that there was no such thing as a clothing store in those years. It would have been a dry-goods store, a general store, with a little bit of clothing such as shirts, sheets maybe, and socks, and things like that.

I would think that he was a fairly religious man—fairly, not too religious—but there was a desire to come to a city where there was a Jewish community, a synagogue, a Jewish butcher. That was important to him: all of the things which I don't think he had there in Boystown. [*I ask, And relatives?*] No. I don't think relatives because, according to his story, when he did come to Montreal it was he who brought his relatives over—brought his brothers and sisters over to Canada. And I guess it was here that he met my mother and got married.

When my father came over here, to Montreal, he started in a store again and then he started manufacturing in the back of the store. All of this is hearsay. But I can remember back when I went to school and I used to come in and help—and this must have been in the late 1920s—when he had a store with a very small manufacturing business. And it was during the Depression years when he had to go bankrupt.

I must clarify though what I meant to say. My father didn't have people working at machines. He had a cutting room and he sent the cut garments out, which was a very acceptable way of doing it then.

I cannot tell you why Jews didn't go into mining or other industries or why other ethnic groups at the time didn't go into the clothing industry. But, for the Jews, this ability must have come from the Old Country, where Jewish people must have known something about clothing or cloth or tailoring. The funny thing is that my father could not cut or sew or even mark a pattern! My uncle couldn't sew, but I did know that he could go in the cutting room and see what was being done, or make sure that it was being done right, or put out a pattern. And I think that has been about as much as a lot of us can do! We can look at a garment, we can see what's wrong with it—in other words, this ability seems to be innate. We have not developed that. It's part of us. We can tell them how it can be altered, but we couldn't sit down and change it. And, as far as I'm concerned, I never want to do it. Once you show an employee that you can do that, especially today when they are not shy, they are not backwards, they will immediately say to you, Well, sit down and do it! So you are leaving yourself open to an awful lot. I can show them how to put out a pattern, I can show them alterations, but I will never take a needle in my hand, I will never sit down to a machine. I can't, though it wouldn't be a problem learning.

In 1932, I was in the woollen business. But in 1935, in Dominion Clothing, I would say there was a good percentage of French and Italians in the business as well as Jews. Jews were in the majority in the clothing industry, but this was the makeup of our place. There was no discrimination here. I do know that my uncle was always speaking French because he sold these eyeglasses. I think he was in Quebec and learned to speak in the small towns and became very friendly towards the French people. He would often answer you in French even if you weren't French. He would *think* in French. It could have been that was the reason for the percentage of French employees. But I don't think it is even that much of a reason. In many cases, it was a matter of the union sending people, and our turnover has always been exceptionally small.

As you came in, perhaps you may have seen a picture there of a trimmer who retired, I believe, after fifty-four years. And it's the only job he ever had. He is a French man—he is still alive. He still calls me once in a while. He started here sweeping the floor and then stayed. It's a halfway decent place to work, and we don't lose employees unless we have to get rid of them one way or another. I'm sure there wasn't any discrimination at all; it just happened that that's the way it worked out. And I'm just thinking of the place that I was most familiar with—the cutting room—and I think there were more French than Jewish people in 1935. At the present time, there happens to be more Jewish than French people. There is, as it happens, only one French person working here right now, a change that took place without any particular reason. The trimmer who had been with us for that length of time was replaced by a Jewish trimmer the union sent to us. He proved satisfactory and we kept him. Had it been anyone else, we would have kept whomever the union sent.

The clothing industry has been exceptionally good insofar as strikes is concerned. We have only had two strikes that I am aware of. One took place this year for approximately two weeks, and the other one maybe eight or ten years ago. They always struck for a short time, and also shops that were struck were the ones that belonged to the bargaining section of the clothing manufacturers. We belonged to that association. We were struck. However, other clothing firms were not struck.

It was piecework in the factory and it was weekly wage in the cutting room, and it remains the same today. There are certain employees in the factory who are on weekly wages.

I know you are interested in the working conditions that existed thirty or forty years ago in the clothing industry, and I understand some of the concerns about exploitation. By "conditions," you are referring to the place in which they worked. The wages were set by the union when the union came in. Before the union came in ... as a matter of fact, many years ago I threw out folders in which I was absolutely shocked to see what the wages were and the rate for piecework! I may look through and see if I can find any—I doubt it, because when we moved I had to get rid of a lot of papers. Since 1903 we have made three moves. We were thirty years on St. Hubert—I'm digressing here, I know—thirty years on St. Paul, and thirty years on St. Catherine, and then here. So in each place we stayed thirty years—it accumulates!

I'm just wondering: were conditions in other industries any different than in the clothing industry at that time? I really think that workers, unfortunately, got very little; and besides that, they were laid off whenever there wasn't enough work for them. So whatever they got, you couldn't consider a weekly wage.

While talking with you, some of this seems to come back to me ... it seems to come back to me. I really think a tremendous urge was this bringing of the family here. There were pogroms wherever they came from, they didn't know how long they'd live. That seemed to be the thing—that you came, you tried to bring someone to this wonderful country, Canada. It still is, as far as I am concerned! And I do believe that most Jewish families did—even the ones from work—that they just kept money for food and sent the rest there until the day they can bring them over. Most of them came over in cattle boats, so the fare was not that out of reach. And I am quite sure that was one of the greatest motivations of the Jewish people: how can I achieve that, bringing family over, the fastest way. Also in those days, you could give a note for the fare tickets and pay later. I know that in the 1930s they even paid labour with notes, you know—promissory notes. Now this I can remember. In other words, you didn't pay individually, if you had a contractor and he did work for you, you would give him two or three notes, for say, thirty or sixty days. Labour is a cash thing because people have to live, they have to eat; and I do know that many, many manufacturers would pay labour that way because they never had the money until they collected for what they sold so they could pay the wages.

I must admit I know these things existed prior to the union coming in; that people worked sometimes for little or no pay, and sometimes months went by without work. But this was all before my time. I know they existed—they existed in every industry and it wasn't until the unions came in, when they tried to bring a little bit of pressure and bring the standard of living up slightly. But I haven't any personal experience of any of those things, so I can't tell you anything.

However, getting back to the question of Jews—I think this was the way everybody worked, because I was only six months on St. Paul Street and it was the dirtiest old building I've ever seen! St. Paul Street is right off the waterfront, and the city of Montreal was built from there. As people landed, the first streets were right besides the harbour. Now St. Paul Street is possibly the fourth street from the harbour, so you can imagine how old a building it is, with narrow streets and the factory was upstairs … certainly conditions were not good. That seemed to be the way and it's an unfortunate thing that in the clothing industry—now whether it's because it was in Jewish hands, I don't know—but it was a very cutthroat, competitive business, and it seems to me that was the only way they could make some money. It's different today; not that much different. I'll go back some ten or fifteen years: it was by saving, skimping, saving cloth, turning lights off, things that you don't hear today at all, not spending anything—and this I've gone through—that you hope at the end of the year you are left with a little bit after paying all your wages and everything else, and hope that the bankruptcies that used to be so numerous in those days didn't take up the profit. And I think that it was just a case of not being able to get out from under and do a little bit more for employees or you will be left without a business.

There was another thing, too. In the men's clothing business, we've always said that men are the last people to buy clothes! When a family is hit, they've got to pay their rent. They must have food! And I would say, the children would be next and if something is left, certainly the wife would get it. And the man can wear a windbreaker. He can have one suit. I can remember when men would come in here and say, You made this suit for my wedding [*laughs*] and now it's fifteen years later! And this is actual fact. It was pretty hard to make a living from people who buy one suit every ten or fifteen years! And I think that, that would be necessity, and necessity is the mother of invention. If there was a ministry where you could go out and command your prices—they do in the steel industry and in others, or have combines—it would be different. But here is a matter of what was the price? Mostly, the bosses went out to sell in the early days and they wouldn't pass up an order.

Sometimes they must not have wondered what had the garment cost that they were selling, just as long as they did business.

My uncle was always closed on Saturdays and open on Sunday mornings. I can't remember in my time the factories ever working on Saturdays—unless it was overtime. Now you remind me. For a little while we used to come in Saturday evening, after dark—and this was just my uncle and myself—to see the mail. It was just a case of seeing the mail. And then we also had, what we called, a peddler's supply, which means that the peddlers would have customers and they would bring the customers in and they would sell them suits from us or made-to-measure. And they would deliver them and they would pay us for them—that is, the peddler would deal with all this, as we had nothing to do with the individual customers. They used to bring their customers in Sunday mornings, and that's why we went in on Sunday mornings. But Sunday morning was not a workday and neither was Saturday.

Insofar as discrimination against the Jews was concerned, I know that it existed in banking and places like that. I don't know about insurance companies. I do know there are lots of insurance agents. Steel, yes, even though in the United States I do know of a Jewish firm in steel—but in the big industry, even to this day ... to what extent there are Jews in it, I don't know.

I often wonder if the desire to go into the clothing business wasn't just the case of the first Jew coming into it and others just following? I don't know; or why the jobbers were Jewish, the storekeepers were Jewish—maybe it was an easy thing to get in. I really don't know the answer to that. Well, it appears that all my uncles were in the clothing industry with the exception of one—and, incidentally, the others helped him become a dentist. He didn't want to be in the clothing business, although he did work. It was hard to go to university then if you didn't have money. You had to work evenings, weekends. The tuition fees were not high, but were extremely high for immigrants at that time and money was not available. I don't know if any of them had clothing businesses in Europe. Now we find that a lot of the people coming here had mills and tremendous business experience in the trade and they follow right through.

Now this is a story I have heard quite often: that all of them were so interested in coming, making money, and bringing the rest of the family over. They couldn't possibly do that by just working at a job; and that could be one of the first reasons why they would get into some kind of a business. They had to get into some kind of a business where they could do most of the work themselves and which would require extremely low capital, because they didn't have it. And by economizing, saving any way they could, they could accumulate a little bit of money and start bringing the family over, which I know happened in our particular case.

The only thing is—and it's away from all this—it's a story that has remained in my mind. It has nothing to do with what we are talking about, but I must tell you. I've told Zelda, my wife, many times. Zelda hasn't gone through a depression. I guess it was in 1929—must have been 1929—there was a chap who used to pass my father's store every day, and I would always go in there after school and I used to see him. His nails were manicured, he was dressed beautifully, and he would always tell us how much money he made in the stock market. And to this day, I have this picture of him in my mind. To me it looks like it could have been two or three weeks after the Crash—or it may have been two or three months later—but looking back, I saw him come in and I saw a man in shreds, his clothes tattered! I couldn't believe it was him! *Because even if he lost all his money, he should have had his clothing.* And you know that has remained in my mind and everything I do with my clothing—it doesn't matter what—that still comes back to me. Whether he pawned his clothing and bought shares? I never knew. But he was really in shreds! And that's hard for a person to imagine unless they've seen it. And that was what the Crash was, and what it did. At that time I was only fourteen years old. It had quite an impact on me and I'll never forget it. Because I never believed—you don't take the clothes off a person. Okay, he's down, he's out—but he's kept the suit, he's kept something!

Conclusion

IN THIS BOOK, I HAVE tried to recount, in their own words, the rich experiences of Eastern European Jewish immigrants who came to Canada between 1900 and 1930. Most of those immigrants went into the garment factories of Montreal, Toronto, and Winnipeg. Listening, I developed three areas of interest: life in the Old Country at the turn of the century; in the factors that conspired to push them out of Europe and pull them toward North America; and, finally, in the adjustments they made in this country.

These immigrants not only carved out the road but paved the way for generations of Jewish immigrants that followed. They picked up and left their families and homes, pioneered a new kind of life and used themselves as guinea pigs. Many generations of Jews would never have been born if these people hadn't found the fortitude to leave. These travellers found themselves at a particular and special juncture in history where so many of them were personally involved in revolutionary activities in Russia. They brought this revolutionary fervor with them when they came to Canada. They watched, very closely, events in the Old Country, which led up to and followed the Russian Revolution of 1917. The USSR, the Union of Soviet Socialist Republics, became a model for a large number of these immigrants and they made a point of knowing everything that took place there.

For these immigrants, to succumb to the poor working conditions in the garment factories of the New World would have been to take a step backward. They had not escaped from the poverty, hunger, dislocation, and fears of Eastern Europe, with its Tsars and Cossacks, only to become slaves in a rich new land. They had not illegally crossed borders, bribed officials, risked jail and death, and survived the agony of crossing the Atlantic Ocean in fetid, overcrowded cattle boats, only to be swallowed up in the quagmire of the sweatshop.

In spite of their efforts to do what they could, many Jewish immigrants blamed themselves for not having done enough to bring others out of Europe.

The pain and hurt of all those who suffered and never got a chance to escape became part of the heritage of those who made it over. Somehow this pain, and this guilt, translated itself into their determination to fight, to save, to struggle—to insure some small measure of social justice. So many of them said to me, We were not fighting for ourselves. We were fighting for our children and grandchildren, so they wouldn't grow up without food and clothes. For us, we knew the Messiah was not going to come in our lifetime! This was their hope. This was their dream.

None of the people who spoke to me ever said: Why me? Or, What did I do to deserve to be here? Self-pity was never on their agenda. It was so close to me, yet I did not realize that the anger, the righteous indignation, the bending backwards of these Jewish immigrants to bring about social change, were their ways of somehow alleviating the suffering, the burden, they carried around inside themselves. Life was not meaningless; it was full of meaning.

Some of the children of these immigrants told me, with a degree of resentment, how their fathers neglected them. Night after night, they didn't see their fathers, who would go straight from the factory to union, cultural, or political meetings. If their fathers were not at meetings, they were out on strike or raising money to feed the strikers. (Many mothers gave a lot of their time to the organizations as well.) On weekends, fathers might have some time for their families. These children, grown men and women, felt their parents gave too much of themselves to the cause of social justice, and too little to the family.

Why? Were they in some way consciously, or unconsciously, paying a debt? Accounting for their being alive? Salving their guilt? I don't think even they could have answered these questions. And, really, does it matter?

In 1975, Lucy S. Davidowicz stated in *The War Against the Jews: 1933–1945* that the Second World War

> brought death to nearly 6 million Jews, to two out of every three European Jews. Though one third of them managed to survive, though the Jewish people and Judaism have outlived the Third Reich, the Germans nevertheless succeeded in irrevocably destroying the life and culture of East European Jewry.

Those who came here brought with them their way of life. Not just the obvious and visible accoutrements like language and dress that came with them, but their strong identification with tradition: their rich sense of the past, and their joy and happiness in celebrating life and its continuance. They also brought, each within his or her own thoughts, the poverty, the hunger, the pogroms, the needless deaths which so many of them suffered through. Some talked about these. Others could not.

The Jews of Eastern Europe were unique in that, within a matter of a decade or two of their departure, the *shtetlekh* and cities from which they had emigrated were gone. The Russian Revolution came and the Pale of Settlement was legally abolished. The Second World War and Hitler came, writing the final chapter of the history of the East European Jew. Today, there are no more *shtetlekh* or cities with large Jewish communities in Eastern Europe; an experience unmatched in its size, scope, or totality by other immigrants to Canada of the time. Where we can say today there are no more *shtetlekh* and cities of Jewish communities in Eastern Europe we cannot say this of other immigrants to this country.

These Jewish immigrants who left Poland, Russia, Romania, Hungary, Latvia, Galicia, and other places, in their struggles in the New World, did not write "The End" to miserable conditions when they came to Canada. Working conditions changed for some trades and industries while others, like the garment industries, remained almost as bad as before for many decades.

As an anthropologist vitally involved in oral history, my purpose was never to establish facts or attempt to test theories. Critics of oral history, like some historians and those who would claim oral history is inherently subjective or biased, claim that the introduction of feelings, impressions, attitudes, emotions, behaviour, and opinions beclouds the historical perspective. However, the human interest aspects of the ordinary, everyday lives of people cannot be submitted as "having happened," or be treated as so much empirical data. The writing of history has been, for so long, an accounting of what happened to the dominant class of people from the point of view of those who wrote that history and not from the perspective of those who participated in it. Studies of the lower classes have a place by reflecting and revealing the history of a people as a whole.

The kinds of lives these Jewish immigrants lived in Eastern Europe do not exist today, whether in the Old Country or in Canada. It is no more. Today, there are no more Jewish immigrants working ten to twelve hours a day in the needle trades. I have tried to capture their lives. To set them down. To make stories come alive for you, the reader, as it came alive for me through the words of these good people.

I was once warned to be ever cognizant of the fact that I hear the voices and the words of these immigrants, and that you will only see them flat on a page; that for me, what they have to say has so many nuances, inflections, meanings, and that for the reader it will always be only one-dimensional; that their sighs, hesitations, laughter, tears, and anger sound only in my ears.

By telling you their stories, I hope I have, in some measure, conveyed how they felt. It cannot be that difficult to grasp because we have all, somewhere inside of us, feared, pained, felt joy, and loved deeply.

Notes

1 There are three things forbidden here. First, the salami was not kosher: that is, not made with kosher meat. Also, it would have had pork in it. Third, mixing meat with dairy (the butter on the bread) was also forbidden.

2 Nicholas II (1894–1917), last tsar of Russia.

3 Now Gdansk, in Poland.

4 Rose had papers saying she was going to work for the Rothsteins, as she had to show she had a job awaiting her in order to enter the country. The Rothsteins were a family living in Vancouver who had a business, probably established at the time.

5 Odessa, in the southern Ukraine, is a major seaport on the Black Sea.

6 Bread present in any form made things unkosher for Passover.

7 Symon Petliura, leader of the Ukraine during its independence between 1918–1920. See Abe Smith's account on page 35.

8 Religious schools to teach Hebrew and the Scriptures.

9 The Jews felt they needed to collaborate and *were* spying for the Germans, as the Russians were killing them. The train took the Jews to Siberia, where life was bad and many died.

10 At this time, Russian Jews lived in the Pale of Settlement, an area along Russia's western border designated by Catherine the Great in the late eighteenth century. The Pale's borders were established several times. Some Jews did live in cities and big towns with the acquisition of permits in order to attend university, for example, or to conduct or carry on a business.

11 Now in Belarus.

12 Alexander Kerensky was minister of justice first, and then the second prime minister of the Russian Provisional Government.

13 In southwestern Russia, near the top of the Caspian Sea.

14 Today Rivne, in the Ukraine.

15 Two of the many sides in the Russian civil war, fought between 1917 and 1923.

16 In 1905 there was a wave of mass political unrest throughout the Russian Empire.

17 Without a trade, one had to get special permission to live in a city within the Pale of Settlement.

18 The "bandits" were Ukrainians involved in the Kiev Pogroms and the uprising of 1919, where they set out to deliberately kill the Jews. Jews would be taken on a boat and thrown into the water with their hands tied and left to drown.

19 Collectively the 1905–6 unrest, uprising, and civil war was known as the Revolution of 1905. It wasn't until 1917 that Nicholas II was overthrown. In 1918, he was murdered with his family. In 1917 as well, Alexander Kerensky became the second prime minister of the Russian Provisional Government, which lasted from March to November of that year.

20 This is a stylistic device for study of the Bible: the Hebrew is given first and then translated into khumesh.

21 Shlomo Yitzhak, medieval rabbi, author of the first authoritative commentary on the Talmud.

22 Tanakh comprises twenty-four books of the Bible.

23 Maimonides, a Torah scholar and philosopher, born in Cordoba, Spain, in 1138, died in Cairo in 1204.

24 Isaac Leib Peretz, along with Sholem Aleichem, is widely regarded as one of the greatest of the classical Yiddish writers. Several schools in Canada and elsewhere in the West are named after him.

25 Prime Minister Stolypin was assassinated at the Opera House, while the Tsar was in attendance.

26 On 21 July 1911, in Kiev, Menachem Mendel Beilis was arrested and accused of murdering a Christian child in a Passover blood ritual. He was eventually exonerated.

27 A weak government, due to the harsh constraints of the Treaty of Versailles.

28 Governing councils, with towns and villages at their base.

29 Wilfrid Laurier became Liberal prime minister of Canada in the general election of 1896.

30 Today Kishenev is called Chisinau, and is in Moldova.

31 A Yiddish cultural organization.

32 Morris Winchevsky (1856–1932), prominent Jewish socialist leader in London, England.

33 The strike was at Shiffer & Hillman. This strike is mentioned by some of the other interviewees.

34 This refers to the split between Amalgamated and the new union. The struggle between the two unions and its effects on workers is something talked about by a number of the people here (see also Max Povitz's account on page 220).

35 A Jewish politician.

36 The unrest gave momentum to the revolution.

37 Conscription at the time was compulsory and you had to serve for five years in the military.

38 The border between Lithuania and Belarus.

39 *Der Kampf* ceased publication at some point and only the *Vochenblatt* remained.

40 See Abe Smith's account of the same events on page 35.

41 Where the ghetto was in 1942–43.

42 A place in Galicia, in the Ukraine.

43 The US Immigration Act of 1924 was aimed at restricting the immigration of Southern and Eastern Europeans, who had been emigrating in large numbers to the US, starting in the 1890s.

44 During World War II, her husband was in the air force. As the Soviets were a member of the Allies, members of the Communist Party felt they were fighting together in the same battle with the Russians against the Nazis, the Germans.

45 Mary is here referring to the Jewish refugees who escaped prior to World War II and the Holocaust.

46 Joe Gershman's account is on page 169.

47 In Manitoba.

48 I feel sure a Jewish relief society must have been involved in paying for tickets at the time, which the immigrant/family later paid back, according to their means.

49 He could possibly be referring to the trench coat, which became popular around this time.

Glossary

Meanings and translations of Yiddish/Hebrew words and phrases are given here to the best of my knowledge. Storytellers tended to explain events utilizing colloquialisms that are difficult to track down in either Yiddish or Hebrew, and are sometimes from another language altogether. My apologies.

I have sometimes given the spellings in both Hebrew and Yiddish, the latter following the prescriptions of the YIVO Institute for Jewish Research, New York, preeminent centre for the study of East European Jewry and Yiddish.

apotheka a druggist

ashtokh a verbal poke, stab, or sarcastic dig

balebos boss; man in charge

bar mitzvah, *also* **barmitsve** the celebration of a boy's religious coming of age when thirteen years old

belfer helper to a *melamed*, a religious teacher

Beglagin Centralle Central Body (not Yiddish)

behilfer a boy who helps a *melamed*

a bisl little

blitzlomp a bright lamp; probably a kerosene lamp

bobe kasha bean porridge

bubes (*sing.* **bubba** *or* **bubbe)** grandmothers

der Bund Jewish Socialist Party

burgrich likely a term for local Ukrainians/Russians involved in pogroms; not a Yiddish word

chachabatoni term refers to the best sort of people; not a Yiddish word

Chassid/Khasid/Hasid followers of the Baal Shem Tov, an eighteenth-century rabbi; this branch of Judaism promotes piety, spirituality, and joy through the popularization of Jewish mysticism

chochow refers specifically to a woman Fanny Osipov's little son called "auntie"; not a Yiddish word

damske for women

danke Gott thank God

dardeke melamed the first or primary level religious teacher

davn (*Hebrew*) pray

Der Kampf (The Struggle), a Canadian Yiddish newspaper

doven (*Yiddish*) pray

droshke a horse cab; can also be a wagon

epicuresh (*also* **epikoyres**) name for a non-observant, secular Jew; someone who attends *shul* or synagogue only on high holidays

fachspracht (*also* **fakh sprakh**) jargon, lingo

far vos? why?

felse (*also* **feldsher**) an old-time barber/surgeon/doctor who, in small towns, practised a form of first aid and who was naturally accomplished in taking care of minor health problems

feter uncle

forsh piz (*also* **forshpayz**) appetizer

Der Freiheit (The Freedom), American Yiddish newspaper

frum religious, observant

frumer a religious person

gerhakte tsuker sugar broken up in pieces rather than in a *hitl*, a cone

goske little bits of sugar

grammatik grammar

greener (*also* **greenhorn**) new immigrant

groschen a small German silver coin

gubernya term for a province in Russia

hent (*sing.* **hant**) hands

hitl tsuker cone-shaped sugar

kabinet office

kamashen shoe tops

kamashen-makher a shoemaker who specialized in making shoe tops

kantshik small leather whip used by a *melamed*

kapote long black robe worn by very religious Jews

kaput gone for good

karke-teyler a man who allots burial spaces in a cemetery

kasha porridge that could be made from buckwheat (*kasha*) or other grain

kehilah organized Jewish community

khaver partner

kheder (*also* **kheyder**) Jewish religious school

khumesh *The Five Books of Moses*

khupa wedding canopy

kibbitz fool around

kleine small, little

kloyz a small, often Khasidic, prayer house

kolonitse a pioneer in the Ukraine

kop head

landsleit (*also* **landslayt**) people from the same area or town

landsmenshaftn (*sing.* **landsmanshaftn**) organizations of countrymen from the same *shtetl* or city

landsman (*pl.* **landsmen**) someone from the same town

landsfolk a variation of *landsmen*

a linke male left-winger

melamed a religious teacher

mensch a person; a decent person

mishma night

mishmorim three parts of the night

moyel a man who performs circumcisions

moykhl toyes a dismissive phrase; lit., "I forgive them," meaning I don't need their favours! I can do without them!

mume aunt

noodged prodded; a "Yinglish," not Yiddish, word

nu well, then, so; possibly Russian in origin

oisgrine (*also* **oysgrine**) no longer a greenhorn

ordn order

ot a hant when the worker

Pesach (*Hebrew*) Passover

peyes sideburns

Peysekh (*Yiddish*) Passover

pimsinholts gopher wood or wood with sap still in it (referred to in the **khumesh**)

Poale Zionist Labour Zionist

pogony probably a colloquialism for epaulets

Polak Polish person

Polishe (*adj. or pl.; also* **paylish**) Polish

Rashi acronym for Rabbi Shlomo Yitzhaki, one of the greatest medieval commentators on the Torah

rebbe rabbi

rikhtik correct

Rosh Hashanah Jewish New Year

rosinkas travelling bags

rov rabbi

ruskayeetas probably a colloquial Russian word used by police to disperse crowds

Shabbes the Sabbath

shifskarte a steamship ticket. See also *shiftcarten* and *siskarten*

shiftcarten ticket. *See also shifskarte and siskarten*

shikse a Gentile girl or young woman

shiur lesson

shmays to hit; to whip

shnayderke seamstress

shochet (*Hebrew*) a ritual slaughterer

shoichet Polish variation on *shochet*

shoykhet (*Yiddish*) a ritual slaughterer

shtapl a rung of a ladder; a level

shtetl (*pl.* shtetlekh) small town

shtibl (*pl.* shtiblekh) small prayer house

shul (*also* sheel) synagogue

shule school; Yiddish school

shuslugen kapital big money; a dismissive term, meaning someone you would not look up to

shver father-in-law

siskarten ship's tickets. *See also shifskarte and shiftcarten*

shmate (*lit., rag*) colloquial term for cloth

svits (*also* shvits) steam bath

somorborona probably a Russian/Ukrainian term for a self-defence group

Succoth (Succah) and Sukes Jewish religious holiday of Tabernacles

tam flavour, taste of something

tallis (*also* tales; *Hebrew* tallith) prayer shawl

Talmud Torah house of learning

Tanakh the Hebrew Bible

tates fathers

taytl a pointer

treyf (*also* tref) unclean, not kosher

tsatskle a toy, sometimes a little cookie

vursht salami

Vochenblatt Canadian weekly newspaper published in Yiddish

yeshiva (*also* **yeshive**) an institution of higher Talmudic learning; in North America, a orthodox Jewish day school

Yidn Jewish

yekes referring to a non-believer or non-observant person

Yom Kippur the Day of Atonement, a religious Jewish holiday

yom tov (*Hebrew; Yiddish,* **yontef**) holiday/religious holiday

yosim (*also* **yosem**) orphan

zaides (*also* **zeydes**) grandfathers

zect a type of apprenticeship board

zibelah (*also* **zibele;** *lit., a seventh*) a child born in the seventh month of pregnancy; premature

zman six-month period between Passover and Sukes; season; school term

Books in the Life Writing Series
Published by Wilfrid Laurier University Press

Haven't Any News: Ruby's Letters from the Fifties edited by Edna Staebler with an Afterword by Marlene Kadar • 1995 / x + 165 pp. / ISBN 0-88920-248-6

"I Want to Join Your Club": Letters from Rural Children, 1900–1920 edited by Norah L. Lewis with a Preface by Neil Sutherland • 1996 / xii + 250 pp. (30 b&w photos) / ISBN 0-88920-260-5

And Peace Never Came by Elisabeth M. Raab with Historical Notes by Marlene Kadar • 1996 / x + 196 pp. (12 b&w photos, map) / ISBN 0-88920-281-8

Dear Editor and Friends: Letters from Rural Women of the North-West, 1900–1920 edited by Norah L. Lewis • 1998 / xvi + 166 pp. (20 b&w photos) / ISBN 0-88920-287-7

The Surprise of My Life: An Autobiography by Claire Drainie Taylor with a Foreword by Marlene Kadar • 1998 / xii + 268 pp. (8 colour photos and 92 b&w photos) / ISBN 0-88920-302-4

Memoirs from Away: A New Found Land Girlhood by Helen M. Buss / Margaret Clarke • 1998 / xvi + 153 pp. / ISBN 0-88920-350-4

The Life and Letters of Annie Leake Tuttle: Working for the Best by Marilyn Färdig Whiteley • 1999 / xviii + 150 pp. / ISBN 0-88920-330-x

Marian Engel's Notebooks: "Ah, mon cahier, écoute" edited by Christl Verduyn • 1999 / viii + 576 pp. / ISBN 0-88920-333-4 cloth / ISBN 0-88920-349-0 paper

Be Good Sweet Maid: The Trials of Dorothy Joudrie by Audrey Andrews • 1999 / vi + 276 pp. / ISBN 0-88920-334-2

Working in Women's Archives: Researching Women's Private Literature and Archival Documents edited by Helen M. Buss and Marlene Kadar • 2001 / vi + 120 pp. / ISBN 0-88920-341-5

Repossessing the World: Reading Memoirs by Contemporary Women by Helen M. Buss • 2002 / xxvi + 206 pp. / ISBN 0-88920-408-x cloth / ISBN 0-88920-410-1 paper

Chasing the Comet: A Scottish-Canadian Life by Patricia Koretchuk • 2002 / xx + 244 pp. / ISBN 0-88920-407-1

The Queen of Peace Room by Magie Dominic • 2002 / xii + 115 pp. / ISBN 0-88920-417-9

China Diary: The Life of Mary Austin Endicott by Shirley Jane Endicott • 2002 / xvi + 251 pp. / ISBN 0-88920-412-8

The Curtain: Witness and Memory in Wartime Holland by Henry G. Schogt • 2003 / xii + 132 pp. / ISBN 0-88920-396-2

Teaching Places by Audrey J. Whitson • 2003 / xiii + 178 pp. / ISBN 0-88920-425-x

Through the Hitler Line by Laurence F. Wilmot, M.C. • 2003 / xvi + 152 pp. / ISBN 0-88920-448-9

Where I Come From by Vijay Agnew • 2003 / xiv + 298 pp. / ISBN 0-88920-414-4

The Water Lily Pond by Han Z. Li • 2004 / x + 254 pp. / ISBN 0-88920-431-4

The Life Writings of Mary Baker McQuesten: Victorian Matriarch edited by Mary J. Anderson • 2004 / xxii + 338 pp. / ISBN 0-88920-437-3

Seven Eggs Today: The Diaries of Mary Armstrong, 1859 and 1869 edited by Jackson W. Armstrong • 2004 / xvi + 228 pp. / ISBN 0-88920-440-3

Love and War in London: A Woman's Diary 1939–1942 by Olivia Cockett; edited by Robert W. Malcolmson • 2005 / xvi + 208 pp. / ISBN 0-88920-458-6

Incorrigible by Velma Demerson • 2004 / vi + 178 pp. / ISBN 0-88920-444-6

Auto/biography in Canada: Critical Directions edited by Julie Rak • 2005 / viii + 264 pp. / ISBN 0-88920-478-0

Tracing the Autobiographical edited by Marlene Kadar, Linda Warley, Jeanne Perreault, and Susanna Egan • 2005 / viii + 280 pp. / ISBN 0-88920-476-4

Must Write: Edna Staebler's Diaries edited by Christl Verduyn • 2005 / viii + 304 pp. / ISBN 0-88920-481-0

Food That Really Schmecks by Edna Staebler • 2007 / xxiv + 334 pp. / ISBN 978-0-88920-521-5

163256: A Memoir of Resistance by Michael Englishman • 2007 / xvi + 112 pp. (14 b&w photos) / ISBN 978-1-55458-009-5

The Wartime Letters of Leslie and Cecil Frost, 1915–1919 edited by R.B. Fleming • 2007 / xxxvi + 384 pp. (49 b&w photos, 5 maps) / ISBN 978-1-55458-000-2

Johanna Krause Twice Persecuted: Surviving in Nazi Germany and Communist East Germany by Carolyn Gammon and Christiane Hemker • 2007 / x + 170 pp. (58 b&w photos, 2 maps) / ISBN 978-1-55458-006-4

Watermelon Syrup: A Novel by Annie Jacobsen with Jane Finlay-Young and Di Brandt • 2007 / x + 268 pp. / ISBN 978-1-55458-005-7

Broad Is the Way: Stories from Mayerthorpe by Margaret Norquay • 2008 / x + 106 pp. (6 b&w photos) / ISBN 978-1-55458-020-0

Becoming My Mother's Daughter: A Story of Survival and Renewal by Erika Gottlieb • 2008 / x + 178 pp. (36 b&w illus., 17 colour) / ISBN 978-1-55458-030-9

Leaving Fundamentalism: Personal Stories edited by G. Elijah Dann • 2008 / xii + 234 pp. / ISBN 978-1-55458-026-2

Bearing Witness: Living with Ovarian Cancer edited by Kathryn Carter and Lauri Elit • 2009 / viii + 94 pp. / ISBN 978-1-55458-055-2

Dead Woman Pickney: A Memoir of Childhood in Jamaica by Yvonne Shorter Brown • 2010 / viii + 202 pp. / ISBN 978-1-55458-189-4

I Have a Story to Tell You by Seemah Berson • 2010 / xxvi + 288 pp. + 10 pp. b&w photos / ISBN 978-1-55458-219-8

We All Giggled: A Bourgeois Family Memoir by Thomas O. Hueglin • forthcoming 2010 / 192 pp. (illustrations) / ISBN 978-1-55458-262-4